MY WOUNDED HEART

The Life of Lilli Jahn
1900–1944

MARTIN DOERRY

Translated from the German by
John Brownjohn

BLOOMSBURY

First published in Great Britain in 2004

Originally published in Germany as *Mein Verwundetes Herz*
by Deutsche Verlags-Anstalt, Munich

Copyright © Deutsche Verlags-Anstalt, Stuttgart München, 2002
Translation copyright © John Brownjohn, 2004

The moral right of the author has been asserted

Bloomsbury Publishing Plc, 38 Soho Square,
London W1D 3HB

A CIP catalogue record for this book
is available from the British Library

ISBN 0 7475 7046 9

10 9 8 7 6 5 4 3 2 1

The publication of this work was supported by
a grant from the Goethe-Institut Inter Nationes.

Typeset by Hewer Text Ltd, Edinburgh
Printed in Germany by Clausen & Bosse, Leck

MY WOUNDED HEART

CONTENTS

Editor's Introduction

Lilli Jahn's fate was never deliberately concealed from her grandchildren, yet her story remained both vague and incomprehensible – indeed, mysterious – and was only ever hinted at in two or three simple sentences. Grandmother Lilli, it was said, had been murdered in Auschwitz. Her husband Ernst Jahn had divorced her, thereby leaving her, a defenceless Jewess, at the mercy of the Nazis.

Lilli's children told their own children no more than that. They would undoubtedly have said more if asked, but they were not alone in being burdened with the traumatic enormity of what had happened; it also weighed on Lilli's grandchildren in the form of an unspoken ban on asking questions.

This taboo prevailed for decades in many families – those that included victims and perpetrators alike – and it was not until the 1990s that it lost some of its force and significance. A new generation began to question the causes and consequences of National Socialism more thoroughly than ever before, and it was this debate that suddenly dissolved the mental block with which many survivors of the Holocaust and their families had sought to shield themselves from their own emotions. That which had for half a century been little more than a past that numbed their minds, overshadowing all else, was now recalled with vivid and often distressing clarity.

When Lilli's son Gerhard died at Marburg in October 1998, his four sisters also embarked on this process. Gerhard Jahn, a Social Democrat politician and minister of justice in Willy

Brandt's cabinet, had left them an unexpected and startling bequest: several cardboard boxes and large envelopes containing some 250 letters written by Lilli's children to their mother in 1943 and 1944, when she was already detained in a labour camp.

Although the sisters naturally remembered these letters, they had no idea that their brother had preserved them for more than five decades. No one had ever mentioned them.

One day early in 1999 Lilli's daughters sat down together and looked through their brother's bequest. They took it in turns to read their own letters aloud, sometimes weeping, sometimes laughing at their childish naivety. Then they replaced them all in the boxes and envelopes and consigned them to oblivion once more.

But memories thus revived could not be suppressed. Ilse, born in 1929 and the eldest of Lilli's daughters, gradually told her three children about what had been found; Johanna, the next in line, also called her four children together and recounted Lilli's story to them. Eva, the third daughter, was initially reluctant to come to terms with her letters and did not read them thoroughly for some time. As for Dorothea, she had been only three years old in 1943 and not yet able to write.

It was a minor miracle that the children's letters had survived at all. Lilli had managed to smuggle them out of Breitenau corrective labour camp, near Kassel, in March 1944, just before she was transferred to Auschwitz. A wardress had probably done her this last favour. And, since Lilli herself had by then written a whole series of letters to her children, most of them mailed illicitly, there now emerged a complete picture of the dramatic events of autumn and winter 1943–4.

Ilse's son, the author of these lines, at first undertook simply to organize and copy the correspondence for the family's benefit. Before long, however, questions arose of which one, in parti-cular, required an answer: Why had Ernst Jahn divorced Lilli in 1942, knowing that this would sentence his Jewish wife to certain death? Or might he not have known it at the time?

Suddenly, the background to their marriage acquired greater

importance. How had Lilli come to marry Ernst, a Protestant? How had he behaved during the first few years after the Nazis seized power?

Further research unearthed still more letters. It soon transpired that each of the sisters possessed documents relating to their mother, or letters from her, of which the others knew little or nothing. Eventually, more than 300 letters written by Lilli between 1918 and 1944 came to light. Together they convey a graphic picture of the stigmatization, isolation and persecution to which she and her children were increasingly subjected.

The question that now arose was whether the correspondence should be published. Gerhard Jahn had been very critical of any attempt to make Lilli's Breitenau letters accessible to a wider public during his lifetime, and had largely succeeded in preventing this. But what were his motives? Was he afraid that it would open old wounds of his own? Lilli's daughters, too, could not at first conceive of exposing their mother's sufferings to strangers. They feared that their privacy would be invaded and their personal emotions and memories despoiled by a Zeitgeist fixated on the Holocaust.

So why should Lilli's story be told at all?

One simple answer is that each new biography or autobiography and each authentic source relating to the Nazi era reaches new readers. If only on that account, they benefit the political culture of the present day and the historical awareness of future generations.

A rather less straightforward answer is that most if not all autobiographies recount the experiences of a survivor. Whether it be Primo Levi, Victor Klemperer, or Ruth Klüger, each of these authors tells of atrocities and tribulations from the standpoint of someone who escaped them. Those who read their books with care can certainly perceive the misfortune of six million murder victims through the good fortune of the handful who survived. What is missing, however, are the experiences and perceptions of those who did *not* survive the Holocaust. Exceptions do exist, of course, foremost among them the diary of Anne Frank, but the typical literary form follows the Schindler pattern: an adventurous escape from direst peril. For anyone unable or unwilling to grasp the dialectical significance of such accounts, these memoirs combine to form the strangely distorted picture of a reign of terror from which the majority did, in the end, escape.

Lilli did not escape it. At bottom her fate is merely representative of the fate of millions, but every victim of the Holocaust has a very special story of his or her own to tell. As Sebastian Haffner says in *Defying Hitler*, anyone wishing to know something about the crucial historical watershed of 1933 must 'read biographies, not those of statesmen but the all too rare ones of unknown individuals'. Lilli Jahn's biography is that of a private individual: a Jewish physician who was an alert contemporary observer of Germany in the 1920s and 1930s; an emancipated woman who loved her profession but was, at the same time, wrapped up in her role as a mother; a literary and musically gifted intellectual who conducted theological and philosophical discussions with her friends. Above all, though, Lilli was an ebullient, high-spirited woman so deeply devoted to her husband that she quickly succumbed to her own illusions about him and suffered severely in consequence.

Ernst Jahn – also a doctor – was morose by nature and utterly unlike his cheerful young wife, who was an enthusiastic dancer and pianist and delighted in going to concerts and art exhibitions. It was only when she married Ernst and was subsequently persecuted by the Nazis that her life became infected with the gloom that now dominates every memory of her.

That, however, was a fate she shared with many of her fellow victims. It is only retrospectively, because of our knowledge of the Holocaust, that the existence of Germany's assimilated middle-class Jews during the first third of the twentieth century has acquired its melancholy patina. Until 1933, in spite of growing anti-Semitic agitation, most German Jews were able to lead lives as contented or happy as those of their non-Jewish contemporaries.

The Nazis' accession to power wrought a change, not only in Lilli's outward circumstances, but also in her personal behaviour: it robbed her of her self-confidence and *joie de vivre*. She abruptly became an apprehensive woman who shunned all contact with strangers. Sensing that all those around her were in the league against her, she no longer left her home – until finally expelled from it. There followed her arrest by the Gestapo, consignment to a corrective labour camp, forced labour in a factory and, ultimately, a one-way train journey to Auschwitz.

The children, who were compelled to witness their mother's slow and agonizing degradation, protested against it in their own way. They struggled to preserve an impression of long-lost normality by writing their imprisoned mother an endless stream of letters. They continued to include her in most of the family's decisions, sent her detailed accounts of their daily lives, and conveyed their sorrow and longing for her in every line of every letter.

Just as Lilli's fate resembles the Calvary of many victims of National Socialism, that of her children is also typical in many respects. Like many millions of other Germans, they experienced the horrors of the so-called home front during the latter years of the war. They trembled with fear in air-raid shelters, were bombed out and evacuated. Gerhard, who became a *Flakhelfer*, or anti-aircraft auxiliary, was compelled to shoot down enemy aircraft, and Ilse and Johanna were assigned to the emergency teams whose job it was to assist other victims of the bombing.

This too forms part of Lilli's story. The children sent her accounts of all these alarums and excursions, which they now had to cope with bereft of a mother's help and loving care. Worse still, Lilli herself was dependent on her children's support. She was hungry – and they sent her parcels of whatever they managed to scrape together in the way of food. She suffered from the cold – and they mailed her parcels of clothes. She begged them to intercede with the Gestapo on her behalf – and they urged their father to do so. Finally, against the possibility of her release, she asked them for the price of a rail ticket home – and they actually sent her twenty Reichsmark.

Outsiders were far from unaware of all these happenings. While Lilli was imprisoned at Breitenau her children continued to lead a largely unaffected social life, at first in Kassel and later back home in their father's house at Immenhausen, the small town where they had grown up. This meant that dozens if not hundreds of friends, neighbours and acquaintances knew of Lilli's fate. Many expressed their sympathy, but most of them simply accepted the reign of terror. They all knew of it, but none of them intervened or protested against this destruction of a woman's life.

This correspondence therefore also teaches us about human indifference in wartime. It exemplifies the disastrous consequences that can, under a totalitarian system, derive from mundane human weaknesses such as cowardice or self-interest. At the same time, it bears witness to absolute devotion, fortitude, and the courage of one's convictions, which were also characteristics and qualities capable of developing under such immense external pressure.

In general, however, this life story leaves such conclusions and interpretations to the individual reader. The editor is largely content to act as a chronicler, supplying explanations of events only where these are essential to an understanding of the letters. There exists such a wealth of informative documents that it would certainly have been possible to write a conventional biography, but respect for authenticity – for the undeniably heart-rending letters of Lilli and her children – made it seem more natural to reproduce the original sources as comprehensively as possible.

Lilli's letters, in particular, were regarded as precious mementoes by their recipients, who cherish them to this day. She had been brought up in the traditions of the educated German middle class, one of which was the art of letter-writing. There was already a telephone at her parental home in Cologne, but its use was confined to the transmission of brief messages. Long phone conversations were not customary, nor – given the technological inadequacies of the day – would they have been a source of pleasure.

So Lilli was an inveterate writer of letters, not only to her friend and future husband and other friends, but ultimately to her children as well. And, because she modelled herself on distinguished correspondents like Rahel Varnhagen and Caroline Schelling, she wrote with a perceptible eye for style. She wrote of everyday matters, but also of her feelings and emotions, of philosophy and politics, and she transmitted this predilection to her children. Ilse's and Johanna's letters are especially indicative of the fact that frequent practice had schooled them in self-perception and observation of the world around them.

Would Lilli have consented to the publication of such intimate documents? Although inescapable, this question is pointless because Lilli herself cannot be consulted. Had her destiny followed a different, happier course, she alone would have determined what was to be done with her correspondence. Now, more than half a century after her death, the decision has devolved on her descendants. In publishing these letters they are shouldering a special responsibility. Nevertheless, the time seems ripe for a reconstruction of this personal tragedy – personal, that is, at first sight only.

A Jewish Family in Cologne

'An indication of our high spirits'
Lilli's parental home, childhood, and adolescence

On 2 March 1897 the Cologne manufacturer Josef Schlüchterer made what was then termed 'a good match': he married his fiancée Paula, a young woman from a very good family.

Paula's father, Moritz Schloss, ran a successful cattle-dealing business in Halle an der Saale. Widely regarded as a prosperous – indeed, wealthy – man, he imported and exported livestock throughout Europe.

Josef's origins were rather humble by comparison. His father Anselm had been a gentlemen's tailor in Zeitlofs, the small Franconian town in which his great grandfather, a rabbi, had lived before him.

Josef had fled these cramped surroundings. He served a commercial apprenticeship in Stuttgart, worked for reputable firms such as Krailheimer of London and Bernard David of Paris, and returned home with a number of excellent testimonials. 'He is an honest and industrious young man,' Mr Krailheimer wrote on 18 August 1882.

Not only industrious but ambitious, because he soon went into business himself. The requisite starting capital was provided by his father, half of it borrowed. On 8 July 1893, three days before his thirtieth birthday, the young man acknowledged receipt of this initial advance:

I hereby confirm that I have received from my father, for

the establishment of my business, 21,000 marks of which I undertake to repay 10,000 after my future marriage. Should this not take place within three years, I undertake to pay interest at 5 per cent on the said 10,000 marks from 1 August 1896 onwards.

Josef Schlüchterer

But Josef was doubtless spared the need to pay interest on what was then a considerable sum, far less repay it. On 29 May 1896, two months before the term of the loan expired, his father Anselm died. The young entrepreneur invested the money in a factory producing household brushes and mowing machines, which he and two other businessmen set up at Solingen. By 1897, the year in which he married Paula, he was living in Cologne.

His young wife had been born at Oberlauringen, Lower Franconia, in 1875. Her parents had given her the somewhat archaic-sounding name Balwine, but she was soon simply called Paula. She was the sixth of eight surviving offspring, her mother Ellen Elise having given birth to no fewer than thirteen children. Ellen Elise ran the cattle dealer's luxurious household. She maintained two kitchens, one kosher for the family and one non-kosher for their many business acquaintances.

In 1887 the Schloss family moved to Halle, where they acquired a house with numerous stables and outbuildings. Paula enjoyed a schooling appropriate to her social status until the age of sixteen, after which her education was limited to private elocution, piano, and singing lessons. In short, Paula Schloss grew up in a respectable middle-class environment, though still retaining strong links with Jewish traditions and religion.

The same could hardly be said of her husband. Josef Schlüchterer participated in the life of the liberal Jewish community in Cologne. He tolerated his wife's religious sensibilities but professed himself more of a rationalist.

His attitude left its mark on his young family and above all on his two children. Lilli came into the world on 5 March 1900, her sister Elsa on 2 June 1901.

The girls were born into a new century of which many contemporaries expected great things: trailblazing scientific discoveries, for example, and an economic boom. They spoke of a 'century of the child', of the dawn of a splendid era of peace. Lilli and Elsa belonged to a new generation that seemed to be provided with all that was required for a successful future. Unlike their parents, the two girls grew up in a small modern family unit, free from many social and religious constraints, and, unlike their mother, were even allowed to study for a profession.

At the beginning of the twentieth century the Schlüchterers of Cologne led a solid middle-class existence. They rented a spacious house in Bismarckstrasse, employed the 'court photographer' to make portraits of their daughters at regular intervals, attended grand musical soirées at the Gürzenich concert hall, and made occasional forays into the social life of the big city. One token of this Jewish family's integration was its formal acquisition of Prussian citizenship on 22 March 1907.

Lilli had first gone to school a year earlier. After attending a private school for young ladies under the aegis of a certain Fräulein Merlo until 1913, she transferred to the Real-Gymnasium of the Kaiserin-Augusta-Schule. This was a privilege: in the late Wilhelminian Empire, only 2 per cent of girls attended a secondary school of this type.

By the outbreak of the First World War in August 1914, if not before, people's rosy, utopian expectations of the new century had evaporated. Paula's younger brother Julius, a landowner whose wedding had been celebrated in style at the Hotel Adlon in Berlin, was sent to the front and died in 1918, probably of syphilis.

Paula devoted herself to the care of wounded soldiers. In company with other female members of Cologne's high society, among them the wives of the regional administrator and the police commissioner, she worked in a Cologne hospital. The symbolic nature of such activities was very significant. By doing her patriotic duty, Lilli's mother was ever so slightly detaching herself from the Jewish milieu and conforming to the ideal invoked by Kaiser Wilhelm II on the outbreak of war: a national community that transcended all social barriers. Paula was awarded a medal for her services.

Meanwhile, Lilli and Elsa were growing up into young ladies. In August 1918, while the war in France was still raging, they went to stay with some family friends at Schierke, in the Harz Mountains.

A noteworthy document survives from this vacation: a postcard, dated 19 August, bearing a photograph of the two sisters with their hosts and the earliest known example of Lilli's handwriting. The making and sending of such cards was very popular during this period, and photographers, especially in tourist resorts like Schierke, did a brisk trade.

Lilli had squeezed into a man's suit for the occasion, whereas Elsa and her girlfriend had dressed up in army uniforms and the young man was wearing female attire. These bizarre outfits show how routine the war had become after four long years. They also suggest that the young people may not have taken it too seriously. Whatever the truth, the facetious foursome sent affectionate greetings to their dear ones back in Cologne. Lilli led off:

> Dearest Parents,
>   Here is an indication of our high spirits. What do you think of it? Many thanks for your card. Fondest love, your Lilli Mouse

There followed messages from Elsa and the other two, and on the front of the card Lilli had jotted down a few brief items of family news.

While political developments were accelerating in the winter of 1918 – the Kaiser had fled to Holland, the republic was proclaimed, and many parts of Germany were in a state akin to civil war – Lilli was preparing to take her school-leaver's examination in Cologne. By Easter 1919 she had passed in every subject and was ready to embark on her studies.

Lilli wanted to become a doctor, medicine being one of

the first academic disciplines to have opened its doors to women, though barely two decades earlier. Her ultimate intention was to join the practice owned by her favourite uncle, Josef Schloss, who had established himself as a paediatrician in Halle.

But a 'young lady' could not simply go off and become a student in a strange city. Lilli's parents considered it absolutely essential to exercise a certain amount of supervision, so she studied under the watchful gaze of her far-flung family. First came two semesters at Würzburg – her father's family lived in Franconia – followed by three semesters at Halle, where she lodged with her grandmother and was so strictly supervised that she sometimes sneaked out over the balcony late at night. After taking her intermediate examination at Halle in November 1921, Lilli spent one semester at Freiburg, where she lived with her somewhat older cousin Olga Mayer. Finally she returned to her parents' home in Cologne, where, after another four semesters, she took the state medical examination in the spring of 1924.

In the meantime, however, dark clouds had gathered over the cosy world of the home town from which Lilli had set off to pursue her studies. Her father's business had run into difficulties because of galloping inflation. Josef travelled the length and breadth of Germany in a not always successful attempt to drum up new customers for his factory.

The atmosphere in the Jewish community had changed too. More Jews had settled in Cologne than in any other Rhineland city, even before the war, and their numbers were steadily growing. By 1925, more than 16,000 Jews lived there.

In the closing years of the war and, more especially, in the early 1920s, some 100,000 Jews had entered Germany from Eastern Europe. The established Jews of Cologne, most of them assimilated and enjoying the lifestyle of the German middle class, saw their social recognition and integration threatened by these outsiders from the *shtetl*, many of whom were uneducated and outlandish in appearance – and this at a time when anti-Semitism had already assumed quite new and blatant forms.

The Jews were blamed for everything – for losing the war, for the humiliation of Versailles, for inflation and a host of other things.

Lilli's father and many of Cologne's long-established Jewish citizens believed that the swelling influx of co-religionists from the East would fan the flames of anti-Semitism. Josef Schlüchterer was at that time a member of the Board of Representatives and one of the leaders of the Jewish community, and in this capacity he strove to stem the flow of immigrants. He was thoroughly exasperated by the Jewish community's plan for a new municipal franchise, which in his opinion had been occasioned simply by 'pressure on the part of foreign and Zionist circles'. This indicates that he had no time for Jewish emigration to Palestine, a policy much discussed and put into effect with increasing frequency.

Above all, however, Josef Schlüchterer was unwilling and unable to accept that the synagogue community should become a kind of catchment area for East European Jews in transit, still less that they be granted democratic rights. On 28 April 1921 he actually broached this matter in a letter to the Prussian ministry of the interior in Berlin. Citing numerous legal statutes and arguments, he expressed his firm opposition to a draft electoral law

> that grants every Jew resident in Cologne, no matter where he has resided heretofore, the active and passive franchise, so that every Jew who has emigrated here has the right to co-determine the destinies, administration, and future of the synagogue community of Cologne, even though, in accordance with his origins and traditions, he has no feeling for or understanding of its living conditions and requirements. Together with the overwhelming majority of members of the Cologne community, I perceive this as a major threat to the existence, future, and prosperity of the synagogue community of Cologne.

Josef Schlüchterer's submission bore no fruit. Alexander Dome-nicus, the liberal minister of the interior, refrained from inter-vening in this internal Jewish controversy. The community of Cologne passed the new electoral law in May 1921, and the senior government administrator in Coblenz endorsed it a few weeks later.

'What is to become of us, Amadé?'
Happiness and heartache

While studying, Lilli was often compelled to leave the Jewish liberal environment. Most of her fellow students and teachers were non-Jews, but her closest women friends hailed from a background similar to hers. She spent much of the time during her four semesters at Cologne with two other budding doctors, Lilly Rothschild and Liesel Auerbach. Liesel's father was also her boss for a time. Benjamin Auerbach headed the Israelitsches Asyl für Kranke und Altersschwache [Jewish Hostel for the Sick and Infirm] in the Ehrenfeld district of Cologne, where Lilli often worked before and after her state medical examination.

In the late summer of 1923, after several probably rather casual flirtations, she got to know a newly qualified young doctor whose family background was initially unfamiliar and quite different from her own. This was Ernst Jahn, originally a Protestant but already displaying a certain penchant for Catholicism.

Born in Bielefeld on 29 March 1900, Ernst was a few weeks younger than Lilli. In 1918 he had seen several months' service as a soldier in the First World War. Prominent among his circle of friends, to which Lilli was now admitted, were two young Catholics whom Ernst had known since his days as a student at Heidelberg: the lawyer Leo Diekamp and the journalist Leo Barth. Another member of his set was Hanne, Barth's girlfriend and wife-to-be, of whom Ernst – incidentally – was also an ardent admirer. A make-believe atmosphere existed among these friends, who gave themselves literary nicknames. Leo Barth was known simply as Posa, Ernst as Amadé, and Lilli, for whatever reasons, was christened Judith.

That was the name with which she signed her first extant letter to her future husband, written in Cologne on 3 September 1923:

My dear Ernst Amadé,

I'm so unutterably tired and worn out today, I'm quite incapable of doing a thing. But I wanted at least to thank you very briefly . . . from the bottom of my heart for your wonderful, warm, sweet, affectionate letter! I can't say more – nor, I suspect, do I need to. We probably revealed more during that silent hour together than we can even hint at in letters.

I was tremendously glad you came at all. I was worried about you, and would have been very uneasy had you failed to turn up. And how lovingly and sensitively you presented me with that book yesterday! I'm touched by so much kindness and look forward immensely to the moment when it can fulfil its purpose. Thank you – and not for that alone! And I venture to hope that you'll finally overcome all your inhibitions and get those big worries off your chest. Please, please do that.

I'm so happy you've found a little peace of mind after the tribulations of recent days. If you go to Barmen on Wednesday, I'll come to see you on Thursday afternoon – if not, let me know if I may come on Wednesday already. And put it down to my physical – and mental – fatigue if I don't go into what you said, in the way you're entitled to expect, and as I would dearly like to. Your letter itself bears some responsibility for my present state of mind. I hope soon to be able to talk with you more.

Yours very sincerely,
Judith

Lilli's very first letter conveys the principal theme of their relationship: Ernst's miserable dissatisfaction with the world and his lot in life, but also with himself. At times he seemed to cultivate this melancholy, pessimistic mood, the more so since it clearly aroused feminine sympathy and solicitude. Lilli's letters to him during the winter of 1923–4 display a pattern of behaviour that would endure in the years to come: she played the maternal friend, he the pitiful victim of misfortune.

Not that his life until then had been an easy one. His father, latterly director of Kaiserlicher Telegrafen, the Imperial telegraph company in Hamburg, had died in 1905, his mother of tuberculosis in 1913. Thereafter the orphaned youth had been shuttled to and fro between relatives. In 1923, the year when he first met Lilli, he lost the money he had inherited from his mother. Inflation had wiped it out.

Now qualified but very poor, Ernst was desperately seeking a permanent post. The young doctor did various locum jobs that would take him to Barmen, to Burgbrohl, and sometimes to Zittau and Dresden.

Meanwhile, Lilli was completing her final semester at Cologne University. Together with her friend Liesel Auerbach she attended a course given by Kurt Schneider, an eminent professor of psychiatry. On 22 January 1924 – by which time the couple had long since adopted the familiar form of address – she wrote about it to Ernst:

> I heard many stimulating, interesting, intelligent and beautiful things on the subject of love and compassion. My mood today was a peculiarly subjective one, and I wished a thousand times that you were there, so that I could discuss it with you. 'Love is a struggle. A struggle for oneself, a struggle for the other person.' That, more or less, was today's quotation from Jaspers. Sometimes, though, this phenomenological, psychological garment became too tight for me, and I couldn't help gasping for air, because it was all so cold, so predictable. No warmth, no passion or life. I'm often tempted to seize Schneider by the shoulders and shake him: You may be alive, yes, but you don't experience things with and through yourself – and it was like that today, too. I don't know if I'm right,

but I couldn't help thinking of art, of music. Surely they teach us far more about the nature of love, and how it subsists and thrills – and I'm not just talking about eroticism. In this context the centrepiece of Rubens's 'Garden of Love' comes to mind with particular clarity. But it was nice for all that, and you could listen to yourself more intently and try to visualize yourself in relation to the person you love. But is it good to dissect and dismember yourself like this?

Lilli, who now had to prepare for her finals, was soon suffering from examination nerves, as she admitted to Ernst on 29 January:

> I just can't get it into my head that I've only got six weeks left. I'm under quite a lot of pressure, and not working half as well as I'd like. What's more, all kinds of people are giving me hell about how unwise it would be for three Jews to take the exam together. I'm really depressed about it, but there's nothing to be done.

When the time came, however, her mood perceptibly brightened. She worked at the Jewish Hostel even during the weeks of her examinations. And on 11 April 1924 – Ernst had since moved on to Immenhausen, near Kassel, and was standing in for a doctor named Keil, who held out hopes that he might take over the practice – she revealed her plans for a future together:

> My Amadé, my dear little Amadé,
> This morning I received your letter with its loving Easter greetings and the wonderful book, which has given me the greatest pleasure. A thousand thanks, my dear, truly. I look forward so much to reading it very soon. 12.4.
> That's as far as I got yesterday – I was so dog-tired after supper, I went to bed at half past nine. And today I'm on duty in my ward and the private wing, standing in for Fräulein Lobbenberg. And, since I won't get much peace

and quiet at home, I'm dropping you a quick line from here.

I wonder what you're doing today, my dear. I wish I had you here and could dispel your gloomy thoughts a little. And now I've got a very serious bone to pick with you: You're a thoroughly obstinate fellow, and I hereby forbid you, once and for all, to brood about your attitude towards me in any way or reproach yourself for it. I'm an adult, after all. I know what I'm doing, and am fully alive to the consequences of my actions. I myself know best of all that superficial things play a part in my life, but you should know me well enough to realize how much stronger is my need for spiritual rather than material riches.

My dear little Amadé, stop making things so terribly hard for yourself and the two of us! I love you so much!! 'Be more acquiescent, don't be so vehement.' You yourself have often lectured me on the subject, so now I'm saying the same things back. Wait a month or two, and have a frank word with Dr Keil. It's quite understandable that the surgery is quieter before Easter – people never like getting sick during the holidays. You'll soon have plenty to do again . . . It's true one can't save much out of 100 marks a month, but things won't stay that way, and after all, I'll be getting some of the furniture from my parents. Look, a practice of one's own is as good as a capital investment, even though there isn't much ready money around at present. And I keep noticing in the case of my friends the Janssens that people can be happy even without money and run a household on very little . . .

Write soon and tell me that everything's still the same between us. Will you? I kiss you, my dear, and thank you once again from the bottom of my heart!

Your Lilli

The same evening, to keep Ernst informed of how the examinations were going, Lilli sat down to her next letter. Her examiners, who included Professors Ferdinand Siegert, Erwin Thomas and Ferdinand Zinsser, seemed more interested in the politics of the day:

My dearest Amadé,

Just as I got home from Siegert the postman handed me your card, for which many thanks. It's very sweet of you to write so often. I'm so delighted every time.

Our examinations aren't going to plan. We didn't get to see Siegert yesterday, Friday, because he's too preoccupied with Reichstag election speeches, etc. He was savagely abused and threatened by the Communists at an election rally in Kalk. If they'd caught him, they'd have beaten him to death. Thomas was away, so we had to go there again today. After he'd explained the significance of the unlucky number, 13, and the unlucky day, Friday, with reference to the New Testament, and delivered a propaganda speech on behalf of the Deutsch-Völkisch Party, he deigned to make an appointment with us for Monday. Let's hope Zinsser takes us on Tuesday instead of Wednesday. Lilly Rothschild and I are feeling very cheerful, now that we've 'emancipated' ourselves.

I'm sure you'd now like to hear about 'Die Kassette'. We had a nice surprise, because dear Schäfer [a fellow student] phoned unexpectedly at lunchtime – he'd come to Cologne to see us – and went out with us in the evening. The performances were beneath contempt, we were speechless and terribly disappointed. No style, no wit or artistry – just trite and meaningless. Nor was the audience as smart and sophisticated as everyone says.

Afterwards, in the restaurant downstairs, there was some splendid dancing to an excellent band on a wonderful dance floor. To begin with we just watched, but then we took the floor ourselves and were repeatedly invited to dance by a total stranger from one of the tables nearby, a brilliant dancer with fantastically good manners. An ex-officer in his late thirties, but with none of the usual blasé attitude and stupidity. Anyway, we felt wonderful, even though we were fully aware that the trivial, positively infantile music and dancing are the most blatant expression of our age. But it was really nice for once, and we didn't get home till three. Thoroughly irresponsible of us while the exams are on, wasn't it? . . .

Incidentally, we're vaguely toying with the idea of going on a week's walking tour in the Bergstrasse after my examination. Everything will be in full bloom then, and besides, they say it's not so far from there into Hessen. For the time being, though, this is just a pipe dream . . .

I miss you terribly, silly creature that I am, and writing to you doesn't improve matters. I often re-read your letters – but more of that another time – or I play some Chopin. That's just what I feel like at the moment. Heartfelt good wishes . . . as always,

Your Lilli

Although *Die Kassette*, a comedy by Carl Sternheim, had evidently proved a flop from her point of view, Lilli thoroughly enjoyed going to the theatre. She took an interest in Wedekind and Strindberg and was a great fan of Bernard Shaw, but she went to classical concerts more often than plays. All the musical stars of the 1920s made guest appearances at Cologne's Gürzenich concert hall. Lilli's jubilant verdict after hearing Furtwängler conduct Beethoven's Seventh was that it was 'her world'. She also heard Bruno Walter conduct Mozart and Mahler with the Vienna Symphony, the violinist Adolf Busch, and the pianist Arthur Schnabel. As for the St Matthew Passion, she wrote on 21 April 1924 that she 'must now have heard it ten times'.

She herself was an enthusiastic pianist. She played a lot of Mozart and Beethoven, as well as Chopin, and would sometimes accompany her sister Elsa, who played the violin, or play four-handed arrangements of whole Beethoven symphonies by heart with her friend Änne.

At this period, however, her examinations naturally took precedence. Lilli was in the midst of being examined by Professors Külbs and Schneider. Külbs, who headed the Augusta Hospital, later supervised her doctoral thesis, twenty pages of typescript 'On the total sulphur content of the blood with special reference to the red corpuscles'.

Meanwhile, Ernst went on working at Immenhausen. The question of his succeeding Dr Keil had still to be resolved, however, so he was considering moving to Honnef, where a new opening had presented itself. Lilli referred to this on 4 May 1924:

My dear little Amadé,

I always look forward to the moment when I've enough time and peace and quiet to be able to write to you. Like now, for instance . . . Is the weather with you just as miserable and overcast? Here there isn't a sign of May, or warmth, or the sun. It's downright depressing!

Yesterday we finally got the 'innards' over. Külbs kept us waiting three hours, tested us on neurology, spouted some incredible rubbish, and then marked us 'Passed'. So that's one stage fewer to go. Now it's full speed ahead for pharmacology.

Änne was with me yesterday afternoon and evening. We chatted a lot with Mummy, spent a long time playing four-handed after that, and had a pleasant evening . . . My parents send their cordial regards. And if you come here at the end of May because of your move to Honnef, and if your room isn't available, my parents warmly invite you to stay the few nights with us. Think it over! You'd be more than welcome, I've no need to stress that!

It was lovely at the Gürzenich on Friday. That Italian has an incredibly beautiful voice, wonderfully soft, warm and capable of endless modulations. In purely musical terms it appealed to me less, because this Italian music can be extremely trivial and superficial at times. The ambience was splendid; the old Gürzenich tribe was there in force. We know one another from all the concerts. A great deal of refinement and wealth and genuine elegance. We felt thoroughly at home.

The semester starts tomorrow. Schneider ran into Fräulein Rothschild yesterday. He spent a long time sitting with her at Bremer's and asked after us all. If Fräulein Auerbach, Fräulein Rothschild and I stopped attending his lectures, he said, Herr Schäfer might well be his only audience. I shall probably go to his lecture from six to seven on Tuesday evening. I'm very much looking forward to his classes again. We're gradually developing something of a personal rapport with him.

I'm just off to 'vote'. All this wretched anti-Jewish agitation by the right-wing bloc is prompting me to cast my vote after all. Our only option is to vote Democrat, though I'd sooner vote more to the left.

Father is nagging me, so I must close. I send you a warm hug and a loving, loving kiss.

Your Lilli

The Reichstag elections on 4 May 1924 did not turn out as Lilli had hoped. The right-wing bloc made substantial gains, and the National Socialists, who had never stood before, won thirty-two Reichstag seats at the first attempt. That Lilli voted for the left-wing liberal Deutsche Demokratische Partei was probably a concession to her father. Her own sympathies lay more with the Social Democrats, particularly as her great role model, Geheimrat [Privy Councillor] Auerbach, was an avowed socialist. Politically, the experiences she underwent as a locum in the working-class districts of Cologne nudged her steadily to the left as time went by. 'On Sunday, when I entered a building that housed more than thirty!!! families,' she confided some months later, 'I understood better than ever how a person can turn Communist.'

Ernst's plan to leave Immenhausen came to nothing. In his depressed state he sought the moral support of old friends, especially old girlfriends – the first, tough test of his relationship with Lilli. Quickly surmising that her Jewish background might be off-putting, she took him to task about it on 24 May 1924.

> My dear, I must be blunt, even if it hurts you deeply. Happy though I am that you're spending a few days with Hanne, it will alienate you from me in the long run, that's quite certain. Then back will come the Other World, the one you never allowed me to share, perhaps because you felt I didn't fit in. What is to become of us, Amadé? The senses alone can't bridge that gulf, and afterwards one feels even colder inside.
>
> I'm in a miserable, chaotic state of mind. Old conflicts have reawakened. I went to the synagogue this morning, smitten with rage and revulsion at everything and myself.

Although Ernst's reaction can be only indirectly inferred from Lilli's next few letters, it is clear that he tried to reassure and mollify her. Their relationship sorted itself out during the summer, at least temporarily, and Lilli, concerned for the welfare of her 'little Amadé', entirely reverted to her maternal role.

Ernst was tormented by financial worries. The Immenhausen practice was doing badly, and there could be no question of asking Lilli's parents for help. As a last resort Lilli herself sold a few engravings – for five marks apiece – and sent him the proceeds: 'So I'm sending you the money – please don't thank me. I find it too distressing to think of you suffering from money worries,' she confided on 4 June. Nor was this her only financial contribution. She did all she could to make her Amadé happy.

'Please understand who I am!'
Doctor, wife and mother all in one?

Lilli herself was finding it far from easy to embark on a professional career. No permanent post was forthcoming at the Jewish Hostel, which she thought of so highly. Employed there for only a few weeks at a time, she doggedly attended a series of job interviews with various Cologne physicians. She, too, had at first to be content with locum jobs, but she had a sizeable number of patients – unlike Ernst. On 4 November 1924 she wrote him an account of her work at a practice in Cologne:

> My dear little Amadé,
>
> So now I've been here for two weeks . . . The surgery was absolutely jam-packed again – half past two till just before six. Luckily, I've got hardly any more calls to make. Let's hope I'm not called out again.
>
> Today I want to thank you again for your splendid letters, to which I could only manage a brief, prosaic reply yesterday.
>
> Those extracts from Ricarda Huch have given me a great deal of pleasure, and have prompted me to send you something of a response on the subject. I've often sensed the mutual affinity and relationships between the arts, and I've pursued them with great enjoyment. What's more, you yourself know how often I've somehow seen an incident or even a person in musical terms. And what Tieck says about Michelangelo, etc., I've clearly sensed again and again when in Italy. Oh, how I wish I pos-

sessed the leisure, the environment, the writing style and expressive faculty of a Rahel Varnhagen or Caroline Schelling, so that I could tell you what I really mean. Incidentally, we're focused on the same literary era, you and I, because I often read one or two of Caroline Schelling's letters in bed at night. I'll send you them soon.

As for what Schlegel says about our relationship to music, I thoroughly agree with him. Conversely I've felt that Bergson's philosophy, in particular, resembles exquisite music – and not because of the language alone. Music has its own ideas just like philosophy, and both – music and philosophy of the same period – display certain similarities. While listening to a modern Russian (Prokoviev) at the Gürzenich recently, I was desperately trying – without having really thought about it – to get to grips with it and other modern music, when I quite suddenly told Änne I had the feeling that the old concept of God was dead here too – not in the sense of some religious formula, but the cosmic idea of God as a whole. Do you see what I mean? Quite intuitively, I'd made the transition from music to philosophy.

Does it surprise you to hear me say all this, when I told you so recently how I hear, enjoy and experience music? That's completely beside the point, however, because these considerations are entirely subconscious and don't come to the surface until much later on. Did you see the Escorial when you were in Spain? I read a really excellent piece on it in the Kölnische Zeitung.

I phoned home just now. Father isn't off till next week. I'm glad. Tell me, my love, do you by any chance know which Masonic lodge your father belonged to in Hamburg? There are several, and it would interest my father.

How are you in other respects, my dear? Do you have a lot of work? Write me another sweet letter soon and tell me about your books and your thoughts . . .

Your Lilli

In 1924 Ernst had gone to Spain to see his half-sister Grete, a daughter from his father's first marriage. To Lilli, who wanted to take the opportunity to interest her own father in Ernst's family, their common interest in freemasonry seemed a potential point of contact. She herself had often visited Josef Schlüchterer's lodge, for example to attend a lecture on the Dutch-Jewish philosopher Spinoza. 'Much of it appealed to me,' she said later, referring to his pantheistic views.

Lilli also had travel plans. She intended to make another trip to Italy in the spring of 1925, this time to Florence with a girlfriend, but trouble was brewing at home in Cologne. Her sister Elsa had fallen for a young man – the wrong one, the Schlüchterers were convinced. On 1 March 1925, shortly before her departure for Florence, Lilli briefly noted how matters stood:

> Well, Hans was here and asked for her hand. Apart from the fact that my parents like him as little as I do, he doesn't make a living . . .
>
> My mother thinks it awful that he isn't a Jew, and she's been on at me for days now: 'Just as long as you don't do the same.'
>
> It's understandable, Amadé – and not entirely easy for me – but still, it's 'the person' that matters, not his 'religion'. But, as I say, I'm feeling rather low. Daddy will get over it a thousand times more easily. C'est la vie . . . So a week from now we'll be in Florence – oh, how your Lilli is looking forward to it! If only she could take you with her.

Undeterred by Elsa's problems, Lilli returned from Florence convinced that she and Ernst had a future together. Not even his love for another woman could shake that certainty. Ernst had known Annekathrin longer than he had Lilli, and their relationship was still fundamentally unresolved. It was only in the course of 1925 that Annekathrin broke with him for good, possibly out of consideration for Lilli. Ernst's first great love married another man, thereby plunging him into another bout of depression.

In fact, there still exist some fifty love letters from Ernst to Annekathrin dated 1922 to 1925, and his estate included some hundred and fifty letters from her to him spanning the years 1922–7.

It is clear that Lilli's love for Ernst was sometimes one-sided. On the other hand, he seemed very confused emotionally and often declared his love for her in no uncertain terms. Lilli, who knew about her rival, tried to alleviate his emotional desolation in a very intimate letter dated 27 March 1925:

My beloved Amadé,

I've set aside a peaceful hour to write you this letter, and now I take my Amadé in my arms and give him a nice, quiet kiss, and love him dearly, fondly, and send him all my devoted good wishes for his birthday. May the second quarter-century of your life bring much sunshine and happiness and innermost contentment and peace, and may you realize, in spite of all the clouds and all your sorrows, how great and wonderful life is!

And now it's time for me, too, to reply calmly and with utter certainty to your own birthday letter to me. I won't desert you, dear Amadé! I know precisely what I'm doing, and – insofar as one can treat these matters rationally – I've weighed them up and thought them over. When I received your letter, I had been thrown off balance by a person capable of giving me a very great deal, and to whom I feel a strong personal affinity, the painter [Heinz] Kroh.

We became very close, but then I told him about you. And, although he himself found it hard, he did all he could, knowing that it could not be, to help us both and bring me down to earth and restore the peace of mind he'd robbed me of. Grateful to him though I was, this emotional conflict distressed me a great deal.

But the fact that I'm writing to you about it today may suffice to prove that I'm utterly and completely over it, and that I now regard it as a pleasant, life-enhancing experience. We haven't seen each other since my trip, and if I were to meet him again I would be quite easy in my mind.

And during the trip, without giving it much thought, I again sensed very strongly how much I love you, and my heart, my whole being, my self said 'yes' to you. And if you'll take me as I am, Amadé, then take me, and all my emotions and love will be yours, and I shall be grateful and content with what you give me, and will always try to ease and help you to bear your sorrow for Annekathrin.

As for my being a Jewess, dear Amadé!!! – of that I shall always remain well aware, and nothing will ever be able to uproot or wrest me away from the community of my forefathers. What scares me more is my parents, who are bound to be hurt, and on whom I shall inflict this disappointment with a heavy heart. But I can't help it! I'm also worried that marriage to a Jewess may cause you problems professionally and hamper your personal advancement. I beg you from the bottom of my heart to answer me frankly on this point.

As for the future, of which you complained in your last letter, my dear, I'm fully aware of how hard you're finding the loneliness there. But shouldn't the certainty that you have, in Annekathrin and me, two people who are very, very close to you in spirit, if not in person, and who will never desert you and will always be there if you need them and call – shouldn't that certainty be worth an immense amount and be soothing and reassuring?! I think so!

And outwardly, too! Don't forget how much progress you've already made, and that the future is no longer a muddle and you've a definite objective to steer for.

After all, you're getting a wife who will work with you, at least for the first few years. I think you'll be able to speak to my parents at the end of this year, and then we'll have taken another big step forward. Right, my Amadé?

And if you feel depressed again, remember that many of your wishes will be fulfilled in the not too distant future, and also that your Lilli is working to that end and dearly longs to be with her Amadé.

I shall get a thorough training in internal medicine, paediatrics and gynaecology, and then settle down with you as a general practitioner for women and children. Don't you think that's the right thing? . . .

I so look forward to the spring! There are some lovely yellow narcissi on my desk, and my bedroom smells strongly of the hyacinths my mother gave me on my return. How much I'd like to bring you a bunch of fragrant spring flowers for your birthday. The cup, which I hope reached you safely, came from an old Italian china factory in Florence. It's to remind you, too, of my trip. The reproductions and cards are also greetings from Italy. Last but not least, the little Gothic print is meant to be a birthday present. I liked it a lot.

By the way, 'Blaue Bücher' have brought out a new volume, German woodcuts up to the end of the sixteenth century, really wonderful, and I've bought it for our joint collection of books. Let's hope we'll acquire some more.

And now au revoir, my Amadé. My parents also send their best wishes and birthday greetings . . . Happiness and blessings,

Your Lilli

This letter was meant to draw a line under Ernst's last, lovesick few months, but his emotional turmoil was too great. He levelled reproaches at Lilli, compared her unfavourably to other women, and accused her of intellectual independence. She countered this criticism by return on 3 April:

But Amadé, dear, sweet Amadé, do you want me as I am? I can't change myself, and neither can you. You can't, for instance, turn me into a simple, uncomplicated person like Hanne. I myself am striving for calm and clarity and hope to attain them, and I hold all my womanly and maternal qualities sacred and cherish them as the finest and best things about me. How can I explain what I mean? Look, I too am very fond of all that's mild and gentle, but it doesn't entirely fulfil me ... I adore Michelangelo, I'm passionate about Faust, and nothing grips me like Bach and Beethoven, like the sea and the Alps. Like greatness, boundlessness, and sublimity!! Like what is timeless, both present and past, old or new. And I also have to get to grips with the art and literature of today. Do you understand? Surely you can't refuse to accept the mental side of the temperament you love so much from the physical aspect. Do try to understand, and realize that I'm naturally talking in extremes just to make you understand what and how and who I am. Oh, my dear, don't be angry, but somehow I was and still am afraid that you want to suppress certain things within me and foster others instead. And then I wouldn't be myself any more!!

Fundamentally, the young couple were striving to indoctrinate each other. Ernst aspired to make Lilli a less intellectual, more maternal companion, whereas Lilli wanted to cure Ernst of his depressive tendencies. Each still believed it possible to turn the other into a different person.

Meanwhile, Lilli's sister Elsa had received a proposal of marriage from her beloved Hans, whom the Schlüchterers still refused to accept. The young man was reputed to be a philanderer, and, besides, he simply wasn't Jewish. On 10 April 1925 Lilli reported the end of the affair – for the time being:

You asked about Elsa. Yes, Father has now rejected Hans W's proposal for valid and thoroughly understandable reasons which she, however, refuses to appreciate. She's very upset by this and thinks she'll never get over it. Being as stubborn and obstinate by nature as she is, she'll certainly find it very hard.

By the mid 1920s the political situation in the Weimar Republic seemed to have stabilized at last. However, this equilibrium was endangered once more by the death of the first Reich President, the Social Democrat Friedrich Ebert.

A successor had to be elected, but Lilli was fundamentally opposed to the only two candidates who entered into her considerations: Field Marshal von Hindenburg, Germany's supreme commander during the 1914–18 war and candidate of the German National and National Socialist Parties; and the Centre Party politician Wilhelm Marx, who was also supported by the Liberals and Social Democrats. The third candidate, the Communist Ernst Thälmann, was beyond the pale from her point of view. On election day, 26 April, she wrote Ernst a brief note:

> I'm going to vote later on – for Herr Marx, the lesser of two evils. It isn't that I've anything against those two personalities, but as for the parties behind them! I can hardly give the German Nationals my vote, being a Jewess, so that only leaves the Centre. A shame these people are so bogus and so ready – more so than others – to trim their sails to the wind.

But Lilli's candidate lost. Hindenburg won by a small margin – a disastrous result, because the elderly field marshal proved incapable of stemming Adolf Hitler's rise to power.

Lilli was becoming steadily more aware of the extent to which her political orientation and whole outlook on life were coloured by her Jewish origins. Sometimes, however, the effect was purely emotional – as, for instance, when she went to an exhibition at Cologne's Kunstverein early in May 1925:

> It's an exhibition by a Russian, a Jew named Marc Chagall. Very imaginative and extremely colourful, but immensely tragic. Much of his work I liked a lot. His pictures appeal to me, which is more than I can say of many modern artists. Is that because he's a Jew? But he's not only modern and revolutionary, he's Russian as well;

and just as I often feel a tightening of the heart when I read Russian authors, so it was when I studied those pictures.

In some small measure, going to exhibitions and concerts helped to take Lilli's mind off the difficulties of embarking on her profession. Although she had passed her finals a year earlier and gained her doctorate, the 'Fräulein Doktor' was still looking for somewhere to train as a specialist. She applied to the children's hospital in Buschgasse, Cologne, and her uncle in Halle held out vague hopes of an assistant's post in Berlin, but nothing was settled. Disheartened and at a loss, she told Ernst of her efforts on 1 May:

My dear Amadé,

I spent the whole morning running around, so far without success. The Buschgasse people were very nice, but there's nothing doing until next year. Then I went to see . . . Dr Franken. She too advised me to go to another women's clinic if I could . . . Now I'm really in a fix. What shall I do? Maybe I'll go and see [Dr] Pankow in Düsseldorf. I miss you terribly, and regret my inability to talk things over properly with you. It's all so crucially important for the future. This general practitioner's training is so sketchy, you know: 'a bit' of internal, 'a bit' of paediatrics, 'a bit' of gynaecology – it's all so half and half and leaves me utterly dissatisfied. You'll tell me you'd have done just the same. I'm sure that's true, but I think I'd be far more satisfied to have had a *thorough* training in a *single* discipline.

Then again, the possibility of my also setting up a practice at Immenhausen strikes me as so nebulous and unlikely. Look, my love, I'm well aware that my primary obligations lie in quite a different sphere: wife and mother – but what of the mental and material outlay on my studies? Is it all to have been for nothing? I should find it quite impossible to play the doctor for another year or two, purely for form's sake and at the expense of my father's health and capacity for work, since I know perfectly well: Sooner or later you'll chuck your profession. *I can't do that!!* You, too, must get that straight. It's all so difficult and I need to decide now, all alone and without discussing it with my parents or with the person I live and want to exist for. Look, wouldn't it be a sensible idea if I went to Berlin after all, became a paediatrician, and eventually took over my uncle's practice in Halle? And if you went on saving hard – because your fears of renewed devaluation are surely quite unfounded – and then came and settled in Halle. Lots of young doctors do this, so why shouldn't it work for you? It certainly wouldn't be any harder than jointly supporting a whole family at Immenhausen for years on end. We've somehow got to come to a decision now, so think it over carefully and give me an answer *soon*. I can't teeter around like this much longer. All I mean is, this solution can't be dismissed out of hand, quite apart from the possibility of living in a big city. For even though I could dispense with a city's advantages because I love you so much, you're as much in need of mental sustenance as I am. But, as I say, those are the last arguments I'm throwing into the scales. What clinches it for me are the unfavourable and – for me, at least – hopeless prospects at Immenhausen.

The letter breaks off at this point, the following page having been lost. Lilli's reservations about Immenhausen grew stronger the more firmly entrenched there Ernst became. He had been officially domiciled at Immenhausen since February 1925, and Lilli could not but feel that settling there herself would be a failure. A small town of some 2,300 inhabitants did not provide enough patients even for Ernst's practice.

What is more, her future husband probably had other objections. He must have found it extremely hard to get used to the prospect of having a wife capable of occupying a professional status equal to his own. More serious still was that, unlike him, Lilli had gained a doctorate. That might just be tolerable in a big city like Cologne, but in a small town like Immenhausen?

Ernst could never have voiced all this openly. He probably fell back on the then still widespread reservations about university-educated women. This, in any case, is what seems to underlie Lilli's letter of 6 May 1925, which was – by her standards – positively irate:

My dear Amadé,

I don't know what to do or how to answer your letter. Even though I've always imagined that I wouldn't practise medicine all my life and would one day devote myself to other, more important obligations, your letter has made this question very acute and unleashed a really violent conflict inside me. And forgive me, but I was rather hurt by your somewhat brusque tone, this 'either/or'. However, my thoughts on the matter are already somewhat calmer than they were yesterday. I understand you so well and fully grasp what you want and how you want me to be. But dear, dear Amadé, you must also pay a little regard to me and my disposition and attitude. You can say and think what you like about university education for women, but I've never studied just for fun, and the longer I spend in my profession the fonder of it I become and the harder I find the thought of being completely unable to pursue it later on.

I'm aware of all your objections and know how justified they are – but it doesn't help me to resolve this dilemma. Oh, how dearly I wish you were here. I think a single day like last summer would help me more than a whole year's letters from you. Amadé, I enjoy being a doctor so much, so very much, in spite of all the depressing inadequacy and all too frequent impotence of our profession.

And who could know better than you that I'm no bluestocking, for all that? That I'm a woman first and foremost, and – oh, I can't write it all down! But you shouldn't be so dismissive of things that have become a part of me. That really hurt.

As far as my own position is concerned, I won't discuss it with my father, not yet, because it would be most inopportune, thanks to this business with Elsa . . . If you insist on my bidding farewell to medicine the moment I marry, then the Halle plan will be null and void, because I was largely counting on my uncle's practice. I'll refrain from interfering in your plans any more and will simply wait to see how your discussions with Keil turn out . . .

It's the Schumann concert today. I was so looking forward to it, but now I'm not in the mood. Mother and Elsa are coming too.

Well, my little Amadé, write again soon and tell me you understand what I've told you today. And tell me whether you love me in spite of it, will you?

I miss you a lot!

All my love,

Your Lilli

Ernst was at the end of his tether. Lilli's obduracy was getting him down, negotiations with a view to taking over Dr Keil's practice were dragging on, and he was still mourning his doomed love for Annekathrin. Lilli, who actually met her rival at this time, did not find the young woman uncongenial. However, Annekathrin passed on some rather alarming news from Immenhausen: Ernst was extremely edgy and in poor shape. On 20 May Lilli confided that she was very disturbed by Anne-kathrin's report on the situation:

So I was shocked to learn that you're smoking thirty or forty cigarettes a day. Amadé, you were always so abstemious and sensible!! And I find it incomprehensible that you're taking morphia for your insomnia! You, a doctor, Amadé, when you're fully aware of all the consequences. Stop it, I beg you.

'Be the water never so deep!'
Lilli's parents try to prevent her from marrying Ernst

Ernst's shattered nerves brooked no further delay. Although
Lilli's parents had still to get over the Elsa affair, she was
eventually compelled to grasp the nettle and inform them of
her marriage plans – the more so since her intensive correspondence with Ernst, now almost two years old, had not been
concealed from them. Lilli was very hopeful of being able to
talk her father round, as she informed Ernst on 29 May 1925:

> I'm almost certain that, all manner of objections and
> counterarguments notwithstanding, he'll never refuse as
> firmly as he did in Elsa's case, because he has always had
> complete faith in me, and has always made a point of
> saying: Lilli goes her own way, and she'll do it right. I
> increasingly regard my father as a friend, and that's the
> spirit in which I shall speak to him.

The time came the next day. She spoke to her father and mother
and wrote Ernst a detailed account of their reactions on 31 May:

> My dearest Amadé,
>   Well, I braved the first step and took it. I spoke to my
> father after lunch yesterday and to my mother last night.
> Outwardly, I myself was completely calm, composed and
> articulate. Father and I had no need to say much. He
> said: I've always found Herr Jahn the most pleasant and
> likable of all your colleagues. That being so, it isn't easy,

of course, and I'll have to think it over. That was all he said, and I didn't question him further. He's never anything but very sweet and affectionate to me.

Mother is very upset. She raised all kinds of objections, tried to draw my attention to the dangers of a mixed marriage, said she'd lose me completely because of it, and more in the same vein. I myself am stupidly agitated and have an almost overpowering desire to see and talk to you. But even if nothing positive has emerged so far, I'm quite convinced I did the right thing. How matters will develop from now on, I still don't know.

Whitsunday, 1 June.

My dear – that's as far as I got yesterday afternoon. Then came a long conversation with my father, who's very understanding with me and very favourably disposed towards you. But, much as he regrets it, he's quite unable to help us. Nor, for the time being, can he see any way out. He says we must both begin by trying to establish a livelihood, then we can discuss the matter again. It has seldom been harder to reconcile the ideal course of action with the financial support that's so essential. I'm to let you know that I've spoken with him, and he advises us not to enter into any binding commitment. I couldn't tell him how strong and indissoluble our mutual commitment is – there wouldn't have been any point.

He warned me against Immenhausen. A big-city child like me, with all my intellectual and cultural pretensions, would never feel at home there, and although he had absolutely no doubt of the depth and sincerity of my feelings, he didn't believe that even my love for you would help me to surmount this incompatibility for a lifetime. But when all was said and done, he said, he couldn't interfere. He didn't know you well, but his impression of you was thoroughly favourable, and he had a great deal of respect for you. But if there was one thing he couldn't bear, it would be to know that I was living in financially straitened and depressing circumstances. Our difference in religion was the last impediment he cited – that and our ages, because a woman ought somehow to heed the laws of nature by marrying a man older than herself. So I should quietly continue to go my own way, and you should too, and if we were still of the same mind in three years' time and had a better chance of making a living, I was to come and see him again. 'I wish I could give you 50,000 marks today, but I don't have them, inflation has ruined me.' So much for my father. I've given you a faithful account of all that was said, to show you how magnanimous he is and how much he loves me. And now to us both. I'm glad my father knows about us, but I'm very, very distressed by his inability to help us. Especially on your account, Amadé. How those deadening, monotonous conditions distress you, and how much strength it takes for you not to be crushed by them.

Your last letter depressed me so much, and my conscience pricks me when I reflect how well off I am in spite of everything, and how starving hungry you are. Amadé, if you don't want to make yourself and me any unhappier, you *must* abandon the Immenhausen project.

Listen to me carefully, Amadé, and please, please have faith in your Lilli. We must both be brave and take command of our future and our lives. I think the goal that beckons us should surely be bright and strong enough to give us the strength to surmount all obstacles and the years that lie ahead of us. After all, we're both young and still have our lives before us, and we love and trust each other and share the same hopes, don't we?!! Amadé, we must seize hold of life and look it in the eye, or it'll devour us and we'll never overcome it. You're more mature, I know, and life has already dealt you some hard knocks, but I wish I could infuse you with some of my own love of life and happiness, with my own spirit of survival, with that optimistic feeling which lends a person so much strength and courage and prevents us from going under!!

I couldn't write any more last night, but tonight I've been doing a lot of thinking. I shall probably write to my uncle this week and go into paediatrics. And my dear, sweet Amadé, would it really be so bad if I continued to practise medicine during the first few years of our marriage, if it gave us the chance to be together all the sooner?!! I think you can safely take that into account, and I promise you'll *never* have to suffer in consequence.

As for you, wait and see how your affairs develop, and it's all the same whether you earn money there or by taking locum jobs. And let me worry about your practice, my dear – there's bound to be a chance of one in Halle or elsewhere. Rely on me for once. I love you so much and promise you again that I won't ever desert you and will stay with you 'be the water never so deep!' Dear, dear Amadé, I miss you . . .

Always your devoted
Lilli

This letter was hardly designed to banish Ernst's depression. During the next few weeks, Lilli made even greater efforts to encourage him. 'I'd like to introduce a clear, bright, ringing note into the sad, dark, discordant strains of your life,' she wrote him on 7 June. Six days later she wrote enthusiastically of having read some essays on Hölderlin, Kleist, and Nietzsche: 'Life is glorious, isn't it, Amadé? I love it so much, and no struggle for survival, however hard, will be able to rob you and me of our delight in it.' Lilli herself had made at least a little progress in the struggle for survival. The Jewish Hostel engaged her as an intern, though still on a temporary basis. On 14 June she was able to inform Ernst that she had been awarded her licence to practise the day before: 'It went very well.'

Nevertheless, the dilemma of her relationship with Ernst was highlighted yet again by the approach of the principal Jewish feast days. She now wanted him to share in her world, as she told him in a letter dated 16 September 1925:

> By the way, it's nearly our New Year (Saturday–Sunday) and in ten days comes the Day of Atonement, and the Feast of Tabernacles isn't until the beginning of October. If you can build a tabernacle it's more than your Lilli can do, but have you ever seen a proper one? On Friday evening I'm going to the synagogue with my parents, then I'll tell you all about it.

The holidays gave Lilli another opportunity to discuss with her family her wish to marry – with rather disheartening results, as she was forced to concede five days later:

> Mother again made it very clear to me that she wasn't reconciled to the idea of a mixed marriage and could never be so. It's going to involve a lot more hard fighting – especially as I can well understand her attitude, which stems from her upbringing in my grandparents' milieu and from her own beliefs and piety.

Admittedly, Lilli's wishes were not her mother's only worry. More dramatic still was Elsa's situation; she refused to be parted from Hans despite her father's resolute opposition. There was great agitation in the Schlüchterer household, and the Jewish New Year and Yom Kippur were overshadowed by both daughters' plans to marry out of their hereditary environment. But Lilli stood firm. On 10 November she was able to send Ernst word of some preliminary successes:

> My dear Amadé,
>   Many thanks for your Sunday letter. My initial agitation has subsided a little; I still hope Elsa will wrest herself away. But I worry day and night about the whole

business, and I'm trying, through Mother, to persuade her to go away for a while. Under present circumstances, though, it's not so easy.

And now I've got all kinds of important things to tell you. On Sunday I spoke with Father again. The upshot is, he'd be glad to have a talk with you and isn't opposed in principle to our getting engaged, but not until we're making an adequate living. He says we couldn't manage on 400 marks a month, and he isn't at present in a position to give us or me a monthly allowance. The whole industry is in such a precarious state that even the best-run firms don't know if they'll be in receivership tomorrow. Just imagine, we've got sufficient orders but not enough money to keep the factory in full operation. Half the hands have been dismissed and the other half are only working a three-day week, and on Fridays it's all we can do to raise the money to pay half the wages. And the three bosses are cutting their monthly withdrawals to the bone. You know nothing of this, of course, if Father mentions it to you.

Under these circumstances, he says, marriage is naturally out of the question. He hopes things will improve by next spring. Well, that's some use to us, and I'm very happy we have my father's agreement in principle . . . Incidentally, he passed through Immenhausen a few weeks ago – aboard the express – and was rather appalled by the place, or as much of it as he could see from the train. But that doesn't deter me.

Sweetheart, I'm so delighted and happy, I must give you a quick kiss! I think we'll stick to our 'Christmas plan' . . . But now you must make some headway with your contract. It's four weeks since you got back from your trip, and still you've got no further. You'd better have it when you speak with my father! Don't be angry, but I sometimes have to put my foot down with you!!

Dear, dear Amadé, all our dreams are slowly coming true. Later on I'll take a couple of locum jobs, and we'll spend the money on furniture and so on. I should be getting 240 marks. I'm not entirely sure what to spend them on – I'll talk it over with Mother again. The surgery is a little quieter today, for the first time in nearly three weeks. It's turned really cold here, but the weather's fine and sunny.

I wanted to tell you about Martin Buber. He's a refined, intellectual person, has an intelligent face, very pale and clean-cut, with a long black beard and gentle, very bright eyes. He talked about the fundamental idea underlying the biblical story of Creation. Starting out from science, and the impossibility of explaining and dissecting what is ultimate and most profound, he quoted a fine example from the Talmud: Three forces are at work in the creation of humankind: father, mother, and God. And then he said that we shouldn't regard Creation as over and done with, but as something perpetual, something that constantly renews itself and occurs again and again, but always in a different form. Nothing created exactly resembles anything else, and every creation is eternal and unique in its own way. And he proved by drawing comparisons with Babylonian and other ancient myths that no Creation story is as comprehensive and exhaustive as the one in the Old Testament, and he ended by reading from it aloud.

None of this was fundamentally new to me, but I enjoyed hearing such ideas voiced for once, because I worship God in all that happens, in every manifestation of life, in disastrous events as well as in the smallest things. I love God in the rustle of the trees and the wind as well as in the most delicate flower, in all that is beautiful, sublime, and noble. And I also love God in Mephistopheles.

But if my God is squeezed into the form of a religion, no matter which, I can't find him. Hence my predicament every time there's a feast day. To me there's no god of the Jews, any more than there's a god of other peoples. To me there's only 'the divine per se'. But I can't pray to my God. I carry him within me, and my faith in him is a help to me – but I can't pray. Can you understand that? Whenever I've sensed this contrast between us, dear Amadé, it has tormented me and I've wanted to write about it – and this seemed the right time. And now my heart quails at the thought of your response to this confession, which has never crossed my lips before. I can only guess at how different your god is and how deep your love can be, but I beg you most earnestly, write me a few words in reply. I'm so tormented by a terrible fear that this may utterly alienate you from me – you, whom I love so much!!! . . .

Your Lilli

The Martin Buber lecture, which Lilli attended with her father at his Masonic lodge, marks an important division in the couple's religious sentiments: Lilli was perceptibly detaching herself from her religious roots, whereas Ernst was increasingly withdrawing into his Catholic world of ideas. Nevertheless, as a token of her concession to this she adorned a wall in her bedroom with a copy of a Dürer Madonna. This veneration of the Virgin accompanied and united the couple for as long as she lived. To Lilli this tradition may have been more of an expression of her love for Ernst; to Ernst it may also, from the outset, have symbolized his ideal of womanhood.

Ernst's reply evidently embodied a sympathetic response to her theological confession, and it also contained another welcome piece of news: his arduous negotiations with a view to taking over Keil's Immenhausen practice had at last been crowned with success. Lilli's letter of 18 November expressed pleasure at this news, and from now on there was no more talk of her moving to Halle.

My dear little Amadé,
    Yesterday afternoon I went to see Dr Cahen, who, after sundry 'ifs' and 'buts', finally accepted me; so on 1

December, provided I obtain Auerbach's permission, I can embark on another three months at the Hostel. To get it I must go to Ehrenfeld right away, because that's where it's best to speak to him, and Fräulein Lobbenberg just called to say today is my only chance.

So I'll at least make a start on answering your long, long letter, for which heartfelt thanks . . . I'm awfully glad the contract business is finally settled, and congratulate you very, very warmly, and Amadé will get a nice kiss for it. I'm sure it's a weight off your mind too. If you come at Christmas, please bring the contract with you – I've forgotten the precise details . . . So, now Lilli must be off. More later.

Well, Auerbach also said yes. He was very nice and asked me all about the practice and how I'd got on there. I'm immensely pleased. I'm going to the Lobbenbergs this evening. Kisch has declined, unfortunately; he had a prior engagement.

And now back to your letter. I think you should write to Father in a fortnight or so. Say that he knows how things stand between us and, since your contract business is settled, you're requesting a personal interview and wonder if 23 December would be convenient.

And when you actually speak with him, it'll be quite unnecessary to adopt any special policy or give careful consideration to what you have to say. You can safely put your cards on the table, call a spade a spade, and speak to my father exactly as you write to me. The more frankly and firmly, the better. In my father's case, I think that's the best and wisest approach.

Then there are our financial affairs, dear Amadé! From January I calculate you'll be earning between 200 and 250 marks a month after all deductions for rent, food, and so on. You'll easily be able to buy a suit and overcoat by April and pay off the desk by May. After all, I'll be getting some wedding presents from my uncles, and I'll ask for a carpet and whatever else we still need. I think we'll be able to equip a home in the course of the year, especially as I can buy kitchen utensils and suchlike considerably cheaper from the wholesalers Father deals with. So don't worry about it so much, my dear . . . And however depressed you are by all our problems and feel they're almost insurmountable, keep your chin up. We'll make it, believe me! . . .

Your Lilli

Josef and Paula Schlüchterer continued to balk a little, and Lilli had to talk them both into the interview planned for Christmas. But then, at the end of November 1925, Ernst received a formal invitation from Paula to stay with the Schlüchterers in Cologne over the Christmas holiday.

'Positively feverish with impatience'
Married with the rabbi's blessing

On 23 December 1925, Ernst asked Josef Schlüchterer for Lilli's hand in marriage. Having been thoroughly briefed by her in advance, he made no attempt to gloss over his financial circumstances but did not convey too pessimistic an impression. Thus the obligatory discussion of Ernst and Lilli's financial prospects left Josef feeling relatively satisfied. He gave the young couple his blessing.

The prospective son-in-law was barely back in Immenhausen when he wrote the Schlüchterers a polite letter thanking them for their hospitality. However, he was injudicious enough to add a few remarks that greatly upset Paula, at least, as Lilli reported on New Year's Day 1926:

> My parents received your letter but were reluctant to show it to me. I had gathered from you what it contained, and was quite absurdly upset that they tried to keep it from me. Then Father gave it to me, and a good thing too, because it caused my parents a certain amount of consternation. I fully appreciate your motives in writing as you did, but whether your frankness was wholly appropriate I tend to doubt, certainly today, because of the effect it had. Well, what's done is done, and I earnestly entreat you not to follow it up with anything in the way of an explanation or defence. That would be a mistake. Father probably understands, but Mother is so worked up about it, she had to go to bed this afternoon.

She plagues herself and me with all kinds of doubts which time alone can dispel. Mother worries about me; she fails to understand that I have to tread this path from inner necessity. To someone incapable of putting herself in my place, perhaps your revelations do sound rather cold and matter-of-fact. She can't understand that I first had – as you put it – to conquer you, and that I fought for you for years. Now she's making things very difficult for herself and me. But please *don't* go writing to her. And what of my reaction to your letter, dearest? Well, Lilli couldn't help shedding some bitter tears this New Year's Day. My old wounds did hurt a bit. But now all is well again, and a pair of happy eyes are shining through the tears . . .

Josef Schlüchterer was also disturbed by Ernst's letter, but he expressed his doubts as to whether his daughter had made the right choice in extremely diplomatic language. On 2 January 1926, in a first extant letter to his future son-in-law, he solemnly besought him to remain faithful to Lilli:

Dear Ernst,

As you see, we're helping you over the hurdle of an unfamiliar form of address by addressing you not by your official title, 'son-in-law', but, as if you were our own son, by your first name, which has become so familiar and dear to us.

If we can make up for what you have lacked from a tender age, we shall do so with joy in our hearts, in gratitude to you for rendering our precious child happy with all your love and true devotion, which she fully deserves. The whole sequence of events, which you described to us in such a lucid and unvarnished but all the more convincing and affecting manner, should guarantee that, come what may, Lilli will steadfastly, resolutely and faithfully continue along the road she has taken, perceiving it to be the right one. And our consent to your union may serve to demonstrate our firm belief that you wholeheartedly, thankfully and joyfully reciprocate and return all her love and loyalty, devotion and goodness. We have given you one of our two dearest and best possessions.

When we entered the house of God last Friday, we were met by the glorious hymn in honour of the Sabbath, the highest, holiest and most exalted day known to our religion. That hymn likens the Sabbath to a comely bride approaching her bridegroom.

From this, dear son, you may infer the respect, love and devotion with which we revere and love your bride and wife-to-be.

If you accept this as the principle that guides the whole of your life together, your hopes and desires will be fulfilled and a kindly providence will bless your union.

Your unclouded happiness and wellbeing will bestow supreme joy on, and best convey your thanks to,

Lilli's, and your, parents

The whole family showed Ernst how pleased they were at the prospect of Lilli's wedding, which was now set for August. Congratulatory messages and gifts poured in from all directions. Grandmother Schloss sent the couple a Blüthner grand piano from Halle, an uncle the handsome sum of $2000 from New York. Lilli, in her exuberance, actually offered to write Ernst a doctoral thesis. Although she dismissed a doctorate as 'nonsense', she said it couldn't hurt him to have one. If Ernst agreed, she told him in January 1926, she could have it finished by the time they got married. Then all he would have to do was come to Cologne for the oral.

Ernst refused to countenance this hoax, fortunately, so Lilli was able to spend the next few months getting a household together and participating in Cologne's social life. On 25 April, for example, she attended a party at the home of her friend Lutz Salomon:

Yesterday's party at the Salomons was rather tedious in spite of all the luxury and elegance. I never feel particularly at home in this rather superficial, impersonal company, nor, unfortunately, do I have the knack of adapting to the situation. Purely aesthetically, of course, it was a delight, what with the fabulous rooms, the wealth of flowers, cut glass and silver, and a bevy of extremely elegant, tastefully attired, and in some cases very beautiful young women! A splendid spectacle! There were thirty of us – and I and a young pianist the only ones with long hair! Also present were numerous colleagues who talked shop in a self-centred way.

Bobbed hair was coming into fashion during this period. Although Lilli temporarily held out against the spirit of the times, photographs from the early 1930s show that she, too, was wearing her hair short.

Only four days after the party at the Salomons she went to another, this time at the home of Privy Councillor Auerbach, the director of the Jewish Hostel.

It was very nice and refined in contrast to the Salomons. We enjoyed ourselves so much, it was two o'clock in the morning before we noticed, and Auerbach was still engaged in the most animated conversation. A delicious dinner, and we danced to music that came through the radio from London. At dinner I had a lawyer from the Higher Regional Court on my left and Löwenstein on my right.

Lilli still hadn't paid a single visit to her future husband in Immenhausen. Now, however, there was no escaping it. Anxious to inspect their future home, she proposed to visit Hessen in May with her mother. For economy's sake Ernst suggested that they spend the night at – of all places – the Christian Hospice in Kassel. Mother and daughter promptly declined, with thanks, and asked him to find them another hotel.

Once that question had been settled, the two women set off on a brief trip to the dreaded provinces. On 17 May, whether out of courtesy or because she was feeling rather relieved, Lilli summed up this first visit in thoroughly favourable terms:

My dear, dear Amadé,

Our postcard will by now have informed you of our arrival. We weathered the journey successfully, and found everything here as it should be, also a message from Father. The beautiful flowers have all perked up splendidly, so they're a real source of pleasure to us. Thank you again for them, and for all your other kindnesses. I expect you could tell how delighted I was to speak with you again on Sunday morning.

I'm so happy, my dear! At last I can form an impression of the surroundings in which you live and work, what your room looks like, where you spend your Thursday evenings, and so on.

All my visions of the future have now assumed tangible form. You'd gone to great lengths to ensure that Immenhausen wouldn't be a disappointment to me. It's already liveable-in, and I greatly took to Kassel. And with my parents being in Cologne, we can always go there for mental stimulation and refreshment, can't we? And once we're together in our little apartment, which you've made so nice and pretty, and for which we've already bought such splendid things, there'll be one more happy couple in the world, won't there, my great big little Amadé child, and then you'll be easier in your mind and more cheerful.

I want to help you in every way, dear Amadé, mentally and physically, and I'll be grateful for every scrap of sunshine and love you give me. And now I'm positively feverish with impatience for everything to be finished, and for us to be together at last!!

I'm especially glad you've found such a splendid person and genuine friend in Bonsmann, whose warmth and kindness thoroughly delighted me. Please give him my very best regards . . .

Earlier we spent an hour on the phone with Elsa. She

asked a host of questions, is in high spirits, and never gets around to reading or writing because she spends the whole time playing table tennis (a parlour game in English country houses!), and there's a party every night . . . My thanks to you, my dear, and a thousand loving good wishes and kisses,

Your Lilli

Lilli's forthcoming marriage introduced some new friends into her life. Among them was Dr Bonsmann, director of the Philipp-stift tuberculosis sanatorium at Immenhausen. Being one of the small town's few intellectuals, he almost automatically belonged to her new circle of acquaintances.

Meanwhile, Lilli's sister Elsa was endeavouring to get over the loss of her Hans by working as lady's companion to a wealthy family. In her case her parents had got their way – a disappointment from which she took years to recover.

To ease the financial situation, Lilli was doing one last stint as a locum in Cologne. Ernst evidently disapproved of this, to judge from a remark in her letter of 26 May:

> I'm really enjoying it again, even though I still feel rather uncertain of many things. But you needn't worry, my dear, I'm still the same old person. Your objections to women pursuing a profession are justified in some respects, but you mustn't forget that the modern education and emancipation of women have aroused a very keen desire in us for brain-work, and that many resulting conflicts are not so easily resolved. No doubt we'll discuss this again later on, won't we, dear Amadé?!!

On 12 August 1926, Lilli's dream came true: she married her beloved Amadé at her parents' home in Cologne. All that marred the occasion was another minor faux pas on Ernst's part: being unfamiliar with Jewish wedding ritual, he went down on his knees in front of the rabbi. Lilli's assembled relations briefly stared at the floor in dismay.

Years of Persecution at Immenhausen

'Your touching concern for me'
The young family

After marrying in August 1926, Lilli and Ernst spent their honeymoon in Munich, where they visited the city's museums in order to take on a little cultural fuel before settling down at Immenhausen, near Kassel.

Although the Hessian town had enjoyed municipal status for over 600 years, it was little more than an overgrown working-class village. Those of its inhabitants who did not commute to Kassel by train, to work in the factories there, earned their living on the land or at Immenhausen's glassworks. Living conditions were modest – indeed, poor – and in 1930, when the worldwide recession forced the glassworks to close and put 190 men and women out of work, the senior government administrator at Kassel proclaimed Immenhausen a disaster area. In the same year, the town council elected its first Social Democratic mayor.

The little town's economic plight impinged on Lilli and Ernst's medical practice, which they initially ran together. The flow of patients was sluggish at first, as Lilli had feared. Pregnant within a few months, she gave birth to their first child, Gerhard, on 10 September 1927. From then on, Ernst mainly practised on his own.

Lilli was soon expecting another child, which would have made the rented apartment too cramped. Her relations came to the rescue once again, enabling the young couple to finance, build, and – in the middle of the bitterly cold winter of 1928–9 – move into an estate house in Gartenstrasse. Ilse was born there on 15 January 1929.

Mounted beside the front door were two nameplates, the one on the left bearing the name of Dr Ernst Jahn, General Practitioner, and his surgery hours, the other that of Dr Lilli Jahn, General Practitioner, and her surgery hours.

They occasionally visited friends and relations, although Ernst could leave Immenhausen only when he found a locum to stand in for him. In June 1930, a Dr Janik fulfilled this function. Ernst went first to the Black Forest to see Lilli's sister Elsa, who had contracted tuberculosis, and then to Freiburg to Lilli's cousin Olga and her husband Max Mayer. Lilli, who was expecting her third child in a few weeks' time, remained at home. The couple promptly resumed their correspondence during this brief separation. On 9 June Lilli wrote to Ernst:

My Dearest,

Whitsuntide is over now, and I hope you found it as lovely and peaceful, satisfying and restful as I wanted it to be for you with all my heart. Did you see much of Elschen? What else are you planning? My dear, sorry though I am that your holiday is speeding by, I so look forward to having you back with us again.

The two days' rest have done me a lot of good. Yesterday Dr Janik had lunch and dinner with his relations in Kassel, so we only cooked simply for ourselves. I lay down for two hours after lunch, then dressed the children smartly and went for a bit of a walk with them. They were in high spirits and very well behaved, and Ilschen is already walking quite well . . .

Today was wonderful! The weather was so heavenly, we spent the whole day in the garden. At half past eight we breakfasted outdoors with the children, and I sat outside all morning. Later I was joined by Dr Janik, who – by the way – is extremely nice to the children. Then we had a very sumptuous lunch, with asparagus and pineapple and whipped cream and a glass of wine. After that I went back to bed – aren't I a good girl!! – and Dr Janik went for a walk in the woods. Fräulein Anna and I had another coffee with the children outside, and then she played with them all afternoon and – most importantly – got into our little boy's good books.

All I did was lounge in the deckchair and idle. Bonsmann had invited Dr Janik to dine at seven, so Fräulein Anna and I had supper outside and stayed there until it got too chilly for us. I haven't looked so well for a long time. Ilschen has already acquired a good tan, but it isn't very noticeable in Gerhard's case.

The practice is quiet. Only two very unimportant house calls yesterday evening, and Dr Janik dealt with those on his way back from Kassel. By the way, Herr Schmidt told me today that his wife is still far from well. She's running a very high temperature again, and a vein in her leg has now been inflamed for some days.

10 June 1930

My dear, three letters and a card from you arrived this morning. I was so pleased to receive such an abundance of lovely mail and thank you with all my heart for your touching concern for me . . .

Dear, tomorrow I shall write to Olga's Freiburg address, because I'm afraid I'll miss you at St Blasien. It's hardly worth sending newspapers, because none turned up today.

I'm glad you're going to see the Mayers. They're such dear, splendid people. I'm really fond of them and I love their straightforward, open manner. Give them my very best regards. Do you plan to look round the town a bit?

Your reports of Elschen are very reassuring. I'm glad you went for a nice drive and were able to spend quite a lot of time together. Give her my fond love and tell her about everything! I've been up the Feldberg too,

49

and I also know the Schluchsee. My dear, I so look forward to the time when we can visit the Black Forest together . . .

Enjoy yourself, my dear, sweet Amadé. All our fondest salutations and all our love and affection,

Your Lilli

Lilli's third child, Johanna, was born on 26 July 1930. Her steadily growing family seems to have made her happier than she had been for years.

She also acquired a new, close friend during the 1930s: Lotte, the daughter of her cousin Olga Mayer. Ten years her junior, Lotte read law at Freiburg and later, like Lilli, married a non-Jew, the literary historian Ernst August Paepcke. The two young women formed a special bond because of their so-called mixed marriages.

Lotte Paepcke, who became a writer after the war, referred to Lilli's fate in 1952 in her book of memoirs, *Unter einem fremden Stern* (*Under a Foreign Star*) and devoted a longish passage to the story of her 'only friend'. She began by recounting Lilli's early years and her move to the new house at Immenhausen:

A lively bustle of activity prevailed in the small rooms. Maidservant, laundress, seamstress and patients occupied the rest of the premises, and Lilli presided over everyone and everything like the cheerful, efficient house-wife she was.

She sympathetically and lovingly conformed to the self-willed ways of her clever but inwardly forever rest-less husband. In addition to running his large and demanding practice, he devoted his nights to the study of art history. A Protestant by upbringing, he was attracted to Catholicism but never quite found his way there, and constantly endeavoured, in a perpetual state of inner tension, to clarify and resolve his spiritual confusion without ever really managing to master it. Like a loving mother clasping her eldest child to her bosom, Lilli

50

soothed and allayed the all too intractable conflict within him.

Although they lived a long way from the nearest city, they owned an excellent library and enjoyed some refined company in the shape of the local clergyman, their colleagues living in the neighbourhood, and the local landowner, a highly cultivated man. They were sometimes able to go to plays and concerts, and derived fresh stimulation and entertainment from their lengthy annual holidays.

Ernst himself knew only too well that his depressive and difficult temperament often took its toll on his young family. He had become 'a prickly crustacean toward those around me', he confessed at the end of September 1931 in a letter to his former fellow student Leo Barth, then the editor of a Mannheim daily: 'I suffer from great nervous irritability – or lack of self-control – and I regret it intensely.'

In January 1932 Lilli's father died of a cerebral haemorrhage, so she now had her mother Paula to worry about as well. To make matters worse, the political outlook was darkening. Owing to the worldwide depression and the substantial gains made by the National Socialists and Communists in the Reichstag elections of September 1930, the Weimar Republic was gradually becoming ungovernable. On 9 February 1932 Lilli sent Leo and Hanne Barth, who had by now become friends of hers, a brief summary of the prevailing mood:

> We're fine. We have no reason or right to complain, and although there are, of course, times when we're particularly aware of the problems and pressures of the day, and when we worry about the future in both general and personal terms, I firmly believe that the natural course of events will extricate us, too, from these difficult times.

In fact the opposite was true. The fateful year 1933 opened at Immenhausen with some fierce political clashes. The outcome of the street fighting which took place on 13 January possessed symbolic significance: after holding a demonstration, local Social Democrats and Communists were brutally beaten up and dispersed by Immenhausen's Brownshirts, who had been reinforced by Göttingen's notorious SA-Sturm 99.

'We've had a shocking time of it!'
The National Socialists assume power

On 30 January 1933 President Hindenburg appointed Adolf
Hitler Reich Chancellor. Two days later the Reichstag was
dissolved and new elections were called for 5 March. It is
doubtful if Lilli realized at first how crucial these political
developments were. Writing to her Mannheim friends, Hanne
and Leo Barth, on 5 February, she began merely by thanking
them for their Christmas presents to her family:

My dear Hanne and Posa,
    I'm using a quiet hour this Sunday morning to start the
letter I've so often written you in my head. If I hadn't
been inhibited by a kind of fatigue and inertia, just as you
are, dear Hanne, you'd have heard from us long ago.
    Our most sincere thanks for Hanne's last dear letter,
for the card you jointly sent with Leo Diekamp, and
again, most particularly, for your kind Christmas parcel
and the letters that accompanied it. The volume of poetry
is so lovely, such a warm and affectionate greeting from
heart to heart, that I often open it and – especially during
these months – derive special pleasure from it. And I
think Amadé feels much the same . . .
    At the beginning of January I accompanied my mother
to Cologne and stayed with her for the anniversary of my
father's death. She's still there now, living at quite a
comfortable boarding-house, and she's trying to find an
apartment by the first of April. It's not easy, because

rents are still pretty high, but I'm hoping she'll find something soon and then be able to spend a few weeks with my sister at St Blasien. A holiday there would do her good.

My sister is still a source of great concern to us. This time her cure is progressing slowly, and she has already been back there for over four months. She herself finds it extremely irksome, and she chafes at being condemned to inactivity.

My five days in Cologne were very full and enjoyable. I stayed with my friend Dr Liesel Auerbach, who did a wonderful job of spoiling me . . . I paid another visit to the Wallraf-Richartz Museum, where I came across various examples of the Cologne school of painting that were quite unknown to me, and also admired two very beautiful portrait heads attributed to Grünewald. Then I went to see the rehung Schnütgen Collection, now housed in the old cuirassier barracks at Deutz, which have been extremely well converted and show it off to far better effect. There was a very mediocre exhibition of modern art at the Kunstverein. I had no idea that pictures by Peiner, Schimpf, etc. – even Nägele! – were on display in another room, and it still pains me that I missed them.

On the other hand, I was able to enjoy a particularly good concert at the Gürzenich. Best of all was a Bach flute concerto with orchestra. The violinist Jascha Heifetz, a fantastic virtuoso, played admirably but left me cold.

One wholly unalloyed pleasure was a performance of [Schiller's] 'Die Jungfrau von Orleans' with Tony van Eyck. I was surprised yet again by the beauty, richness and profundity of the play. Although rather ashamed of this old (yet new) realization, I went home happy . . . You can well imagine how I drank in and savoured the whole atmosphere of our beloved Cologne with every fibre of my being.

Our little house, just as it is, transferred with all its contents to Cologne – that would make me supremely happy! But I'm simply being too presumptuous and expecting too much of this life . . .

From time to time we have friends for dinner or are invited out, but as a rule we stay at home, and Amadé, particularly, is glad not to have to go out (except to work, of course) in these times of political agitation. There are only two extremes here, 'The National Front!' and the Left. We've been following recent events in the Kölnische Volkszeitung with some indignation. I've said to Amadé so often: 'How nice it would be if I could hear Posa's voice for once!!!' We assume, no doubt correctly, that you're exceptionally busy at present.

Amadé reads a great deal and is working hard. I expect he'll soon be an expert on German monasteries and the history of monastic orders. I greatly envy his energy and mental capacity. My days are so taken up with the house and children that I'm tired out by nightfall . . .

And now, a loving hug to you both from your affectionate Lilli

It was the extremists on both sides that enraged Lilli and Ernst. They believed that the power struggle between the National Socialists and the Communists was still undecided. Two days later, in another letter to the Barths, Ernst complained only in passing about the uncertain political situation: 'And on top of it all this Reich Chancellor, and this attitude towards the Jews – incredibile [sic].' The situation was indeed incredible. Fundamentally, however, Lilli and Ernst still had no idea what to make of current events.

The fire at the Reichstag on 27 February triggered an enormous wave of arrests, mainly of Communists, who were the alleged perpetrators. But even the Reichstag elections of 5 March, in which the Nazis made substantial gains, failed to clarify the situation entirely. In little Immenhausen the Left again won appreciably more votes than the Right, and in the local elections a week later the Social Democrats actually maintained their majority on the town council, winning six of the eleven seats.

But then the Nazis asserted themselves. The Act of Enablement, which the Reichstag approved on 23 March 1933 despite the opposition of the Social Democrats, stripped parliament of its authority. Hitler's cabinet now possessed almost unlimited powers, and it took only another two days to bring this home to Immenhausen's Social Democrats and Communists: Brownshirts forced their way into the houses and apartments of some twenty left-wingers and hauled their victims off to a former button factory in the neighbouring town of Hofgeismar. There, after being tried by a bogus court, they were beaten up and tortured throughout the night.

The next morning Ernst Jahn treated these men, some of whom were in a bad way. Lilli was thus, for the first time, brought face to face with the consequences of the Nazi reign of terror in her own home. In addition, anti-Semitic outrages had occurred in neighbouring Kassel. The windows of several Jewish-owned shops were smashed, and squads of Brownshirts beat up Jewish shopkeepers, lawyers and bankers, one of whom actually died of his injuries.

Lilli also received some bad news from her relations in Freiburg. Max Mayer, her cousin Olga's husband, a Jewish leather merchant and Social Democrat town councillor, had been arrested. Together with all the other SPD councillors, he had been imprisoned on 20 March and was not released until the 30th.

Great agitation reigned in the Jahn household. It was clear that the Nazis were systematically trying to intimidate their political opponents. This was made even clearer by the so-called 'Judenboykott' on 1 April, a nationwide boycott of all Jewish businesses, lawyers and doctors imposed from ten o'clock in the morning onwards. The inhabitants of Immenhausen, who did not adhere too closely to the terms of this campaign, extended it to Ernst's practice. He was thus, for the first time, publicly penalized for having married a Jew. The next day, already under considerable strain in the days preceding the birth of her fourth child, Lilli informed her friends Hanne and Leo of what had happened:

Dear Ones,

Just a few lines to tell you how delighted we were by the good news of Hanne and your baby. We think of you so often and so fondly! Special thanks to you, dear Hanne, for your thoughtful card. It did me good to know that you also take such an interest in the little, everyday things in life. But since 1 March I've had a new home help who has settled down well and is hard-working and conscientious. And yesterday evening the nurse arrived, because our child is due next week . . . We're all well, the children are fit and behaving themselves, and I can be happy with the way things are going at home!

But otherwise we've had a shocking time of it! Can you imagine how I'm feeling? Can you understand how heavy-hearted I am and how bitterly hurtful it all is? So much so that it's utterly blighting my joy at the prospect of the baby!!

Just imagine, they also boycotted my Amadé because he has a Jewish wife! I can't find the words to tell you how profoundly shocked I was. And of course we are now very fearful: Will there be other repercussions on us? We don't dare to speculate . . .

All the very best, and spare an occasional thought for your very depressed and isolated friend, who misses you more than ever,

Lilli did not sign her name to the letter, but Ernst added an imploring 'Christus vincet nonetheless, Sincerely yours, Amadé.'

Christus vincet, Christ conquers . . . Lilli, who lacked this faith in God, was at least as distressed as Ernst by the humiliation to which he had been subjected, and she was powerless to help, especially as Eva, her third daughter, was born a few days later on 10 April.

Before long her nameplate on the right of the front door had to be taken down. After that, so as not to give offence, Lilli refrained from practising her profession. Nor could she hope for any political protection. At the end of March, Immenhausen's Social Democrat mayor had been compelled to vacate his office in favour of a National Socialist.

Lilli's sister was also affected by the harassment of the Jews. Having studied chemistry at Cologne and obtained her doctorate, Elsa had been hoping to pursue an academic career, but Jewish scientists were now tolerated at universities only in exceptional cases. This put paid to her ambitions.

Leo and Hanne were quick to respond to Lilli's letter of 2 April and offer her a little consolation. Lilli replied on 10 May:

Dear Hanne and Leo,

Heartfelt thanks for your good wishes on the birth of our baby . . . for the booklet on the Jesuit Church, which greatly invigorated me during my confinement, and above all for your kind words, those tokens of your sympathy and love, which did my wounded heart so much good. I'm quickly endorsing what Amadé has written and ask you myself, most sincerely, to bring Ursula and spend Whitsun with us if you possibly can. Can you imagine what that would mean to us? We should be so grateful . . .

Our little Eva is progressing well . . . The older ones watch every washing and feeding procedure with great interest and simply couldn't do without their little sister now. Other than that, of course, they're far too busy with their own activities, especially as they spend the whole day outdoors and are supremely interested – our boy in particular – in the SA and SS. They march and drill and favour us from dawn to dusk with the Horst-Wessel song. We let the nurse go last Saturday, for certain reasons, so I've been looking after the baby myself, and my days are naturally very full. A good thing too, because all else – everything congenial and pleasurable –

has been thrust into the background by events, and our thoughts continuously revolve around the same subject . . . Ever your devoted

Lilli

It was true that Gerhard, who had only just turned six, had found a small imperial flag somewhere. In company with his sisters Ilse and Johanna, he now strutted proudly round the garden, blithely singing the Nazis' notorious marching song.

'The fate imposed on us'
Lilli and her family are ostracized

Having passed her first public examination in law at the end of March, Lilli's friend Lotte Paepcke was then debarred 'on racial grounds' from becoming a civil service probationer. In July the Nazis put her in prison because of her membership of the Red Students' Group. She languished there for three weeks until a friend of her father's, a non-Jewish lawyer, vouched for her and she formally abjured her communistic ideas. On her release she travelled by way of Zurich to Rome. Emigrating to Italy was out of the question, however, because her future husband, Ernst August, could neither speak the language nor find employment there as a German literary historian. In January 1934 the couple returned to Germany and hastily got married. It was foreseeable even then that the Nazis would sooner or later prohibit mixed marriages.

Meanwhile, everyday life at Immenhausen had undergone a complete change. Widely respected until shortly before, Ernst and his family were all of a sudden shunned and ostracized by the local dignitaries. Here is another extract from Lotte Paepcke's memoirs:

> Although they regarded the doctor and his family with a certain affection born of dependence, the townsfolk could not resist looking on with a smug, voluptuous shudder as a member of the prosperous upper class was demeaned by the state and they themselves . . . rose in status as a result . . .

One day the local landowner appeared at the surgery with a minor cut and asked the doctor to dress it for him. Purely in passing, as one friend to another, he wanted to make it clear that he and his wife would, alas, be temporarily compelled to sever relations with the doctor and his family. 'You understand, my dear doctor, it's just a formality, and doesn't in any way affect our high esteem for you and your lady wife. In my exposed position, however, I simply can't afford . . .' The doctor understood. With a courteous bow, he escorted the landowner to the door.

Soon afterwards a colleague and neighbour telephoned to say that he had a few professional matters to discuss and would be passing by in his car. No, he couldn't, unfortunately, spare the time for a congenial evening together, he could only drop in for a quarter of an hour. It was just enough time in which to inform his colleague that, sadly, their respective families' friendly relations had been disrupted by the political situation, and that he owed it to his own and his family's existence to back off. 'Knowing me as you do, my esteemed colleague, you must realize that nothing could ever detract from my respect for you and your lady wife, but circumstances . . .' The doctor got the message. With a courteous bow, he saw his colleague to the door.

Six months later the clergyman came to say that he had now received his third warning from Party headquarters, and that their pleasant chats at the doctor's home must unfortunately cease . . .

The doctor politely escorted his last visitor to the door. Now they were very much alone.

Lotte was describing episodes from her friend Lilli's life in literary form. Although the snippets of dialogue are probably authentic in tenor only, events in Gartenstrasse must have followed this or a similar course.

Contemporary observers also recall citizens of Immenhausen

taking part in isolated outrages. As early as 1933, Brownshirts surrounded the Jahn house on the pretext of having to 'protect' the Jewess Lilli Jahn from public resentment. However, the Party's well-organized 'national fury' was probably far more intense than any genuine antipathy felt by the small town's inhabitants.

When Lilli left the house to go shopping, so it is said in Immenhausen today, she steadfastly kept her eyes lowered to spare others the embarrassment of having to bid her good day. Very few people breached this barrier of isolation and went up to her of their own accord; most cared little about the personal fate of this stigmatized woman and her family. In other respects they were dependent on Ernst Jahn's medical expertise. Despite all this official harassment, his practice was doing better and better.

In 1933 Lilli's sister Elsa emigrated to England. She had no ties, her academic career was at an end, and tuberculosis had compelled her to undertake several lengthy cures. She went to Birmingham, but her German qualifications were not recognized there, so she had to repeat her school-leaver's examination and her academic training in a hurry, this time concentrating on pharmacology.

Elsa paid her sister a few visits from England, but Lilli was becoming more and more isolated. Of her friends, two couples initially continued to maintain contact from afar: the lawyer Leo Diekamp and his wife Lise in Bochum and, more especially, Leo and Hanne Barth in Mannheim. They exchanged letters a few times a year and visited the Jahns during the holidays. On 4 February 1934 Lilli informed the Barths of the current situation at Immenhausen:

> My dear, dear Leo and Hanne,
>   This time we're deeply in your debt, and I sincerely apologize for our silence, which verges on the discourteous. We still haven't thanked you properly for your sweet and affectionate good wishes at Christmas and New Year, but we've hardly come to rest, let alone collected our thoughts, since then. Amadé and I are both

worn out: Amadé by his busy and tiring practice – thank God for that, I have to say – and I by all kinds of housewifely exigencies and fairly frequent ailments affecting various children.

The only one that still worries us is our little Gerhard. He's very frail, not at all robust, and pale and thin . . . Last Wednesday I took him to school for the first time. I didn't feel too happy about it – you'll understand, I'm sure. He himself was very interested, but one could also sense a certain reserve on his part. Back home, without being asked, he suddenly came out with a lucid and accurate description of the three pictures on the classroom wall. Even his daddy, who's very critical of the children and sparing with his praise, couldn't but register this with satisfaction.

Anyway, he isn't – insofar as one tell at this stage – the 'collective type'. In later years, if his character continues to develop along these lines, he'll probably accept with equanimity the fact that he's debarred from marching with the 'brown columns'.

Ilschen and Hannele would like nothing better than to go to school with their brother. They're fit, strong, and high-spirited. Ilschen a proud little housewife, Hannele a little imp. Eva is a law unto herself. If you saw her now, Leo, you'd never believe she's the same placid, contented child she was last summer. The other three were never as wild and temperamental . . .

Christmas was lovely, really lovely. The children's touching faith and radiant happiness lightened and rejoiced our hearts too, rendering us richer and more receptive to the mutual affection and love we constantly have to build up as a bulwark against 'the outside'.

I think I've simmered down a little since the autumn. The wound we've been dealt is still there, and it smarts, but I'm trying, if only for the sake of my husband and our children, to view the fate imposed on us from a higher standpoint. There may also be a good side to the fact that we're now compelled to come to grips with questions which we were once too lazy, or perhaps too cowardly, to acknowledge. But those are things that don't really belong in a letter – we should be able to discuss them quietly together.

We had some quiet time to talk while Lise Diekamp was with us. What a boon that was – what an oasis in our otherwise lonely, isolated existence! And what a splendid person she is . . . We can now, for the first time, fully appreciate what being together with Lise means to you too.

My sister has now passed her school-leaver's examination in London and is continuing to study pharmacology in Birmingham. Her health is still a worry, however. We're expecting Mother to stay for a few weeks before long.

Our ostracism here in Immenhausen is now more complete than anyone could have dreamt. SA headquarters has forbidden Bonsmann to cross our threshold!! The fact that he obeyed this prohibition requires no comment. Personally, I very seldom leave the house. How are things with you, my dears? How is Leo's mother doing? We often think of her and wish her well. And is Leo's life a little less hectic? We follow all the developments that specially affect you both with the greatest interest. We found Cardinal F's Advent sermons very comforting and enjoyable. I wish we could discuss those too . . . Don't repay evil with evil, but write to us again soon. Heartfelt good wishes from your devoted

Lilli

The five Advent sermons delivered prior to Christmas 1933 by Cardinal Faulhaber of Freising were construed at the time as signs of opposition to the National Socialists' racial mania. In reality, however, Faulhaber's sole intention was to defend the Old Testament as part of a common Christian and Judaic tradition. Far from publicly opposing political discrimination against the German Jews, he later made common cause with Hitler.

Lilli's social ostracism was exacerbated by numerous personal disappointments. Among those who severed contact with the Jahn family was the man who had so impressed her during her first visit to Immenhausen, Ernst's friend Dr Bonsmann. He did so out of political conviction as well as personal opportunism. As early as July 1934 a letter written by the Party's district director at Hofgeismar described him as a 'senior SA [Brownshirt] officer'. At Immenhausen, Bonsmann had attained the rank of 'Sanitätsobersturmführer' (medical first lieutenant).

In the anonymity of a big city like Cologne, Lilli's Jewish origins might have been quite unknown to many of her neighbours. In a small town like Immenhausen, on the other hand, everyone knew of them, so those who failed to observe the politically imposed boycott could expect to attract sanctions of their own.

Lilli's complete outward adaptation to a Christian family life was no help at all. The children had received a Protestant baptism and were later confirmed in succession. The Jahns hung up an Advent wreath every year as a matter of course, just as they decorated a Christmas tree and sang carols. Lilli even embroidered an elaborate Christmas cloth for the family dinner table.

She never accompanied her children to church, however, and sometimes attended the synagogue in Kassel on her own. A Jewish prayerbook in a silver cover sat on her bedside table, and her children occasionally saw her saying prayers at night. And once a year, on the anniversary of her father's death, a candle would burn on her desk for twenty-four hours.

It almost seems that her hitherto tenuous attachment to the Jewish faith had grown stronger as a result of her isolation at Immenhausen.

Meanwhile Ernst was drawing away from Protestantism. His Catholic mother had secretly, and against his Protestant father's wishes, taken him and his sister to Catholic Mass. The more his marriage to Lilli cut him off from colleagues, friends and acquaintances, the more he diverged into the orbit of Catholicism, which to him seemed sound and morally firm. A regular reader of *Das Hochland*, he cherished a great and certainly not fortuitous enthusiasm for literary works by Catholic converts. One of his favourite authors, as evidenced by his letter to the Barths dated 27 February 1934, was the cultural critic Theodor Haecker, who had converted to Catholicism in 1921, and whose works, despite their very conservative outlook, were not allowed to be printed in the Third Reich from 1938 onwards. Another was the Norwegian Nobel laureate Sigrid Undset, likewise a convert to Catholicism, who wrote the medieval epic *Olav Audunsson*.

Dear Hanne, dear Leo,

Many thanks for kindly lending me the books, which I'm finally returning to you. These last few weeks I've been reading 'Olav Audunsson'. It's art of the very highest quality, possessing a realism and spiritual greatness and profundity such as can only, it is clear, derive from the forces of religion. Books of that kind and Theodor Haecker's ethos, 'Das Hochland', and our art books – those are our guests and helpmates in this era, which deems it right to treat people like us as abhorrent and to be shunned. It's so grotesque that any discussion of the fact seems pointless. We parents would bear this fate . . . with some equanimity, in the knowledge that we have committed absolutely no crime against our nation and state, but it all weighs heavy on us because of our children. They will be protected – if God is willing – for as long as we live, but thereafter . . .

Lise Diekamp's visit was a great and undeserved blessing which we gratefully accepted. Our awareness of our attachment to you and to them [the Diekamps] is now even more of a support and comfort to us.

So how are you, your parents, and Ursel and Vroni? . . . I would so much like to send Lilli to you, but something always intervenes. All the children have had

Lilli Jahn, 1918.

Lilli and her sister Elsa in carnival costumes, c. 1903.

Lilli and Elsa in Cologne, 1905.

Lilli's mother Paula (*to the right behind the bridegroom*), at the wedding of her brother, Julius Schloss, to Lotte Kirschbaum-Springer, at the Hotel Adlon, Berlin, in 1911. Lilli's uncle, Dr Josef Schloss, is on the extreme right of the front row.

Lilli's father, Josef Schlüchterer.

Lilli's mother Paula (*second from right*) attending a Christmas party at a military hospital during the First World War.

Lilli in the summer of 1916.

Lilli (*right*) and Elsa (*left*) with Frau M. Wrede and Helmuth Wrede
at Schierke in the Harz Mountains, August 1918.

Lilli (*third from right*) with her medical colleagues at the Jewish Home for the Sick and Infirm in Cologne, c. 1924.

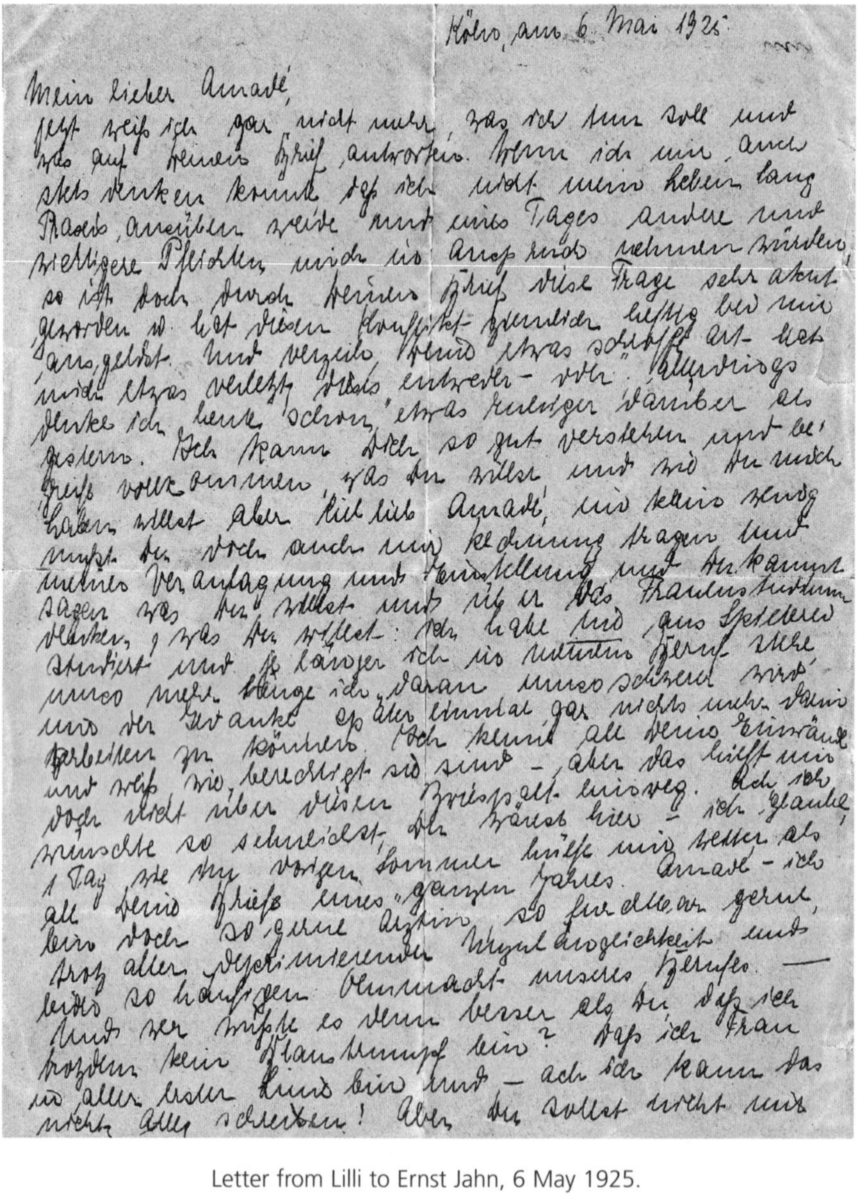

Köln, am 6. Mai 1925

Mein lieber Amadé,
jetzt weiß ich gar nicht mehr, was ich tun soll und was auf Deinen Brief antworten. Wenn ich mir auch stets denken konnte, daß ich nicht mein Leben lang Praxis ausüben werde und eines Tages andere und wichtigere Pflichten mich in Anspruch nehmen würden, so ist doch durch Deinen Brief diese Frage sehr akut geworden u. hat diesen Konflikt ziemlich heftig bei mir ausgelöst. Und verzeih, Freund, etwas schroff ist – hat mich etwas verletzt, dies „entweder – oder". Allerdings denke ich heute schon etwas ruhiger darüber als gestern. Ich kann Dich so gut verstehen und begreife vollkommen, was Du willst und wie Du mich haben willst, aber lieb lieb Amadé, wie [illegible] mußt Du doch auch mir Rechnung tragen und meiner Veranlagung und Einstellung und Du kannst sagen, was Du willst und [illegible] das Frauenstudium [illegible], was Du willst: ich habe nicht aus Spielerei studiert und je länger ich in meinem Beruf stehe umso mehr hänge ich daran, umso schwerer wird mir der Gedanke, später einmal gar nicht mehr darin arbeiten zu können. Ich kenne all Deine Einwände und weiß, wie berechtigt sie sind – aber das hilft mir doch nicht über diesen Zwiespalt hinweg. Ach ich wünschte, so [illegible], Du wärest hier – ich glaube, 1 Tag wie im vorigen Sommer hülfe mir besser als all Deine Briefe eines „ganzen Jahres". Amadé – ich bin doch so gerne Ärztin, so furchtbar gern, trotz aller deprimierenden Unzulänglichkeit und leider so häufigen Ohnmacht unseres Berufes. — Und wer wüßte es denn besser als Du, daß ich trotzdem kein Blaustrumpf bin? Daß ich Frau in aller erster Linie bin und – ach ich kann das nicht alles schreiben! Aber Du sollst nicht mit

Letter from Lilli to Ernst Jahn, 6 May 1925.

Lilli and Ernst Jahn, 1926.

Lilli with her children Gerhard and Ilse, c. 1929/30.

Ernst Jahn with Gerhard and Ilse outside their home in Immenhausen in 1931.
Flanking the front door are the plates bearing Ernst's and Lilli's surgery hours.

Gerhard and Ilse outside the house at Immenhausen in 1936.
Lilli's plate had by then been removed.

Gerhard, Ilse and Johanna, May 1933.

Ernst Jahn's letter to Hanne and Leo Barth, 27 February 1934.

Elsa Schlüchterer with her godson Gerhard Jahn at Immenshausen, August 1936.

tonsillitis, one after another, and Lilli herself has a bad sore throat and a temperature. Tomorrow we change maidservants, then we're expecting Lilli's mother to stay. Will we see each other this year? . . .

A thousand good wishes from

Your Amadé

Lilli, too, expressed more and more misgivings about her children's uncertain prospects. She confided in a letter to the Barths on 16 May 1934 that she was very depressed by 'fears for their future'. National Socialist terminology labelled her children 'half-Jews', which excluded them on principle from almost every profession and opportunity in life. Although Gerhard, Ilse and Johanna would be permitted to go on to secondary schools in Kassel in the next few years, it was foreseeable that their paths through life would sooner or later be blocked. There was no question of Gerhard's joining the Hitler Youth, and Ilse and Johanna were denied admission to meetings of the local equivalent for girls, the 'Jungmädel', after only a few weeks. Lilli's children chafed at their outsider's role. At roll call in the school yard they always stood to one side, the only pupils not in uniform.

'In his last speech, Herr Goebbels once more ensured that we don't pitch our expectations too high,' Lilli noted in her letter of 16 May. A few months later, on 25 October, she had some 'rather disagreeable news' from Cologne and Birmingham to impart:

It's impossible at present for my mother to send my sister any money, not even for her college fees, let alone for living expenses. There are no grounds for it, either culturally or from the aspect of foreign policy – that was the official ruling. What now? We're very concerned. Isn't this immensely, monstrously unjust? First they deprive us of every opportunity at home, and now they prevent us from making a living abroad.

With this letter Ernst enclosed some material published by the Party's 'Department of Racial Policy'. The Jahns and their

friends were still trying to detect some kind of logic in the Nazis'
reign of terror. Growing outside pressure was clearly welding
Ernst and Lilli more closely together at this period. Lilli often
mentioned her husband's little tokens of affection, for instance in
the following account of her thirty-fifth birthday addressed to
the Barths on 22 March 1935:

> Amadé spoilt me again so much. He conjured up a whole
> garden of spring flowers and gave me some lovely books,
> among other things . . . The children have already made
> the very most of these first fine spring days – the weather
> agrees with them splendidly. Yesterday Amadé and I
> went for our first walk across the fields, and delighted in
> the catkins and the early skylarks. We're both worn out
> and much in need of a holiday. It isn't just the work that
> fatigues us. So many things keep weighing us down, not
> least our great concern for the children's future. We're
> also, of course, in need of a change and some mental
> stimulation.

Lilli sent similar lamentations to her Mannheim friends at ever
shorter intervals. 'Our uncertainty about the future is agonizing.
Believe me, we're very, very depressed and disheartened,' she
wrote on 20 July 1935. And on 23 August: 'There are times
when I don't know where to find the strength to bear it all.'

Political pressures were accompanied by various personal
problems: Ernst was overworked, Lilli was finding it ever harder, as a Jewess, to engage nursemaids and housemaids, and the
children had countless ailments, some of them serious. Johanna,
by now five years old, was a particular source of concern. She
suffered badly from asthma, which twice confined her for several
months in a children's sanatorium. But not even that was
straightforward. Her parents had each time to ascertain in
advance whether their 'non-Aryan' daughter would be admitted
at all.

The summer of 1935 did inject a little variety into their lives:
Lilli's sister came over from England and stayed for several

weeks. Quickly recognizing that the family's position was almost hopeless, Elsa worked out a rescue plan with Ernst and Lilli in which a central role was to be played by Ernst's half-sister, Grete Jahn de Rodriguez Mateo, who lived in Madrid. Grete was married to a Spanish journalist named Alfonso de Rodriguez Mateo, who was probably employed at this time by Madrid's Department of Education and wielded a certain amount of influence. Elsa hoped that this might be of help to the family.

Mail in Germany was censored, so she waited until she was back in England before writing to Grete Jahn. This is the letter she sent her on 29 August 1935:

Dear Frau Jahn de Rodriguez Mateo,

My sister and brother-in-law, Herr and Frau Ernst Jahn of Immenhausen, have asked me to send you their warmest regards from here, and to give you a detailed account of them and the situation in Germany. As you're probably aware, mail in Germany is very strictly censored, so it's impossible, when writing from there, to describe conditions openly, and Lilli and Ernst earnestly beg you, when you reply, not to make any reference to the contents of this letter, but simply to answer my questions without comment.

Conditions in Germany have deteriorated to such an extent that your brother is seriously worried about his livelihood. Being married to a Jew, he is constantly subjected to slander. His colleagues in the district communicate with him by phone, and only when absolutely necessary. He cannot join the NS [National Socialist] Medical Association, and the doctor from a neighbouring village has been enlisted to treat children at the NS kindergarten and women members of the NS Public Welfare Organization. In short, efforts are being made to exclude him wherever possible.

Socially, the couple are completely isolated. Even loyal friends in Mannheim and Bochum have now been compelled to distance themselves from the Jahns for fear of endangering their own livelihoods – both couples are active members of the Catholic movement.

I can't tell you what Lilli and Ernst are going through in spirit and how they are suffering from these incessant slanders, nor the human greatness with which they are bearing their incredibly hard lot. It's heartbreaking to see how these two people strive to support and console each other, and, above all, how all their efforts are directed towards easing the lot of their children.

It is also consideration and responsibility for the children that has made them stick it out until now, for Ernst cannot abandon his hitherto profitable practice before he is certain of being able to make a new life abroad. It seems to be German government policy to gradually cut the ground from under the feet of all Jews, non-Aryans, and people related to Jews by marriage, thereby prompting them to leave the country.

Permit me to give you some details of the Germans' unbridled behaviour. There isn't a village or small town in the whole of Hessen where you won't find notices bearing venomous inscriptions such as 'Jews Not Wanted Here' or shops displaying placards reading 'No Goods Sold To Jews'.

A good friend of Ernst and Lilli who was a doctor in a small neighbouring town – he's a Jew married to a Catholic – has been remanded in custody for eight weeks, allegedly for violating Aryan girls and women with the aid of hypnotism. As witnesses for the prosecution they've scraped together an epileptic and a woman who has been in a lunatic asylum for years, and they're trying to drum up further witnesses by sending the local policeman from patient to patient to question them. In today's Germany, any statement can be had for money! And there isn't a word of truth in the whole story! But those are the ways and means whereby they're trying to destroy every last Jewish livelihood.

I tell you all this to show you how imperative it is for

Ernst to make a new life abroad, and to make it clear to you how entitled he is to fear for his livelihood.

The purpose of my letter is to ask you, on Ernst and Lilli's behalf, if it might be possible for Ernst to find employment in Spain through your and your husband's connections. He would naturally prefer to obtain a position as a doctor, but he would also be willing, painful for him though this would be, to work in another capacity. He hopes that your husband may enable him to secure a post at a large hospital or obtain permission for him to settle in Spain. The fact that his patients remain loyal to him, and that his practice continues to prosper in spite of all the agitation, may demonstrate to you that he is a competent and reliable doctor. But the uncertain and precarious nature of his livelihood, and the spiritual humiliations to which they are both being exposed, have prompted him to give serious consideration to the idea of leaving Germany.

I returned to England yesterday to continue my studies. Although our life over here is very difficult and full of hardship, I'm happy to be out of Germany. I spent two weeks at Immenhausen, and although we enjoyed a harmonious time together, it was overshadowed by the intense pressure that weighs us all down. The children have come on splendidly. They really are the only pleasure Ernst and Lilli have left, but we're very worried about their future as well . . .

Forgive me if I have depressed you by writing this letter, but I should be only too happy if it were in your power to help Ernst and Lilli. And I would ask you again to make no allusions to this letter in your response, but simply to discuss what chances there are of their making a new life with you in Spain. You would get Ernst and Lilli into the greatest trouble if you so much as mentioned the ordeal they're undergoing.

I also spoke with your sister Lore and her two children this year. She was back in Herzhausen am Edersee, and we and the three older children went to see her from Immenhausen – but not before Lore had been forced to inquire whether we non-Aryans would be served lunch at the hotel! That's what things have come to in this Germany of ours! . . .

Please convey my respects to your husband, although we haven't met, and please don't take it amiss that I've written to you so frankly.

With warmest regards, yours very sincerely,

Elsa Schlüchterer

Grete Jahn's response is not on record, but the plan evidently came to nothing. Alfonso de Rodriguez Mateo fled to the South of France with members of the Republican government when Franco assumed power. He later returned to Spain, lured there by the promise of an amnesty, but was promptly detained and, according to his brother, murdered by the Fascists.

Elsa, who refused to give up, found some friends in England who were prepared to vouch for the Jahn family. Dr John Henry Crosskey and his wife Evelyn, two wealthy physicians belonging to Birmingham's upper crust, undertook to send an affidavit to colleagues in Germany, and Evelyn Crosskey, who was related to the British premier, Neville Chamberlain, successfully lobbied a relief committee for German refugees.

This removed all official obstacles and rendered emigration possible, but Ernst refused to leave. His Immenhausen practice was doing so well, in spite of all the Nazis' harassment, that making a fresh start in England struck him as too risky and arduous. As for Lilli, she was naturally unwilling to go on her own, still less without her children.

Before long she was Immenhausen's only Jewish inhabitant. In 1933 the little town had been home to two Jewish shopkeepers and their families: the grocer Bernhard Friedemann, his wife Johanna, and their three children – the Friedemanns maintained loose social contacts with the Jahns – and the chemist Max Goldin. Both families were regularly checked on by the authorities. The mayor had to send the district administrator in

Hofgeismar a monthly political report which also covered the town's Jewish residents. They themselves never gave any cause for reproach, unlike the rest of the inhabitants, who did not always toe the Party line. Both shops were supposed to have been boycotted, but the mayor conceded in November 1934 that 'once again, more Christians are shopping at the Friedemanns'. As time went by, however, the Jewish families were compelled to abandon their businesses. The Goldins emigrated to Palestine in 1934, the Friedemanns in 1937.

Lilli never appeared in the mayor's reports, being still protected by her marriage to Ernst.

She was profoundly depressed by the feeling that all her friends were gradually deserting her. 'The only close acquaintances we have left are off to South Africa in the middle of January – a very palpable loss, because then we'll be completely isolated here,' she wrote to the Barths on 2 December 1935.

The Jahns' growing isolation also affected their children, whose status as 'outsiders' could no longer be ignored. The older they became the more questions they asked, so their parents felt they owed them an explanation. In the spring of 1938 – when Gerhard was ten years old, Ilse nine, Johanna seven, and Eva five – Lilli and Ernst strove to make it clear to them why the Nazis found their origins objectionable. Lilli informed her Mannheim friends of this on 16 April 1938:

> We've now told them the truth about their origins and their special status within the 'national community'. It passed off without any great emotional upset, thank God, and they're trying, to the best of their childish abilities, to understand these things and jointly bear our common lot. I'm glad we've reached this stage, although it changes nothing.

After attending Immenhausen's primary school for only three years, Ilse now moved on to the Jakob-Grimm secondary school in Kassel, where she had her first taste of political harassment. 'In Ilschen's case,' Lilli wrote to Hanne Barth on 23 August

1938, 'the hurtfulness and discrimination I've been dreading are now making their appearance.' She still hoped to put a stop to it 'by vigorously protesting to the principal' – but she was deluding herself, as it soon turned out. Ilse and, before long, Johanna were regularly subjected to anti-Semitic intimidation and derision by teachers faithful to the Party line.

'The Jewish grandmother'
A tribute to Lilli's cousin Olga

By enacting the Nuremberg Laws in September 1935, the National Socialists had systematized their racial mania in an absurd manner. These statutes embodied a whole list of discriminatory measures aimed not only at German Jews but at so-called 'Mischlinge' (racial hybrids). Lilli's family was as much affected by them as that of her friend Lotte and every other Jewish-Christian family in the Third Reich. The Nazis precisely defined who was to be exposed to what forms of discrimination. Your grandparents' origins were the factor that clinched your membership of the 'Aryan race'. A Jewish grandmother classified you as a Mischling Grade II, two Jewish grandparents as a Mischling Grade I, and thus as a 'half-Jew'. 'Jewish grandmother' became a standard term. Those 'penalized' by it were not members of the Aryan master race and had to endure limitations on their civil rights that became more and palpable with every passing year.

Lotte's son Peter was born into this lunatic environment in 1935, when the Paepckes were still living in Freiburg. Three years later Lotte's husband Ernst August was transferred to Bielefeld, and his young family had to accompany him there. On 9 May 1938 Peter's grandfather, Max Mayer, made their impending separation the occasion for writing him a long letter. Being only three years old, Peter would naturally have been unable, as yet, to read his grandfather's heartfelt and perceptive remarks. Max doubtless intended his letter for other eyes, for instance those of Ernst August, his non-Jewish son-in-law, whose fortitude and strength of character were to prove of ever-increasing importance. In fact Max Mayer never sent the letter. He did not entrust it to his daughter and son-in-law until 1948, ten years later, by which time it had become a historical document.

It is doubtful whether Lilli knew of this letter, but absolutely certain that she would have endorsed every word of it. After the war it became an icon in the Mayer, Nördlinger and Schlüchterer family circles, testifying as it does to the German-Jewish self-confidence that characterized many assimilated Jews during the first third of the twentieth century.

My dear grandson Peter,

A few days ago, on 3 May, you turned three. You have hitherto been the light and daily delight of my life and that of your grandmother Olga. You owe this statement not only to the natural love of grandparents for their grandchildren, but to our sympathetic and knowledge-able participation in your awakening, your steady ad-vance into a world of impressions, your instinct for play and the directions it can take, and the development of your character. That is how we have come to know our boy Peter's nature and disposition, and that is how we should like to accompany you further on your way.

And we, your grandmother Olga and I, enjoy your love in return. It has not been wheedled out of you with chocolate, nor by pampering or other forms of bribery. Nor does it exist only in our imagination; it is real. You still regard us as key figures, recipients of your radiant smiles. You still take an interest in us. We have yet to become elderly supernumeraries. That is how matters stand today, 9 May 1938. Nothing will ever affect the loving bond between us. However, I wish to speak to you of two events that have occurred almost simultaneously.

The first is the regrettable probability that your dear father's firm is going to transfer him from here to Bielefeld, and that he, your mother Lotte and you will therefore be leaving us. This will be decided within the next ten days. If it comes to it, we – we and your parents – will find ourselves deprived of a wonderful family life founded on absolute harmony and mutual devotion. Although our physical separation will not affect this, we shall no longer be able to enjoy and contribute to it as we have until now. Daily experience of its joys will be replaced by exchanges of letters and the annual holiday visit. However, such separations are normal in all sections of the population.

The second event, which took place on your third birthday, is the one that has occasioned this letter:

Yesterday, 8 May 1938, you were baptized in the chapel of the Lutheran church in Stadtstrasse, Freiburg. Your parents had informed us of their intention in advance. It came as a shock to me in my Jewishness, because the latter – previously no more than an accident of birth which I never denied but made light of – has become my stronghold during these last few years of persecution. I saw you going off to be christened from their balcony. But I promptly came to the conclusion that your father's motives were apt, not to say compelling. At present, in this German era of mass humanity, a standard is demanded of every German. He requires a number, a pigeonhole, a category, an identifying mark; he must fit into some subcommunity. I have no desire to analyse the type of person which this modern, standardized German becomes. I shall also refrain from pointing out the route opened up for you by baptism and, therefore, inclusion. In any case, a young person cannot be guided by his grandfather in questions to be posed and answered by a new generation.

But there is one matter on which you must listen to my voice, and on which I desire to be heard. Listen to me, my grandson Peter! For five years now, Jews in Germany have been subjected to a relentless process of expulsion from the body politic. After years of preparatory agitation by the party that sustains it, the government of the

Third Reich has postulated – and invested that postulate with the force of law – that the Jews constitute a foreign body within the nation, and one that is inhibiting the German nation from legitimately affirming its status as a chosen people. This people, it is said, needs to be cleansed and liberated from Jewish members and elements.

In fulfilment of this theory, which is dressed up as an 'ideology', an orgy of racial hatred has been instituted, together with a process whereby Jewish persons are subjected to total and systematic disqualification. The entire Party machine, the press, vocational training, broadcasting, official propaganda, the political education of the young, the whole of national life – all have been harnessed to the task of stripping Jews of their good name and social acceptability, regardless of personal standing. They are being ousted from their homes and livelihoods and compelled to emigrate destitute of means, and the belief in their human inferiority is being duly incorporated in the Aryan world of ideas.

This is not the place to describe the tragic fate of those affected, nor to defend them in objective terms. Confronting them are the 'Aryans', some of whom readily accept this persecution of the Jews and mindlessly recite the slogans supplied by propagandists. To a very large extent, however, people reject this persecution, aware of the falsity and injustice of such slogans, but unable to assist their victims.

To complete his dissociation from the Jew and legitimize his place beneath the Aryan roof, the Aryan citizen has been awarded a 'certificate of Aryan descent'. No stage in a civil career can now be traversed without proof of half, three-quarters, or full Aryan status. In order to obtain this conclusive legitimation, people in Germany are currently procuring certificates of Aryan descent and family trees.

And it is about your own family tree, my dear grandson Peter, that I wish to speak to you now. The foregoing description of the position of the Jews was a preamble indispensable to your comprehension of my ensuing remarks about your family tree. The appointed time for them was your baptism yesterday. In undergoing this, not that you realize it yet, you have reached a point in your journey from which you will henceforth make your own way towards a sphere of life in which the chorus of hatred will quickly come within earshot. I want you to hear my dissenting voice and my affirmation of your family tree.

The paternal branch of your family tree, being the Aryan branch, requires no advocacy. When your father announced his decision to marry our beloved daughter Lotte, we dutifully and urgently drew attention to its gravity and to the manifold burdens he would be shouldering through his union with a Jewish wife. He utterly dismissed those considerations. In his affection and esteem for Lotte, but also because of his fundamentally humane cast of mind, he stood firm and erect in the face of the anti-Semitic tempest that had already been pumped into the German people for several years.

In standing by Lotte he passed his storm test and thereby proved that he had kept his mind and soul untainted by this epidemic of hatred. He has not become pro-Jewish because of his marriage, but has reaffirmed his original objectivity and lack of prejudice towards the Jewish world. The fact that matrimony later became the exalted human union your father hoped for – which it is today and will, I hope, continue to be – not only lends him and his marriage their due justification but demonstrates your mother's fine qualities, in which your father's hopes have been fulfilled.

Your mother, if her health endures so that you yourself are privileged to have her with you until well into your mature years, is so very close to you that her great goodness and selflessness, her purity of desire and her guidance will, in themselves, enable you to sense the sacred, mysterious power of maternal love and grasp that it far transcends all loveless human activity. Your mother's superior place in your family tree will be held sacred by you yourself. No matter how people change over the years and decades, their mothers retain an undiminished place in their hearts. Mothers perpetuate our childish existence, so I hope that in later years, dear Peter, you will refer to 'my little Mama' as affectionately as you do today, in the fourth year of your life.

As things stand now, you are unavoidably subject to the new German legislation that brands you a half-breed because your mother is of Jewish blood. This puts you half a rung above your mother, and your mother is classified as inferior to you in terms of human merit. You are legally subject to these regulations. It is up to you whether you acknowledge this classification and order of precedence. I venture to assume that you will stand by your mother from a sense of filial duty. But you should not base your attitude on the law of nature alone, whereas your Aryan fellow Germans, with their family trees, infer the merits of their parents from the number, merits, and names of their Aryan forebears.

If it is necessary to examine the mothers of the past, you should be aware that the historical superstructure of your maternal line will withstand any amount of investigation. The names Nördlinger, Leser, Levi and Schlüchterer in your family tree occupy the same moral and human status as the names Lederle, Klausmann, Thorwaldsen or Finkbeiner in an Aryan family tree. For I have come across no single one of your forebears who could be denied the reputation of a moral person – moral in the personal domain and moral in keeping with the requirements of co-existence with the German national community. Submitting our kinsfolk to critical scrutiny, I discern none that falls short of a universally valid standard of personal and professional integrity, sense of duty, and purity of family life. This statement would retain its validity even if a lapse had occurred somewhere in our ancestral line, but I know of none.

But control of one's racial alloy is vested in the person of the grandmother. In order to establish the German people's Aryan exclusivity and expel the Jewish element, the German government employs the grandmother as a trigonometrical point. For all those who come across a Jewish grandmother when retrospectively focusing on this point, that grandmother acquires fateful significance. She devalues her grandchildren – unless, like you, they have one Aryan parent. In that case the grandchild is worth fifty per cent more than its Jewish grandmother. Several different percentages are possible, depending on the extent of the mixture. Racial content expressed in percentages, with one's grandmother as the focal point, is what currently dominates the masses who aspire to be legitimately housed beneath the Aryan roof. 'Jewish grandmother' is the catch phrase, both humorous and serious, of the present time. That is why I consider it important, my dear Peter, to introduce your Jewish grandmother to you.

Your grandmother Olga is a woman of exemplary character, opposed to all that is technically and objectively false. Although devoid of social pretensions, she is distinguished by her exceptional dependability, her sense of duty, her trustworthiness in matters great and small, and her simple, steadfast way of life.

Your grandmother Olga is self-sacrificing, fair and lenient in her judgement of others, and conciliatory towards all human weaknesses, provided they do not run counter to her own conception of loyal and upright conduct. She confronts life's difficulties with courage, but Germany's persecution of the Jews is gnawing at her heart.

Your grandmother Olga dispenses love from the clear

and abundant wellsprings of her profound and genuine goodness – but she is utterly unsentimental and uncomplicated, candid and transparent, pure and fine in the extreme. She has an unclouded mind, and is severely critical of herself. Although naturally selfish in her maternal solicitude for her children and family, she has always maintained a lively and genuine relationship with the interests of the nation as a whole, whose ideologies – when they did not compel her to discard her own, independent views – she has sincerely shared. She looked upon the world war of 1914–18 as a matter of national concern and her conduct throughout could not have been bettered.

In every country in the world, a woman endowed with these qualities would be called a truly moral person. In Germany, pretentiously, she is termed 'a genuinely German woman'. The former description is sufficient, dear Peter. You can be proud of your Jewish grandmother, and have no need to feel that she is the weak spot on your certificate of descent. You may regard her inclusion with total confidence; no nobler grandmother is inscribed in any Aryan certificate. She herself would reject this description in a resolutely self-critical manner, or accept it only with the reservation that there are millions like her in every class of society. True enough, and this equivalence is precisely what I wished to affirm.

Greetings, my grandson Peter,

Your grandfather, Max Mayer

On 9 November 1938, exactly six months to the day after this letter was written, the Nazis staged the so-called 'Kristallnacht' (Night of Broken Glass), a new high-water mark in the persecution of Germany's Jews. Like many other Jewish citizens, Max Mayer was dragged from his home and put in a concentration camp. Sixty-five years old, he had to endure a month's detention in Dachau, where he was bullied and tortured. He returned home to Freiburg a broken man, still hoping to the last that the Germans would come to their senses. Belatedly – almost too late, in fact – Max and Olga decided to emigrate. On 1 September 1939, the first day of the Second World War, they crossed the frontier into Switzerland.

'Charity never faileth'
Lilli and Ernst's marriage disintegrates

The Friedemanns and the Goldins had long been in Palestine when the Immenhausen Brownshirts initiated on their own 'Kristallnacht'. Lilli and her family seemed to be the only suitable objects of 'national fury' left. On the night of 9 November 1938, a few Nazis, some of them drunk, climbed on top of the garage in which Ernst's Opel was parked and smashed a window. Lilli and Ernst and their children, who were at home, waited anxiously for still worse things to happen, but the men simply blundered around in the garden for a while, yelling abuse, and then withdrew. Ilse did not go to her secondary school in Kassel the next morning and stayed at home. Gerhard made his way to the Friedrichsgymnasium but was promptly sent home by a concerned teacher.

A week later the SS corporal in charge submitted a report of events in the Hofgeismar district on 9 November. His cynical summary included a reference to the incident in Gartenstrasse:

> In the local area only the synagogue at Meimbressen was destroyed. Unfortunately, the synagogues at Hofgeismar and Grebenstein have already passed into Aryan hands, so destroying them would have been inappropriate.
>
> In the Hofgeismar district a total of eight business premises were wrecked. In addition, the windows of three private residences were smashed . . .
>
> In some cases, Jews of particularly bad reputation had their backsides kicked. The next day, with black eyes and

aching limbs, they were made to clean the streets. No looting occurred in this district. In this district a total of seven Jews were arrested.

No religious objects or records were secured, most of them having been burnt or destroyed. However, the Jews' account books were confiscated and will be examined by the competent authority.

Unfortunately, no suicides or other fatalities involving Jews occurred during this period.

The Nazis had wrought worse havoc in Cologne, where Paula's apartment had been completely wrecked. Lilli went at once to help her mother clear up the mess. By then, if not before, they must both have realized that any further hope of an improvement in the political situation would be futile.

In November 1938, Jews were forbidden on principle to attend public functions, notably theatrical performances and concerts – a severe blow to Lilli in particular. On 31 December 1938 she was issued with an identity card, a document bearing a large 'J' which all German Jews had to carry from then on. In accordance with the new regulations – Jewish men and women had, respectively, to adopt the additional forenames Israel and Sara – Lilli signed her card, which was issued by the municipality of Immenhausen, 'Lilli Sara Jahn'. She also had to affix the imprints of her left and right index fingers.

Paula, who went through the same procedure, had already taken the preliminary steps required for emigration. Aged sixty-four and with a very poor command of English, she had only one recourse, which was to join her daughter Elsa in Birmingham.

Elsa obtained the requisite documents in England. Paula had to procure a birth certificate from the Protestant parochial office in Oberlauringen and use it to apply for a passport in Cologne. Above all, however, she had to pay through the nose: on 7 March 1939 the senior inspector of taxes at Cologne issued her with a 'clearance certificate' confirming that she currently owed the authorities nothing in the way of 'state taxes, surcharges, fines, fees, and expenses'. It also recorded that she had previously paid a 'Reich desertion tax' of 20,144 Reichsmark and a 'Jewish assets levy' of 21,400 Reichsmark. Moreover, she could only take her furniture to England after paying the exchequer yet again for each item belonging to her. These outgoings largely depleted her assets. On 15 May 1939 Paula left Germany for good.

Lilli remained behind. During the next few months she bade a tearful farewell to several friends and relations who stopped at Kassel station on their way to Hamburg or Bremen before sailing for America or Britain. In the end she was forsaken by nearly everyone close to her.

In the summer she and her family paid a last visit to the Black Forest. The Jahns had holidayed there in 1936 and 1937, and had always made excursions to Freiburg to see the Mayers and the Paepckes. In 1938 they began their summer tour in the Sauerland before driving down to Garmisch and the Zugspitze, but their trip to the Black Forest proved a disaster. The hotel at which they had originally booked rooms refused to accept them: Jews were not wanted. Only after a lengthy search and with Max and Olga Mayer's help did they at last find a hotel that graciously overlooked Lilli's Jewish identity card. This odyssey had a thoroughly traumatic effect on her children. It brought home to them, not for the first time, that they were among the despised outsiders of German society.

These holidays were made possible because Ernst's practice was now doing so well that the family could afford such little luxuries. Everything depended, however, on whether Ernst could find a locum to look after his Immenhausen patients. In the summer of 1939 this post was filled by Rita Schmidt, a young female colleague from Göttingen whom the whole family, and Lilli in particular, initially welcomed and regarded as a friend.

The first snapshots of Rita in the family album are dated April 1939, when Ernst's young colleague was photographed with Eva on her very first day at school. She soon started coming to Immenhausen outside the holiday season and helped out at the surgery, which was often inundated with patients.

Lotte Paepcke, who visited the Jahns at Immenhausen around

this time, found Lilli rather subdued and apprehensive. Shortly after the war, in a letter to her parents, who were by then living in New York, Lotte recalled a memorable evening she and her husband Ernst August spent at Immenhausen with Rita, Ernst, and Lilli. The party became quite lively, she wrote, and they even indulged in a little dancing.

> For Lilli it was the first time in years [that she had danced], and she was so girlishly delighted and animated that it really touched us. Ernst can't dance and was very embarrassed, but Lilli was simply thrilled.

Lotte – who also found Rita thoroughly likeable at first – became a major source of support to Lilli during this period. She occasionally arranged brief meetings on the autobahn near Kassel, where the Paepckes would call a brief halt on their holiday trips or when visiting relations in Rostock. Lotte was probably the first to learn that the Jahn family's friendship with Rita had taken a disastrous turn. Here is a final extract from her memoirs:

> Lilli's only source of news from the outside world was a young woman physician who occasionally stood in for the overburdened doctor. To Lilli she was another child whom she cared for and admired; to the children a young aunt from the city who always brought them nice gifts; and to the doctor an appreciable respite from his excessive workload. She was soon his friend and then his lover, for she became his route back into life – back into the world of all those who dared to point their finger at him, to shun and deride him.
>
> After a bleak, orphaned childhood the doctor had laboriously fought for a chance to study, and, disadvantaged by his lack of means, had watched his fellow students leading easier, happier lives. At last, however, he seemed to have attained his goal: the security of a well-ordered existence began to beckon. It was that security

which he had sought in his wife. He sought it in the ever-growing band of children that surrounded him. He sought it in the bosom of mighty Mother Church. And then? Then along came those who wanted to wrest it all away from him – cut the ground from beneath his feet just when he had underpinned it. They jeered at him, they threatened his wife with stones! They pointed their grubby forefingers at the ancient Madonnas in his books, at the pictures in whose smiling faces he hoped to discover the eternal order of things. Were they seeking to destroy him? No, no, no! He couldn't endure it.

He felt harassed and persecuted, became irritable and suddenly prone to furious outbursts. He began to find his once beloved wife intolerable. The way she sat there so innocently, sewing, as if she didn't know what was happening to him – him, whose one desire was a quiet life, respect and security.

Oh yes, she knew it. She could see the terrible thing that was happening to him, to them both, but she was powerless to prevent it. All she had left was her work by day and her tears by night.

The husband began to criticize his children – no, they weren't blond, they weren't radiant like the Hitler Youth lads who marched past him on the roads. How miserably that half-breed son of his sat around at home on Sundays instead of marching outside with the rest of them. And he became so sad and embittered about them all as they stood around him – a fivefold misfortune – that the children began to be afraid of him.

Just as he was thirsting for the life of the majority of Germans, who were secure, along came Rita, the compassionate Samaritan, who brought him his first drop to drink. To give him something else to think about for once, she invited him to accompany her to the theatre. Lilli gladly gave her consent. What joy it was to sit in a box again, to stroll round the foyer with a pretty companion at his side! The doctor came home feeling more self-assured but slightly embarrassed. And Rita gave the thirsty man still more: she arranged a little outing together, since Lilli could no longer go. She then made him a present of a long excursion. And, in the end, she gave him herself.

This is Lotte's account, which broadly covers 1939–40, the first year of the war. However, Lilli's daughters maintain that Lotte was mistaken in one respect: today, Johanna and Ilse flatly deny that they were ever afraid of their father. Lotte's account is exaggerated, they say, and in some respects quite wrong. Ernst never regarded his son and four daughters – the fourth, Dorothea, was born on 25 September 1940 – as a 'fivefold misfortune', nor did he consider his children's Jewish blood a blemish. They maintain that, in spite of all that happened, he remained a loving father.

The autumn of 1940 brought Lilli another piece of bad news: the death of her favourite uncle, Josef Schloss. The Halle paediatrician whose practice she had once hoped to take over had for years been subjected to systematic pressure by the authorities. In the autumn of 1938, like every remaining Jewish doctor, he had his licence revoked. In April 1939 he was compelled, under the so-called Aryanization programme, to relinquish the house he had inherited from his father. Finally, he developed heart trouble. On 14 October 1940 he made his will, which expressly bequeathed a large proportion of his remaining assets to his 'non-Jewish' great-nephews and great-nieces. On 25 November 1940 he took his own life.

Josef's sister Marie Klein, who had kept the dying man company during his last hours, informed his nearest relatives the next day.

Lilli promptly went to Halle and helped to wind up the household. One or two heirlooms including some Biedermeier furniture, medical equipment, and a fur coat for Ernst, were sent to Immenhausen. The Nazis subsequently bore Marie off to Theresienstadt concentration camp, her last known whereabouts.

Lilli and Ernst were more worried about the family than ever. Their correspondence with the Barths was not resumed until the end of 1940, but only by Lilli and Hanne: Leo had been called up and was stationed in France. On 11 December 1940 Lilli sent her Mannheim friend a Christmas greeting:

My dear Hanne,

It's an absolute age since you heard from me last, but it's simply and solely down to that incurable disease, lack of time. Although my work is piling up sky-high, especially now – and Amadé's no less so – we want to send you some news of us at Christmas, together with a little book for you and Leo.

We very much hope that Leo will get some holiday leave, and wish you all a happy Christmas. This year, as ever, we shall think of you beside the twinkling Christmas tree with friendship and gratitude for your loyal and enduring sentiments, which are always such a comfort and pleasure to us . . . Leo's letter and affectionate good wishes from France warmed our hearts.

So that you too will know what the baby who'll wear the dear little bonnet looks like, I'm enclosing two little snaps for you. Many thanks for your kind good wishes on the birth of our Dorle [Dorothea]. She's making excellent progress and is, of course, the focal point and favourite of the whole household. Even the baby's big brother takes an affectionate interest in her. I myself have recovered very quickly and am able, thank goodness, to work hard again from early in the morning till late at night. All the children are fit and cheerful and have grown a lot. It won't be long before Gerhard overtops us.

I could tell you plenty more, but how much nicer it would be if you could come and see them again in person. I'm not abandoning hope that you'll be able to do so when peace is restored, hopefully in the not too distant future.

And so, dearest Hanne, let me close for today with this burning and heartfelt desire for peace which we all share.

May the year 1941 be good to us all, and may all of us, whom life is giving so much to endure, have courage and confidence and stout hearts – and God's blessing.

All my fondest love, also to Leo, the children, and Grandpa and Grandma.

Yours ever, Lilli

The everyday life of the family now became Lilli's sole *raison d'être*. For her, everything revolved around the welfare of Ernst and the children. She seldom left the house.

On 23 March 1941 Gerhard was confirmed. The obligatory photographs of the boy in his confirmation suit show him standing with his parents in the garden of the house in Gartenstrasse. Taken on the same occasion, however, is a grim-faced photograph of Ernst: On his right is Lilli, looking unmistakably run down, and on his left is his mistress, Rita. There was clearly an attempt to simulate normality at almost any price. This snapshot is reminiscent of Ernst's double life in the early days of his relationship with Lilli. Then it had been his girlfriend, Annekathrin, who cast her spell over him; now it was Rita who held him in thrall.

Once again, Ernst's emotional dichotomy did not prevent him from giving Lilli small gifts. At Easter 1941 he gave her a reprint of Jakob Grimm's *Hausbüchel*. There was plenty of room in it for personal jottings. Ernst started off with a dedication and a series of quotations:

To my dear Lilli
filled with gratitude on Sunday, 6 April 1941
with all good wishes,
so that she may, for once, have a little book of her very own,
for her personal delectation and for the benefit and
enrichment of us all

Amadé

Inside the book Ernst inscribed a quotation from Dante's *Divine Comedy*, and on the first blank double page he stuck a postcard of a Madonna with a quotation from Goethe beneath it:

Great ideas and a pure heart;
that is what we should ask of God.

The next double page Ernst filled with two more quotations from Goethe's *Italienische Reise* (*Italian Journey*). One of them read:

That which at first gave blithe pleasure, when superficially accepted, tiresomely obtrudes thereafter, when one perceives that, without thorough knowledge, true pleasure is lacking.

Lilli later added a Schiller quotation which meaningfully developed Goethe's somewhat schoolmasterly dictum – indeed, fundamentally commented on it:

To combine the greatest abundance of artistic pleasure with the pleasure of the heart has always been my supreme ideal in life, and to unite the two is also, as I see it, the most infallible means of bringing each to its greatest abundance.

Ernst and Lilli were still united by their interest in literature, music and philosophy, though each laid stress on different aspects. Ernst strove primarily for true faith and a knowledge of art history, whereas Lilli went in search of love and its peculiarities. She filled the next twenty-three pages with quotations that turned on this one great subject. Even when she opened with a biblical quotation (from *I Corinthians*), she remained true to what was, for her, a vital matter:

Charity [in German: *Liebe*] suffereth long, and is kind; charity envieth not, seeketh not her own; beareth all things, believeth all things, hopeth all things, endureth all things. Charity never faileth.

Lilli jotted down ideas and aphorisms drawn from Hegel, Hölderlin, Schopenhauer, Albert Schweitzer, Werner Bergengruen, and Rainer Maria Rilke. Her literary diary breaks off after a quotation from Ernst Jünger.

In September 1941 she also finished her work on the family photo album, which she had probably given Ernst shortly before, perhaps on the occasion of Dorothea's birth. Her dedication read: 'For Daddy, a picture book of his five children.' The last two photographs show little Dorle on 25 September 1941, her first birthday.

It was probably prints of these photographs which she sent to her friend Hanne in Mannheim on 23 November:

My dear Hanne,

I'm sure I needn't keep emphasizing that, even in default of any outward signs of life we think with warm and undiminished affection of you, Leo, and your four splendid children. We were immensely pleased – indeed, delighted – to get those little pictures you sent me in the summer. You can justly be proud of having such an enchanting, radiant brood of children, Hanne! I'm sure little Michael is a strapping boy by now, and laughing and talking. As with us, so with you, the nestling must surely be his older siblings' pet.

The enclosed snaps will show you what our Dorle looks like now. She's a little dumpling, but scuttles around like a weasel and is immensely lively. We're having a tough time with her at present, because nothing is safe from her chubby little hands and we have to keep a close eye on her. It's high time she became potty-trained, but it's always such an effort. Yet every day renews the happiness one feels at having such a dear, affectionate little creature.

The four older ones are growing fast. Gerhard is enthusiastically learning Latin, Greek and English, and still feels very much at home at his school. Ilse, who finds learning harder, works diligently and conscientiously but with less enjoyment. On the other hand, she's a good little housewife and does a lot of the shopping by herself, which is a considerable relief to me, given all the restrictions I'm subject to. She, Gerhard and Hannele have very open, receptive minds and clearly betray the influence of their father's art-historical and intellectual interests.

Hannele's health continues to be a worry, alas, because of her asthma. She was at a children's sanatorium in Kassel from 1 September until mid-November, and has recovered quite well, generally speaking, but her attacks persist. As for our Eva, she's a real little tomboy – always outdoors helping here and there, but preferably in the nearby carpenter's yard, where they let her wield hammer and nails to her heart's content. She's never still, and Sundays, when the others devote themselves to reading, are a torment to her.

Today Amadé went to the theatre in Kassel with Gerhard to see 'Troubadour'. I look forward to hearing what they say about it. Amadé is always far too overworked. We managed with great difficulty to get hold of a locum for two weeks in July, and Amadé went to the Ruhestein near Baden-Baden. He said that the holiday should have been twice as long.

Rita Schmidt . . . spends a good deal of time with us. She is very well. She sends her best regards and the enclosed book of tickets.

There's nothing much to tell you about myself. I'll spare you my familiar song of woe about domestic servants – and I no longer lead any kind of life outside this house. Why should I waste many words on the subject? Sometimes it's harder than you may think.

After this long bulletin about us, I must be entitled to ask you to tell us soon about yourself and all of you, especially how the children are coming along and what they're up to . . .

All the very best to you, Hanne, and fondest love to you and yours from

Your Lilli

Why had Lilli become so reclusive? Technically, there were no restrictions on her freedom of movement outside the house, nor, thanks to her marriage to Ernst, was she compelled to wear the yellow star that had been obligatory for all Jews since 19 September 1941.

This was anything but a privilege to be relied on, however. Lilli went in constant fear of abuses of power by Nazi thugs or bureaucrats, who would certainly have gone unpunished. Above all, though, large-scale deportations were now under way throughout the Reich. Who could guarantee that she might not be picked up and bundled off to the East by train?

The first consignment of Jews left Kassel's main-line station on 9 December 1941. In the days beforehand, the head of the 'Jewish section' of Kassel's Gestapo, August Hoppach, had seen to it that as many Jews as possible were herded into the city from the surrounding area so as to fill the thousand places made available to him by the Reichsbahn, the state railway. This first round-up was transported to the ghetto in Riga; the second, on 1 July 1942, to Lublin/Maidanek concentration camp; and the third, on 7 September 1942, to Theresienstadt. All this happened under the noses of Kassel's citizens. Long columns of their Jewish neighbours straggled through the city centre to the railway station, and the personal belongings they left behind were publicly auctioned.

The Nazis of Immenhausen could not understand why Lilli should escape this fate. On 20 January 1942 the incumbent mayor and deputy district director of the NSDAP (National Socialist German Labour Party), Karl Gross, wrote as follows to his superior at Hofgeismar:

To the District Director of the NSDAP at Hofgeismar:
Further to your communication No. 138/42 dated 17 January 1942 regarding privileged mixed marriages, I hereby inform you that the local inhabitants have taken great exception to the fact that the local woman doctor (a full-blooded Jewess) is not required to wear a Jewish star. The Jewess takes full advantage of this in that she often

95

goes to Kassel by train, second class, and can travel free from interference without the star. The entire population would welcome it if this state of affairs could be remedied in some way.

I inform you at the same time that consideration might be given to deporting the local Jewess because her husband (a doctor) is having an affair with an Aryan woman doctor, who is expecting a child by him in the next few weeks. If the Jewess were deported, the Aryan woman doctor could continue to run Dr Jahn's household. It might be appropriate to discuss the said circumstances [with him] in person. This could bring about the disappearance of the only Jewess still resident here.

Heil Hitler!

Gross
Dep. District Director

It is debatable whether the citizens of Immenhausen really took offence at Lilli's train journeys. The inhabitants of the little town probably had quite different concerns at this time, the third winter of the war. Doubtless it was primarily the Party machine that sought further victims.

In any case, Lilli was forced to discontinue her trips to Kassel two months later. At the end of March 1942 the Security Police issued a directive prohibiting German Jews from using public transport. They were allowed to travel by train only if they could produce a special police permit.

Although it is uncertain whether Party officials personally interviewed Ernst Jahn about his marriage to Lilli, they probably suggested, at least, that he divorce her.

Lilli and Ernst's was a so-called privileged mixed marriage. In December 1938 the Nazis had accorded this status to 'half-Jewish' married couples who did not bring up their children in the Jewish faith. As the war progressed, so the social and political pressures on such marriages increased. Divorce was considered desirable but seldom enforced. Moreover, Lilli and Ernst's union was the most advantageous of the possible variations: the marriage of a Jewish man to a non-Jewish woman was generally subject to harsher sanctions.

In 1942 there were still some 28,000 mixed marriages in the Third Reich. If one of the partners became unable to resist political pressure and asked for a divorce, Nazi judges always hurried the proceedings along. Custody of under-age children was almost invariably granted to the wife, and this applied also to Jewesses in mixed marriages. Jewish mothers were generally exempt from arrest and deportation after such a divorce, although their immunity became eroded towards the end of the war.

During 1942 Ernst took Rita to Bochum to discuss the modalities of divorce and remarriage with Leo Diekamp, his friend and former fellow student. The lawyer strongly advised him not to dissolve his marriage. No one could tell how long Lilli would continue to benefit from her existing protection, especially as the rights of Jews in Germany were being steadily and manifestly curtailed by the Nazi legal system. However, Ernst was confident that the Nazis would show consideration for his five children, and that no harm would come to Lilli on their account. Apparently, or so he always reiterated in later years, the competent authorities had assured him of this.

In fact, the Nazi bureaucrats continued to train their sights on Lilli. On 22 May 1942 Mayor Gross submitted another report on the current situation in the Jahn household:

> To the District Directorate of the NSDAP at Hofgeismar
> Re: Dr Ernst Jahn, general practitioner at Immenhausen.
>
> In the above matter I hereby inform you that Dr Rita Schmidt . . . has given birth to a daughter in the home of Dr Jahn. Jahn is the father of the child. According to Jahn's wife, the child was delivered by Jahn himself, Frau Jahn being present in an auxiliary capacity. The local midwife was called in the next afternoon and visited the mother twice a day for a week. The mother was thereafter attended in the Jahn home by a qualified obstetric nurse from Göttingen.

Dr Schmidt has often stood in for Jahn at his surgery. Before giving birth she resided in the family home for a considerable period. Jahn himself has five other children by his wife, who is a full-blooded Jewess.

p.p. Gross

How must Lilli have felt as she helped Rita to give birth to a child fathered by Ernst? The medical association also took exception to this proceeding, albeit for a grotesque reason: Rita was reprimanded for having brought her child into the world with the assistance of a Jewish colleague.

Some weeks after the birth Rita and her baby daughter moved into an apartment in Kassel. Ernst visited her there regularly – from Lilli's point of view, an almost intolerable state of affairs. The children were also naturally distressed by the unmistakable disintegration of their parents' marriage.

Lilli had had little contact with her mother and sister in Birmingham since the outbreak of war, it being impossible to correspond with them direct. To begin with even the British regarded the two German immigrants as suspect, and Elsa lost her job as an industrial chemist. When Lilli wanted to communicate with them she did so by way of an 'Aunt Paula' living in Geneva, who forwarded her letters and messages to England from neutral Switzerland.

On 27 September 1942 Lilli wrote once again to this woman (who has never been identified). Her letter must have been checked by the censor, because all the place names had been obliterated – a mandatory but wholly nonsensical measure, given that Lilli confined herself to giving news of her family at Immenhausen and describing the interests and aptitudes of her growing children. Nonetheless, this roundabout route did enable Lilli to send her mother and sister a coded message. The following passage occurs near the end of her letter:

> I have had no news of my family either, since all my aunts have moved house. I was very, very interested to read what you wrote about your namesake in your last letter.

You know how very fond I always was of her and her daughter. I was terribly sorry to hear that the hard-working doctor has been ill again. If you write to them, please send them both my very best and most cordial regards.

'Aunt Paula's' namesake was none other than Lilli's mother, and the hard-working doctor was her tubercular sister Elsa.

Lilli's aunts had not simply 'moved house'. Also deported to Theresienstadt like Marie, who has already been mentioned, were Eva and Margarete Schloss, Helene Nördlinger, and Ottilie ('Tilly') Schlüchterer. None of them ever returned. After the war, Lilli's mother Paula counted no fewer than twenty-three victims of the Holocaust among her relations.

One reason why they numbered so many was that Jewish members of the middle class seldom considered emigrating to Palestine. Most of Paula's kinsfolk shared Josef Schlüchterer's anti-Zionism, and the nationalistic sentiments of these assimilated German Jews rendered them fundamentally hostile to the idea of abandoning their native land. Moreover, reports from Palestine indicated that life there was rather hazardous. Those who were too old or immobile, like Lilli's aunts, remained in Germany and fell into the hands of the Nazis, and anyone who managed to escape to New York, like Lilli's cousin Olga and her husband Max, did so with the firm intention of some day returning to Germany.

Lilli was also immobile in this sense, but for different reasons. In 1942 she was compelled to make over her entire bank balance, some 10,000 Reichsmark, to Ernst, as well as the share of the Immenhausen property registered in her name. On 8 October she formally consented to the divorce. A few weeks later, on 14 November 1942, Ernst and Rita got married.

'Infinitely lonely and forlorn'
Under the same roof but separated

The divorce did not at first bring any change in the domestic arrangements at Immenhausen. Ernst joined his new wife in Kassel nearly every night and at the weekend; for the time being, Lilli continued to live at Immenhausen with the children.

Meanwhile, she had new worries to contend with. Ernst's sister Lore and her family lived in Essen, and the Ruhr was being subjected to heavy air raids at this time. Lore had stood by Lilli ever since the outbreak of war and, more especially, since the divorce. On 19 January 1943 Lilli invited her sister-in-law and her husband, Dr Wilhelm Sasse, to move to Immenhausen with their children, Marilis and Wilhelm:

> My dear, dear Lore,
>   There seemed no hope of getting through to you on the phone, or we would have called you as soon as we received your letter. We want you to know, you and yours, that we're thinking of you with the greatest sympathy. I hope that you've had a little more peace and quiet in the last few days and can relax a bit. It's really awful, what you're having to go through.
>   I shall carefully preserve your list and all your particulars and requests, and you may rest assured of this, Lore: You can rely on us to the hilt at all times. We shall always be there for your children. You must surely know that I love them like my own. I shall always be a true and understanding friend to Marilis as well as a helpful aunt.

God grant that all your anxieties and precautions prove needless. Ernst sends his special love. He wonders whether you shouldn't leave Essen. It ought to be easy enough for Willy to obtain enough doctor's certificates to show that he's no longer capable of running his practice, and that life in Essen is injurious to his health. Come to us – we'll put you up. Wilhelm can go to school in Kassel for a few months. You surely can't put up with it indefinitely! Or at least come for a few weeks – you're more than welcome any time. We'd so much like to be of help! At least write again very soon, even if it's only a brief line. Did you receive the parcel of peas and cornflour? Meantime, Ilschen asks me to thank you warmly for your birthday greetings and the very, very fine art book. Give our suggestion some thought – we really mean it. Good-bye for now. All the very best!

Fondest regards to you all from all of us,

Lilli

And a postscript:

Wouldn't you like at least to send us a few suitcases of clothes, silver, etc.? Shall I send you a big, new Mädler suitcase for the purpose? Really, see if you can get out of that hell. A big, affectionate hug, dear Lore!

Your Lilli

In spite of the divorce, Lilli and Ernst still attended to many everyday matters jointly, whether they involved helping Lore and her family or making decisions about the children's future.

Meanwhile, the war was drawing steadily closer to Immenhausen. In August 1942 Kassel was subjected to its first large-scale raid by Allied bombers. Lilli's son Gerhard, by now fifteen, was drafted with his classmates into an anti-aircraft unit based at Obervellmar, near Kassel. The young air-force auxiliaries, who reported for duty on 15 February 1943, underwent basic military training and attended a few school classes on the side. They went into action a few weeks later. This meant serving the anti-aircraft guns – from Gerhard's point of view, a welcome mark of recognition. Although he had hitherto suffered little discrimination at the Friedrichsgymnasium in Kassel – unlike his sisters Ilse and Johanna, who had already been subjected to numerous forms of harassment and threatened with expulsion by the principal of their secondary school – he regarded his incorporation in the war machine as a form of rehabilitation. He could not become a member of the Hitler Youth, but now, thanks to the exigencies of war, he was evidently needed after all. It suddenly seemed that he had ceased to be an outsider: he 'belonged' at last.

Was Lilli equally pleased? If not, she never let her son feel it, but always evinced the greatest interest in this transformation of his daily life. Gerhard was allowed home only at weekends, if at all. When he did come to Immenhausen, he was cosseted and fed and had his clothes laundered and darned.

Lilli strove to conceal her heartache from the children, and for a long time she said nothing about the divorce to her few remaining friends. On 11 March 1943, however, she finally informed Hanne Barth in Mannheim:

My dear, dear, faithful Hanne,

First, heartfelt thanks for all your kind messages, which have, to my shame, remained unanswered. Yet they always bring us such joy, and me especially, as tokens of your unaltered feelings and friendship. And I was absolutely delighted to receive the charming notebook at Christmas, which was really sweet of you. Extra special thanks.

Believe me, I'm immensely interested to read of everything to do with you and the children, and of what you can tell me about Leo. I share your joy whenever you write about the happy days when he's on leave, and try to imagine what it must mean to have to let your beloved husband go away again. You're a brave woman, Hanne, and I hope from the bottom of my heart that your father recovers, and that you can all be reunited in the not too distant future. To think of all you've been through in the way of illnesses and worries about yourself and the children! That was why I was particularly glad that your card today contained nothing but good news.

Please don't think me lacking in concern for you. I've written to you again and again in my head, but it was a long time before I could put this letter down on paper, and even today it comes terribly hard. In view of our long friendship, however, I feel obliged and compelled to inform you of something so serious and unpleasant that it's almost impossible to say in a letter.

I've undergone some very hard and bitter experiences in the past two and a half years, and I haven't got over them even now. Hanne, on 8 October 1942 Amadé and I were divorced, and on 14 November 1942 he got married again to Rita Schmidt, whom you know, after . . . the birth here of their child, a baby girl named Magda.

How am I to explain it all – above all, how am I to render Amadé's behaviour comprehensible to you, so that you understand and don't condemn him?!!

Hanne, I wish I could sit beside you now, take your hand, and say something very quietly: Hanne, do you remember the first time I visited you both at Mannheim in the summer of 1925? Do you remember that Sunday afternoon when Amadé, who was my only reason for coming, left me alone and fled to you on the pretext that he was on duty at the hospital? Do you recall how shocked and hurt I was when you told me the next morning?

You see, that should have been a warning to me, and I shall now, after many years of imagining that I and we both were happy, have to spend the rest of my days atoning for my failure to heed that warning. For Amadé's fateful meeting with that other woman, Rita Schmidt, brought it home to him that, in marrying me, he had been untrue to his innermost self.

And then, suddenly, he found this woman, a fellow creature who brought him an inexpressible happiness he had never felt before, who became a home to him, and who led him, whom you also know to be a seeker after God, back to himself and to God. To Amadé, this love has profoundly religious roots. He had to affirm it, or he couldn't have gone on living in the deepest sense. Knowing Amadé as you do, you must realize that his gentle, sensitive nature would have made it impossible for him to develop and mature inwardly had he renounced his love and suppressed it. His best and most valuable qualities would have perished.

I'm sure I've no need to stress that this experience and this development have also cost him much heart-searching, and that he tried again and again to call himself to account before having to affirm this love with every fibre of his heart and soul.

You see, Hanne, Amadé and Rita attend church together, and it's probably just a question of time before he converts. She's a woman of German blood, and more his own kind. The unhappy, almost intolerable circumstances under which he was compelled to live with me counted for a very great deal, although they were not the decisive factor, but this you will not be able to gauge fully until I can describe them to you in more detail.

Will you try to understand Amadé and not judge him too harshly? He doesn't deserve it, because he can't be accused of thoughtlessness or heartlessness or wickedness. Even Lise and Leo Diekamp, who know the full story and have witnessed it all for over a year, have been convinced by personal conversations with Amadé and letters from him. I myself, emotionally torn in the extreme . . . have confided in Lise – I couldn't and didn't want to come to you with my troubles, dear Hanne, because you yourself have enough to bear. But Lise has been a disappointment to me. In all this time I have received only *one* letter addressed to me personally, and it was so very cold and businesslike that it hurt me. As for the brisker correspondence between her and Amadé, that has long been kept from me.

What am I to tell you about myself, Hanne? Inwardly I feel infinitely lonely and forlorn. I'm fighting hard against bitterness and disillusionment and for faith in humankind, and it's only in the last few weeks that I've very slowly found my way back to myself and to faith in God's dispensations. You, dear Hanne, will sympathize and understand how sick with sorrow . . . I was, and how much I grieve for my children – the three older ones have also suffered a great deal – and myself. Look, Hanne, I grasped and understood from the first what was going on inside my Amadé. From the beginning I let him go his own way, not always with an easy mind but confident that our relationship would survive in spite of everything. And when I saw that I'd been wrong – that marriage to me was just a burden to him, and that he couldn't endure this life of twin commitments – I gave him back his freedom.

I can't say anything about Rita – I fear I'm not sufficiently objective, and I cannot rid myself of the reproachful feeling that she had it in her power to prevent the worst from happening. I've come to know her as an inconsiderate and self-centred person in all things, big and small, in matters of the heart as well as everyday trivia, especially during the three months she spent here in the house before, during, and after the child's birth. I tried for Amadé's sake to establish an amicable relationship with her, but all my efforts failed, partly because of my great sensitivity to her, no doubt, but not for that reason alone. Nothing is ever more than skin deep with her, and she doesn't hit it off with the children either.

On a practical level, our circumstances are such that the youth welfare office has granted me physical custody of the children. We remain here in the house, Ernst continues to practise here, Rita works as an assistant physician at a children's hospital in Kassel, where she has a charming little apartment, and Amadé spends all his free time, many nights a week and all weekends and public holidays, with his wife. It goes without saying that he's providing for me and the children in the most generous manner, and far in excess of his legal obligations. But nothing, absolutely nothing, can make up for our having lost him.

I've often wanted to visit you, dearest Hanne, and also to have a talk with Leo, but it's impossible. Amadé's sister has preserved her great affection for me and the children, but I don't have any family or close friends left.

Gerhard has been an air-force auxiliary for the past four weeks, and is serving with an anti-aircraft battery near Kassel. He seldom gets any leave. The four girls are well and enjoying life, Dorle being a true godsend and my one joy all day long, when the others are out of the house. I live entirely within my own four walls.

Dear, sweet Hanne, no doubt you will now comprehend my long silence. Give my love and a thousand good wishes to Leo, and tell him everything, so that he understands my seeming disloyalty to him. If you wish to, and think it right to do so, send him this letter. And now you, too, will have a better understanding of how very gratified I am by your renewed affection, for which I'm so very grateful to you.

Goodbye for now. All the best to you and the children, and a big, affectionate kiss,

Your Lilli

In the meantime, Lore had taken Lilli up on her offer and sent her children from Essen to spend a few weeks in the safety of Immenhausen. On 30 April Lilli thanked her for doing so:

You're not angry with Marilis and Wilhelm for staying here so long, are you? If you only knew what a rare and great pleasure it is for me to have your children's company. Heartfelt thanks for sending them to me. We welcomed Wilhelm with great rejoicing . . . And send the children to me as often as possible – as often as they like and for as long as you can spare them.

Lore's son Wilhelm, a charming youth of eighteen, was rather idolized by his girl cousins. On 28 May 1943, a few weeks after visiting Immenhausen, he and his father were killed in an air raid on Essen.

Banishment to Kassel

'Saying goodbye was very hard'
Lilli and her children are ousted from Immenhausen

The Nazi authorities found it intolerable that a couple who had been divorced for nine months should continue to share the same house. They demolished this peculiar domestic set-up with two swift blows. Early in July 1943, Ernst was drafted into the armed forces and assigned to medical duties at a military hospital near Kassel, his classification being 'k. v. Heimat' (employable for war service on the home front). His duties at Immenhausen were taken over by another physician, Dr Karl-Werner Schupmann. Ernst himself regarded his conscription as a form of official harassment, especially as he was given the rank of Unterarzt (medical lieutenant), a comparatively junior rung on the military ladder. He was doubtless being punished for lack of consistency, because his new wife lived alone in Kassel with their child, whereas he and Lilli resided under the same roof.

Soon afterwards, Mayor Gross decreed that Lilli should leave Immenhausen and move to Kassel with her children. There was plenty of vacant accommodation in the city, many of its inhabitants having abandoned their homes because of the frequent air raids.

On 21 July 1943 Lilli and the five children moved into 3 Motzstrasse, an apartment house. The relevant entry can be found on page fourteen of Kassel's 'Household Register No. 431'. Lilli's religion is specified as 'Jewess' and that of her children as 'Lutheran Protestant'.

The building was largely unoccupied when they moved in, and the ground floor was not let at all. The Jahns' apartment was situated on the second floor. Much of the Gartenstrasse furniture was transported there from Immenhausen, including the handsome Blüthner grand piano that had been a wedding present to Lilli from her grandmother.

The family was accompanied to its new abode by a 'domestic servant', Julia Maguestiaux, then thirty-seven, a foreign worker from Belgium. The household register listed her as Catholic and married. This indicates that Julia – the family called her Julie – was certainly not in Kassel of her own free will but had been deported to Germany by the Nazis.

The inhabitants of the occupied countries of Western Europe had since October 1942 been subject to a compulsory labour edict under which, if the authorities so decreed, they could be made to work in Germany. Because Lilli, being a Jewess, had been precluded from employing a German housemaid since the end of February 1943, she was allocated the young woman from Belgium. Her daughters still recall that Julie was always – unsurprisingly – 'sullen' and 'uncooperative'.

Where Ilse and Johanna were concerned, the move did have one advantage: they no longer had to travel by train every day to their secondary school in Kassel. Their sister Eva, on the other hand, could only attend an elementary school there. In the spring of 1943, when she was supposed to enrol at the same secondary school as her sisters, she was rejected because of her Jewish mother.

On 12 August 1943 Lilli described the circumstances of her move from Immenhausen to Kassel in a letter to her friend Hanne Barth in Mannheim:

My dear Hanne,
    This is not only to thank you for your sweet letter, but first and foremost to express the hope that you're all unscathed after the raid on Mannheim. Anyway, I want you to know that my loving thoughts are with you.
    I was absolutely delighted to hear your news. Leo's leave must be up by now, I suppose, but this time your goodbyes won't have been half as distressing. I fully

share your happiness at his transfer to Berlin, I assure you. Now you're bound to be able to visit him from time to time. How incredibly relieved you must feel, knowing that he isn't in the East any more. And let's hope the war will soon be over!!

Just imagine, I've now been living in Kassel with the children for three weeks. It all happened very suddenly and was none of my doing, still less what I wanted. It's all so complicated, and so many factors were involved that I just can't explain it all on paper. We have a nice, light, spacious, comfortable apartment. For the schoolchildren it's a great relief in many respects, but it was very, very hard to say goodbye to the house, into which Rita has now moved. What's more, I'm finding the mental and physical adjustment extremely difficult, especially as my whole situation is now very much worse.

To crown everything, Amadé was unexpectedly called up at very short notice a few days before the move. He's now doing a month-long medical lieutenant's course here in Kassel and is sometimes badly harassed, which comes very hard at his age. He takes his medical lieutenant's examination at the end of next week – what will happen to him then is anyone's guess. Although he's only classified as employable for war service on the home front, he could still be sent God knows where. At Immenhausen they've engaged a doctor ten years his junior.

In the meantime, we've already had two daylight raids on Kassel and plenty of air-raid warnings. We live in a state of constant apprehension. You know, dear Hanne, it sometimes takes my breath away when I think how these strokes of misfortune never end, and I often can't help feeling terribly sad. One good thing is that the children, with all their physical and mental demands upon me, unwittingly replenish my energy.

Don't be angry if I don't write at greater length today, but I can't bring myself to write a long letter, I'm far too tense and edgy – and unable to come to terms with myself. It's a struggle not to become hard and bitter.

And you, dear Hanne, please don't misjudge Amadé unfairly – I must ask you that again and again. Write me a nice letter if you have the time, but perhaps address it as if from Ursula to Ilse . . .

Many thanks for being a true friend.

With very best wishes to you and yours,

Lilli

Lilli knew only too well that she was under surveillance. Her letters were censored, and she even had to allow for the possibility that they might harm their addressees. Those who corresponded with her, a Jewess, might themselves be penalized on some pretext, and it seems doubtful that the censor would have been duped by her suggestion that Hanne's daughter Ursula address the envelopes in future. In any event, her correspondence with Hanne and Leo evidently ceased at this point. No further letters are on record.

'Into another witch's cauldron'
Arrested by the Gestapo

On moving house, Lilli had put a visiting card beside the doorbell to act as a makeshift nameplate. The brief inscription, 'Dr. med. Lilli Jahn', contravened a Nazi edict dated 17 August 1938, which decreed that Jewish women had to add the name 'Sara' to their forename. Lilli had also omitted to delete the 'Dr. med.', a title of which all Jews had been stripped.

This minor act of omission – or was it deliberate non-compliance with discriminatory measures? – must have been spotted by some visitor to the building in Motzstrasse, or by a resident. Lilli was reported to the Gestapo, who summoned her to their headquarters in Wilhelmshöher Allee. She was questioned, then allowed to go home. A few days later some Gestapo officers turned up at Motzstrasse. Lilli's children anxiously watched the men in long black leather coats as they searched the apartment and rummaged in the cupboards – with no perceptible result. During these tense days Lilli wrote of her Gestapo summons to her friend Lotte, who was now living in Leipzig. Lotte replied on 29 August 1943:

My dear Lilli,
I would have answered your sweet but very serious letter by return, had I not been ill again. I've had an awful dose of flu . . .
And you, you poor dear, are in the thick of more problems. We hoped so much that, in spite of your distressing loneliness, you were gradually recovering your peace of mind.

And now you've landed in another witch's cauldron. We debated whether it would or wouldn't have been right for Ernst to go to the Gestapo himself and set out the facts of the matter. But one can't judge such things at this distance. Surely it ought to be possible to get the case shelved for the duration of the war?

Now we're back where we started, and can do absolutely nothing for you. It really is too much, what you've been burdened with. This ought to be the end of it. Not a day goes by without my thinking of you . . .

Please, please write at once and tell me how your last interview with the Gestapo went and how everything stands at present. Do me a favour and drop me a line at once to say how things are. I'm so worried, and I haven't heard from you for too long, thanks to my own lengthy silence. You will write at once, won't you?

I can well imagine how much you miss the countryside in town. When I made a couple of excursions into the mountains from Freiburg, I sensed again how very much easier life is when you can spend it in natural surroundings. You then have something that won't let you down, even in the worst kind of turmoil. I also found it hard to bid all that farewell, and I've nothing left of it but a bunch of heather!

If you ever felt like it, I'd be very interested to hear how you've furnished your apartment. I'd so much like to be able to form a rough idea of it . . . I can imagine that living in the city has many advantages from the children's point of view. Just so long as their situation doesn't worsen in other respects.

What has your sister-in-law decided? Would it help if she came to stay with you? It would be a great relief to me.

Everyone here is nervous because of the danger of air raids, and there's talk of evacuating the schools. Preparations are being made in any case. You can imagine how awful it would be for me if we had to give Peter up again. – We're going to send off some parcels and a crate. Personally, I'm a great fatalist and not so terribly attached to material possessions, but I feel obliged to.

I shall at least see to it that this letter goes off today, so you can write as soon as possible and tell me about your present situation.

Please, my dear, stick it out for a bit longer, the way you've already done through such bad times. The darkness will lift, believe me!

And remember we think of you every day with concern and affectionate good wishes and love. Hugs and kisses

Yours, Lotte

Lilli probably had to report to the Gestapo again the very next day, 30 August. 'I'll be right back, children!' she called to her daughters. Then she set off for Wilhelmshöher Allee.

After a while, Ilse, Johanna and Eva became uneasy. They went out onto the apartment's small balcony and leant over the parapet so as to spot their mother as soon as she turned into Motzstrasse. Lilli was wearing a blue dress that day, and the girls' hopes initially rose at the sight of every woman in a blue dress.

But Lilli didn't return. Instead, the phone rang at some stage. The Gestapo, they were told, had arrested their mother. Just that, no reason, no explanation. Lilli had in fact been taken to Königstor police station after her arrest and confined in a cell there.

The children, who were initially left to their own devices, hoped at first that it was all a misunderstanding and would soon be cleared up. Maria Lieberknecht, a Kassel acquaintance of the Jahn family, learned of Lilli's arrest from her brother-in-law, who was in the Gestapo. Her husband, a minister of the Confessional Church, later described the course of events in a letter to Ernst Jahn. Paul Lieberknecht's letter, published in January 1947, documents his resentment at the behaviour of Ernst Jahn and his new wife:

The day after this arrest my wife came dashing into the library and told me that her brother-in-law . . . had urgently requested us to get you to take the five children into your home at Immenhausen, otherwise the Gestapo might bundle the orphaned children off to a camp. My wife spent a long time telephoning around in the presence of the officers in his department . . . until she finally got through to you. You refused at that time, saying: 'I can't, I don't know how my wife at Immenhausen would feel about it. Try to get her to agree to the children's coming back to Immenhausen.'

My wife then called her and received the following response: 'It's completely out of the question, the children can't come here. I shall write and ask Aunt Lore to come – she doesn't have anywhere to live in any case. Then she can keep house for the children in Kassel.'

My wife replied that it might be too late for the children by then. She said she would think over . . . what could be done for the children so that they weren't taken away too. My wife then went to the Gestapo and asked Hoppach to release the woman for the children's sake. I imagine I need not repeat the whole of what he said to her. Anyway, he told her that I was known by them to be a Jewish lackey and that the children would be treated like Jews, that is to say, would also have to wear a star. My wife stated that the children were half Aryan, and that she would, out of gratitude, look after them daily until a relation turned up.

August Hoppach, who headed the Kassel Gestapo, did not carry out his threats. Lilli's children were not compelled to wear the Jewish star, but their mother remained in custody.

Ernst and Rita did at least ensure that an adult spent the night in Kassel with the children from then on. Ernst himself came at first. His sister Lore, who had been bombed out in Essen, and whose help Rita had primarily hoped to enlist, then returned to Kassel and temporarily took their mother's place. At this time

Ilse was fourteen, Johanna thirteen, Eva ten, and Dorothea two. Gerhard, who was nearly sixteen, came home only at weekends, if at all.

Before long, however, Lore became so preoccupied with finding somewhere else to live that she was less and less able to take care of Lilli's daughters. When Lore went off to Essen and later to the south of Germany, therefore, it was usually Rita who had to spend the night at Motzstrasse. And when Rita either couldn't or wouldn't do so, this task was undertaken by Lore's eighteen-year-old daughter Marilis.

Although everyone adapted to the new situation, the children couldn't understand why their mother had been taken away from them. Ilse went to the Gestapo twice in the days following Lilli's arrest and asked when she would be released, but to no avail. On the second occasion one of the uniformed men told her: 'If you come again, we'll keep you here too.'

Breitenau Corrective Labour Camp

'Some bread and a little salt'
Cold and hunger in the 'institution'

A few days after being imprisoned in a police cell at Kassel, Lilli was transferred to the corrective labour camp at Breitenau, a Gestapo institution. Sandwiched between a female labourer named Valentina Iwaschkewiteck and a teacher named Luba Jutschenko, she is listed in the camp records as 'Detainee No. 1764, Lilli-Sara Jahn, housewife'. Date of admission: 3 September 1943.

The family were not informed at first. It was not until 10 September, a week later, that the Gestapo notified the children of where their mother was incarcerated. Ilse, the eldest, wrote to Lilli the same day:

> Dear Mummy,
> Today we heard where you are. Please write soon and tell us when you're coming home. We so look forward to seeing you. Are you getting enough to eat? May we send you something to eat? We'll send you some clothes. Today was Gerhard's birthday. It was very nice, but also not nice. There were apple yeast cakes and pancakes . . . Have you got a room of your own? Have you got a decent bed? All my thoughts are with you, dearest Mummy. Marilis came today. Marilis sleeps at our place and not at Immenhausen. I'm learning a lot of Latin and French. Otherwise, there's no news. We now have curtains in all the rooms.

I hope you're well. Do write soon . . . Please write and say exactly what we can send you. Daddy stays with us every night and Aunt Lore during the day. Dorle and Eva and Hannele are all very cheerful. Gerhard was very pleased with his books. There were sweets for children up to fourteen. We gave Gerhard some of them. Let's hope you come home soon! So lots and lots and lots and lots of love and kisses from your Ilse!

And a big hug

Like many of their contemporaries, no doubt, Lilli's children had no idea of what went on in a corrective labour camp, even though the Gestapo had begun to set up such camps throughout the Reich in 1940. Ultimately there were over 200 corrective labour camps, and they all had one main function: to punish and discipline those who failed, in the view of the Nazis, to fulfil their quota of work. Most of the prisoners were foreign labour conscripts who had allegedly or actually resisted forced labour.

A workhouse for beggars and vagabonds had been established in the former Benedictine monastery of Breitenau at Guxhagen, south of Kassel, back in the nineteenth century. From 1933 to 1934 it briefly served as a concentration camp. Finally, in May 1940, the corrective labour camp was set up. The Kassel Gestapo regularly sent detainees to Breitenau. The monastery-prison was now officially termed 'a preliminary to a concentration camp'.

Breitenau could house up to 350 prisoners. Most of them remained there for only three or four weeks and were then returned to their places of work. Apart from labour conscripts, most of whom came from Eastern Europe, German men and women were imprisoned there, either because they had opposed the Nazis politically, or because they had violated 'wholesome National Socialist popular sentiment' by having affairs with foreign workers or Jews – or because, like Lilli, they were Jews themselves. The Breitenau admissions register lists the names of at least 145 Jewish detainees, roughly half of whom were later deported to concentration camps and killed there.

Needless to say, Lilli had neither a room of her own nor enough to eat. She was accommodated in the women's building, which contained dormitories and cells. The women slept on wooden planks, palliasses, or plain beds of straw. Like all the other prisoners, Lilli had to work twelve hours a day. The food was worse than meagre and the treatment almost invariably harsh. Warders from the regional penitentiary usually functioned as guards, and many were feared for their brutality and ruthlessness. Their disciplinary repertoire included corporal punishment and solitary confinement. 'Punching and kicking were the order of the day,' former inmates testified later, and several prisoners were allegedly murdered by guards. In the summer of 1943 the district administrator at Fulda assured the camp authorities – and he meant it as a compliment – that several former inmates had said 'they would sooner be dead than do another spell in Breitenau'.

On 12 September 1943, before Lilli had received Ilse's letter, she was permitted to write to her family for the first time. The front of the letter bears two notes made by a wardress named Steinmetz, who was assigned to censor mail: 'via the institution' and 'Jahn, 13.9.43/St.' Lilli's address was given as: Breitenau, near Kassel, Guxhagen Post Office, 6 Adolf-Hitlerstrasse.

My dearly beloved children *all*, including Marilis and my dearest Lore,

Tomorrow I shall have been away for two weeks – I've been here ten days, and I welcome the passing of every day. But I don't yet dare to count the days until I can be with you again. Don't worry about me, I'm really fine. I'm fit, and your Mummy has always been good at getting up early, as you know, and the work is a blessing. I still have far too much time to think and brood, and then, of course, I miss you and feel homesick.

But now, children, you can write to me as often as you wish. So *please* write a lot and very soon, and tell me about everything, good and bad, about your joys and your sorrows. I won't be able to reply for the moment, but please write to me for that very reason. You can write to me too, Lore, and if there's any mail from Lotte or Uncle Georg, please send it on.

What is my Dorle up to? Is she being good? I won't be home in time for her birthday, but you'll find her big birthday candle and three little handkerchiefs in the bottom drawer of the front cupboard in the hall, and a few sweets in the sideboard.

Are you better, my little Eva? Have you missed a lot at school, and do you now have your books? Are you enjoying school, and do you still go to Immenhausen?

And Hannele, what is Heidi doing, and what of the violin? What's it like in Confirmation class? Will you be getting your little bird soon?

And you, my great big Ilse Mouse, I'm sure you're being a great help to Aunt Lore! How are you and Ulla and Gisela? Do they still come and see you? How is the Latin going?

To you, my Marilis, warmest good wishes and congratulations on your name day. Are you going to Göttingen? Will we see each other again soon?

And what is my Gerhard doing? Does he come home regularly, and how did his birthday go?

Lore, my dear, how are you? Isn't the work too much for you? Are you managing all right? How is Julie behaving? Give her my regards if she deserves it.

And how is Daddy? Where is he? What is he doing? Give him my very warmest regards. Oh, how much good it would do me to get a nice, comforting letter from him, but I don't suppose that will be possible.

And now I've got many, many requests, and my thanks to you in advance for all your trouble. Perhaps you could make up several small parcels, they may come quicker. Above all, please send me some newspapers regularly, and a book to read (Daddy will pick something out), possibly Stifter's 'Nachsommer'. I'm sure you'll find a less precious book for my room-mates on the bookshelf in the hall. Also, please: my nail file, my tweezers, the mirror from my red handbag, a box of Vasenol powder and the two sachets of talcum powder from the little cupboard in the children's chest of drawers, my slippers and a pair of *old* black shoes, and also, just occasionally, if you can, some bread and a little salt, and maybe you can spare a little cheese or jam, and put in one of the old silver knives (right-hand drawer). And might you possibly have a few apples? – we *only* get soup or boiled potatoes here. Also, but only if you can spare it, four or five packets of plain custard powder. And now goodbye for today. Hugs and kisses to you all. My thoughts, best wishes, and all my longings are with you day and night. With love!

Mummy

Certain words in Lilli's letter, for instance 'nail file', 'tweezers', 'mirror', 'talcum powder', 'slippers', 'bread', 'salt', and 'custard powder' were evidently underlined in pencil afterwards, either by a wardress or by the recipients. It may have been the children's way of identifying all the things they had to obtain for their parcels to Lilli.

Her appeal to write regularly unleashed a flood of letters. The children promptly grasped that this was the only way of keeping the virtually fatherless family intact. For six whole months, Ilse and Johanna wrote to Breitenau almost every other day, Eva about twice a week, and Gerhard every weekend. Initially limited to brief questions and items of news, their letters increasingly assumed the character of diary entries from which Lilli could form a very accurate picture of her children's daily life, their worries and their little pleasures.

Ilse apparently answered Lilli's first letter from Breitenau by return. Her reply, so a wardress noted, reached there on 17 September 1943:

Dearest Mummy,

How happy I was to get your news. Mummy, write

and tell us what sort of work you have to do. Do you get enough to eat? Are you allowed to smoke? We can easily spare what we're sending you. I sent Aunt Lotte four pounds of bread and one and a half pounds of cereals. Could you do with some cereals too? We're sending you the old slippers, because the other ones are surely too good. I hope the shoes are all right. We'll send you everything bit by bit. . . . The custard powder is all ready, you only have to dissolve it in milk. So now good night, dear Mummy. A thousand loving kisses from your Ilse, who never forgets you.

Johanna, too, wrote regularly to Breitenau from this point on. On 17 September she sent Lilli a postcard depicting a Madonna. The thirteen-year-old girl knew the importance her mother attached to this subject.

My dear sweet Mummy,
I hope you get this card by Sunday, I'd be so pleased . . . It's a pretty card, isn't it? I'm afraid I couldn't write yesterday. Our form, only ours, had to write an essay overnight on one sheet of paper about the women's RAD [Reichsarbeitsdienst, or Reich Labour Service]. This will be forwarded to the head of the Reichsarbeitsdienst, who wants to know what people think of the women's RAD We had to describe bad or happy experiences. Marilis helped me a lot. The three best ones will be published in the newspaper, but mine won't.
Evchen got some apples from the Rösches and some onions from the Wittichs . . . Just put your faith in the Almighty!
Masses of good wishes and kisses, and all the best from your Hannele

Unlike her two older sisters, ten-year-old Eva was a child of nature. Even from Kassel she visited two farmers' families in Immenhausen several times a week. She helped in the farmyard, tended the animals, and was recompensed with food, which she brought back to Kassel. Here is one of her first letters dating from September 1943:

Dear Mummy,
   How are you? We're all fine. I hope you're fine too. Lots of people have asked me to send you their regards. The Bäckers, the Hirdes, Neuman, Minna, and so many other people, I can't remember them all. In school we're sewing dirndl aprons. Last Saturday I picked apples for two hours at the Rösches, and I've already been given masses of fruit. Many, many thousands of good wishes and kisses from your Eva.

At ten, Eva was too young to see through people's cordiality. It is unclear, even today, why the townsfolk of Immenhausen asked her to remember them to her mother – as if Lilli had simply gone away for a day or two. Did it verge on an act of resistance to send an imprisoned Jewess their regards, or was it rather a symptom of thoughtlessness? In fact, no one in all those months uttered even a surreptitious word of sympathy for the four girls. Yet every inhabitant of the small town was aware of what had happened to Lilli: that the once respected woman doctor had been wrested away from her children and locked up for no good reason.

   While Eva was always remunerated for her help on the farms with fresh vegetables and fruit, meat and sausages, Ilse went shopping in Kassel with the food ration coupons to which the family was entitled. Her father supplied her with the requisite cash, and she herself ran the household with her Aunt Lore's help.

   Meanwhile, another (not extant) letter had arrived from her mother. Lilli had evidently complained again of being hungry. Ilse replied on 19 September:

My dearest Mummy,
   Oh, Mummy wrote to us, and our joy was indescrib-

able. We were absolutely delighted about nearly everything, but not about the fact that you still don't know when you'll be back with us, not about that, nor that you don't get such good food. We'll send you all we can spare, and not only that, but also what we know you like. I hope you'll enjoy everything we've got for you. Would you like some cereals to put in the soup? We'd have liked to send you some jam before now, but we thought the jar might get smashed. That's why we looked for a can first.

We've bottled a lot of stuff. Several jars of apple puree, stewed apples, pears, grapes, tomato puree, spinach, and pumpkin. We bought a pumpkin a few days after you went away, and another one with the Kunzes. When the Kunzes bottled their half of the pumpkin, we had to bottle the other half. I got hold of the recipe and bottled it myself. Mummy, it's scrumptious! The little ones wanted to eat it right away and asked me not to put it in jars, they thought it was so good when I let them taste it. The only thing is, you need an awful lot of sugar . . .

All children between three and eighteen are getting 200 grammes of nuts. We've got enough cheese and bread. Julie's being awfully rude. Aunt Lore cooks and darns, and I do all the shopping, and I have the housekeeping money. It's all a lot of work.

To begin with I found it awfully hard to go to bed and get up without your being there. But now I've chosen this motto: 'What do our dismal cares avail / and what our melancholy cries? / What use it is that we bewail / our fate each morning when we rise? / All that we gain from our despair / is a far heavier cross to bear.'

Oh, Mummy, it's so hard without you. Come back soon.

Aunt Lotte wrote me an awfully sweet letter. I've already written back and am waiting for a reply. Frau Zschiegner nearly fainted, she went as white as a sheet.

Ilse deliberately refrained from explaining her allusion to Frau Zschiegner, who was the wife of her and Gerhard's piano teacher in Kassel. She had, in fact, turned pale on learning of Lilli's arrest, but Ilse did not spell this out because the Breitenau censor might have taken exception to the information, and her mother might have suffered as a result. Although the matter was never raised, the children knew full well what they could afford to tell Lilli and what would be better left unsaid.

Ilse's letter of 19 September goes on:

Aunt Rita has given me a red necklace. It's quite nice, but Aunt Rita! I don't exactly get on very well with her. She's always trying to make up to me, and what can I do? I have to co-operate for Daddy's sake . . .

Dorle is very much looking forward to her birthday. Daddy has bought her a sweet picture book. She's also getting a doll from Immenhausen. I hope that's all right with you.

Gerhard is coming home on leave tomorrow. Today I sent him, via Marilis, four apples, one tomato, some grapes, five walnuts and some cakes. We had some apple cakes and some cheese. For supper there were open fish sandwiches and sausage. Fish is very plentiful at present. We've registered at the fishmonger's as well. We got some sardines once. We're very well off for food.

Let's hope you come back soon!!!!! Daddy isn't at the garrison hospital from today. From today he's at Lindenberg military hospital. That's out past Bettenhausen, at the back of beyond. That's why he won't be able to see us so often. Daddy has an officer's uniform and looks more presentable. He has a room of his own and eats in the officers' mess.

Do you want any more books? Should we send you some more? Be sure to write and tell me!!! . . . We're all sitting in our bedroom, writing to you. Afterwards we'll make up a parcel for you. Let's hope you like it. I only managed to get a small sachet of powder for you. There's very little around . . .

127

Please forgive me for writing so seldom, but I have so little time. You mustn't think you're the person I think of least of all. I'm going to make Hannele and Eva's school and breakfast sandwiches in a minute, then I won't have to get up at half past six.

So goodbye for now, dearest Mummy, and masses of good wishes and kisses from your Ilse, who never forgets you.

After this letter from Ilse came a short break occasioned by illness. Now it was Johanna who had to keep their mother up to date with news of the family. Her letter dated 22 September:

My dearest darling Mummy,

How are you? You'll wonder why I'm the only one writing. It's because Ille is in bed with a touch of flu, but it's not too bad. She may even get up tomorrow. Evchen is a bit lazy, so I'm writing to you.

First, I've a confession to make: I've cut the straps off my satchel. Now Heidi has taken the satchel with her to Hümme. The saddler there is making me a handle for it. Another thing: I went to your darning drawer and . . . took a piece of white material (not linen) for the dirndl apron. Was that naughty of me? Aunt Rita has just come back. She's sitting with Ilschen, and they're talking. Evchen is asleep already, and Dorle is chattering to herself. For supper this evening we had noodles and apple puree.

Lots of love and kisses for now, your Hannele

It was a rite of passage, even in those days, for children to give up wearing their school satchels on their backs and carry them like briefcases instead. For Ilse, who was a year older, this farewell to childhood came of its own accord: Lilli's absence compelled her to assume the role of surrogate mother. She now had to look after her younger sisters, a function that abruptly promoted her to adult status.

Having organized Dorle's third birthday celebrations on 25 September, she reported this to Lilli a few days later:

My dearest Mummy,

I couldn't write any sooner, I'm afraid, because I was ill. It wasn't too bad, but I'd have got better much quicker if you'd been here with me. I got up today for the first time. We tried on our winter things today. We don't really know what's what. Mummy, listen: I'm sure you're getting cold now. Shouldn't we send you a dress or a pair of gloves? Darling Mummy, are you really getting some sleep?

I was supposed to go to Gisela's in Nienhagen last Saturday, but I couldn't because I was in bed. That night Dr Stephan's maid came and asked if I'd taken the 1.45 bus, because that bus had come unhitched from its trailer, which was why the Stephans were so terribly worried. On Sunday morning Aunt Lore sent a telegram to Nienhagen saying I was still alive and kicking. I shall go there next Sunday. Let's hope nothing gets in the way.

We're getting three hundredweight of potatoes to last us from 21 November to 21 July 1944. That ought to do us. We've now got nine pounds of apples apiece, so things are getting steadily better. We have hot bathwater every Saturday and Sunday or Friday and Saturday.

There was quite a shindig on Dorle's birthday. Dorle was very pleased with her things . . . And now, a big kiss and masses of love from your Ilse, who's always thinking of you.

During the early weeks of Lilli's absence, Ilse's letters were still tinged with pride at her evident success in keeping house for the youthful family largely unaided. This accounts for her letter of 1 October, in which she enthuses about a sumptuous meal:

My very dearest Mummy,

I've just got up from a fantastic supper. We started

with some left-over baked noodles, then came potatoes in bechamel sauce with mixed pickles, and then smoked eel. It was delicious. We really enjoyed it, Mummy, and Marilis and I were glad we had something so good today because Gerhard was there.

He came around half past one and ate an apple with us for pudding. Then he went to Lindenberg to see Daddy and had a long talk with him. Daddy showed him over the whole place, and Gerhard is very surprised at how neat and nice it all is up there at the hospital.

Mummy, before I forget: Where is Gerhard's blue, high-necked sweater? And where is the key to the cupboard where our winter coats are? Please write and tell us. If you don't have much room to write, just write: The k. is in such and such a place, the s. is in such and such a place. Do it that way, all right? Now Gerhard is sitting talking with Marilis.

I hope you aren't too cold!! Yesterday, wonder of wonders, the heating came on. But only 20 cm of the radiators is hot and all the rest is cold. They were quite cold again from this morning to around six o'clock this evening. Very funny, I don't think!!! Tomorrow you'll be getting another parcel. I hope you like everything.

Ilse's letter, which has not survived in full, breaks off at this point. It marks the end of the children's almost untroubled certainty that Lilli would soon return from Breitenau. From then on their letters contain one simple, reiterated expression of despair. 'When are you coming home?' Eva asked on 3 October 1943. Her apprehensive rider: 'Soon, let's hope.'

'The more I miss you'
Lilli's clandestine letters to her children

Because Lilli was generally permitted to write home only once a month, she looked for ways and means of sending her children further communications in secret. Not having any notepaper of her own at Breitenau, she had to improvise. On Sunday, 3 October 1943, she used the backs of five labels for Sanatogen, a 'tonic for general physical debility' and 'exhaustion'. Written in pencil, the letter was meant not only for the children but also for her niece Marilis, who was spending a few weeks at the Kassel apartment prior to enrolling at Marburg University.

> My dearly beloved children, all six of you,
> Although I'm not allowed to write to you again for another week, a *kind* person has given me some stamps and an envelope and will post this for me tomorrow. So I hope you'll receive these bits of paper on Tuesday or Wednesday. But you must *not*, when you reply, disclose that you've had a letter from me – not under *any* circumstances, or I'd get into very serious trouble. I wrote to you a week ago, but had no opportunity to get the letter off until Friday, *without* stamps. I hope you got it all the same. I think of you so often day and night, my dear children, and the longer I'm away from you the more I miss you! If only I knew when I'll be allowed home! Oh, if only it were *soon*!
> My greatest and only pleasure here is your letters and loving messages, and I can't thank you enough for them!

Whether it's the dear long letters from Gerhard or Marilis, or the almost regular letters from Hannele telling me about Dorle and sending me her love, or Evalein's postcards, I'm always happy and sad at the same time, then happy again.

As for Ilse Mouse's letter, I particularly looked forward to it this week because I was worried about her flu. That's why I was doubly glad to get it. Thank you all from the bottom of my heart!

But you mustn't send me all your lovely postcards. *Please, please* keep them for yourselves. Oh, and yesterday evening Evalein's parcel of apple slices and biscuits arrived – a regular Sunday salutation. You dear girl, it gave me such pleasure. I've had two batches of newspapers and three parcels this week (eleven in all now), one with bread, one with some apples and two little nuts, one with apples and cheese. A thousand thanks. Could you really spare the cheese? And the bread? Anyway, I'm very grateful for everything you send, because we don't get much to eat, never any butter, never any meat, a small piece of sausage once every two weeks, just soup otherwise, and Sundays are especially bad. At half past six in the morning we get a slice of dry bread and this awful dishwater coffee, at eleven either some thin soup or jacket potatoes with gravy and gherkins, and at four another slice of dry bread with either a little sausage or a spoonful of cottage cheese and some coffee, then nothing more till the next morning. So I'm very thankful to have some bread and cheese at night and, between times, some of your really delicious apples. But for goodness' sake *don't* mention any of this in your letters.

Please send me some more salt if you can, and a little jam, but *no* cereals and, as soon as possible, some sanitary towels.

Wouldn't it be more practical if you sent bigger parcels after all? Maybe on Mondays, then it'll probably get here by the end of the week and you won't have to go to the post office so often and will also save postage. But just as you wish.

Has Aunt Lore gone to Essen? I had an idea she was going this month, but only on Wilhelm's birthday at the end of the month. I think of her a great deal, and never forget her grief and sorrow.

Please write to Aunt Lotte and send her *lots* of love! I was so pleased to hear from her, and she can safely write more often. All the letters get here, it's just that I can't answer them. And I'd like to know how she and Peter are.

A shame Daddy can't come to see you as often. Is he looking a bit better these days? Give him my special love, and I've got a request for him: Can he get me a book by Karl H. Ruppel, whom I so much admire: *Berliner Theater – Dramaturgische Betrachtung*, published by Paul Neff (Berlin-Vienna). There was a good review of it in the *Kölnische Zeitung*, in which I always find something nice and enjoyable to read. I don't manage to read anything else, I'm afraid, this place is too noisy.

Did my Ille go to Nienhagen today? The weather is really glorious. I also thought a great deal about Hannele at ten o'clock during morning service. Did the poem go well? When are you going to Heidi's? When are your autumn holidays? Marilis must have been to see Gerhard, I'm sure. Oh, I just don't dare to think of him coming home next weekend – *how* much I'd like to be with you then. But I'm glad Marilis is with you. Have you decided on Marburg? I'm sure it's nice there too.

Evchen, are you hard at work harvesting potatoes? And Dorle will show me her new picture book when I'm back home, won't you, my little treasure? Oh, if only I could hug you tight again, you and all of you.

You've no need to send me any warm clothes, we wear institute clothing. I can well imagine that you were stumped by the winter things. In the mothball cupboard at Immenhausen there's an old red woollen dress of mine, and there's some more material among my patching offcuts; one of you should get a dress out of it. Perhaps Aunt Lore could also buy some material on my clothing card, I've enough for the winter. There are also some old pleated skirts in the cupboard at home, maybe some of them can be used for Dorle.

Now my paper's run out and I must stop. Give Aunt Maria my love too. Can't she help me? May God protect you, my beloved children! I send you my heartfelt good wishes and a loving, grateful kiss.

Your Mummy

In the letters she smuggled out, unlike those that were officially censored prior to posting, Lilli could give an unvarnished account of the wretched conditions prevailing at Breitenau, but she was always restrained in her descriptions so as not to shock the children too much.

Her question at the end of the letter – whether Maria Lieberknecht couldn't help her – was repeatedly taken up by the children in the months to come. Maria's brother-in-law was in the Gestapo, after all, and it was he who had informed them of Lilli's arrest at the end of August. All Lilli's hopes and those of the children now rested on this one contact: Couldn't Maria, with her brother-in-law's help, persuade the Gestapo to release her?

It may have been thanks to this brother-in-law that most of the children's parcels were delivered. Jewish and Polish prisoners at Breitenau had, in fact, been forbidden parcels since 1941, but Lilli was clearly exempt from this restriction.

The same night, 3 October, the city of Kassel was once more the target of a large-scale British air raid. It was probably because of this that Lilli added a marginal note: 'We always have air-raid warnings at the same time as you do, and then I think of you very much.' Most of the bombs hit the suburbs, however, and the city itself was almost undamaged.

Ilse, who had spent the night of the raid at Nienhagen, where the parents of her Kassel girlfriend Gisela Stephan owned a weekend house, described the course of events on 6 October:

My dearest sweetest Mummy,

I hope you didn't come to any harm during the raid. I was with Gisela at Nienhagen that night, and we had a good view of everything from there. Lucky nothing happened to us. I was very worried about everyone the night I was at Nienhagen – firstly about you, secondly about everyone in Kassel, and thirdly about Gerhard. But we're all fine including Gerhard, thank God, and I very much hope the same applies to you. On the assumption that you're all right, I'll tell you all about it.

On Monday morning I went from Nienhagen to Kassel. It was a very nice trip. We didn't have any classes because our school is an assembly point for the homeless. Aunt Rita came to see how we were the morning after the raid. Daddy got some leave today, from lunchtime till tomorrow night. Aunt Lore is coming back on Thursday or Friday.

We've now bottled the big pumpkin as well. It made four two-litre jars and a half-litre jar. One of them we ate right away. The children are awfully fond of pumpkin, but we used a great deal of sugar. We're trying to save some for next year, but we haven't got very far. Frau Stephan gave me a big basket of apples that had been bruised during picking. We shall probably make some apple jelly out of them when the new sugar ration becomes available. We're really well off for food in general. You get so much on the ration cards at present. I hope you also get enough to eat?!

We sent off another little parcel today. The tinned sardines were on the ration card for over-fourteens. I have one of those cards, so I got a tin. We recently had eel, and I thought you'd be bound to enjoy some. I hope it doesn't go astray in the mail in spite of being registered. The powder is Fissan [baby] powder, but I think you'll be able to use it all the same. I'm sure you'll also find a use for the other bits and pieces. Write and tell us sometime where Julie's papers are. We ought to know in case we ever need them. You can shorten it again: J's papers are . . . Will you manage to open the tin of sardines? I *hope so*!!! . . .

I'm writing everything higgledy-piggledy because I've got so much to tell you. Dorle is being very good. Daddy was here yesterday evening, and he washed her and put her to bed. Dorle was terribly pleased. Dearest Mummy, aren't you cold? Do you get some sleep at nights? Don't worry too much, understand? I'm doing everything as well as I can, and my work is gradually coming to resemble yours. I can't do things the way you can, of course. I always keep you safe in my heart, my little Mummy, so that you don't worry too much. Good night. A thousand good wishes and a loving kiss from your Ilse

Johanna also wrote to Breitenau the same night. A little dream of hers had just come true: she was at last going to get the budgerigar she'd set her heart on. This plan had been agreed before Lilli's arrest. Now Ernst had to help in obtaining the bird.

My dear darling Mummy,

How are you? Guess what I'm getting? A budgerigar, a pale yellow one. Now listen carefully: At 6 Motzstrasse there lives a civil servant named Weber whose son is a medical probationer at Daddy's hospital. He's in his eighth semester and does practical work here in Kassel during the vacations. He's very nice. He once told Daddy that he'd acquired a young budgerigar. Daddy, the dear, knew I was looking for one, so he promptly asked the man how and what and where! The probationer said I should come to see him at seven on such and such an evening, so I went. He was very nice and gave me the address of some people in Wilhelmshöhe. He promised me he would get a bird cage from his girlfriend and would tell Daddy when he got it.

So the next morning I went to Wilhelmshöhe, to the stop for Kunoldstrasse. You have to go down a street to the right, then you come to Lange Strasse. No. 76 is a bit further along on the left. It's a kind of express delivery business, but the man has a tremendous number of birds. I'd taken Dorle with me. On the door was a note: Back in a minute. So we stood there and waited. There was a loud twittering sound everywhere. I managed to peer through a window. There was a huge cage containing a big, brightly coloured, gorgeous parrot. A magnificent creature! Then the man turned up. He showed us three budgerigars including a green one for fifteen Reichsmark. It couldn't fly because its wings had grown too long, but I didn't want that one anyway. In the same cage was a pale yellow budgerigar for twenty-five. I liked that one best. Then there was another for thirty, but it was also green. I don't know why, but the dear little yellow one was nicer and cheaper. It was healthy, too. All three were only five weeks old. So I asked the man if he'd keep the yellow one for me, and said I would come to collect it in three or four days' time. I told Daddy all this, and he agreed. So tomorrow evening I'm getting the cage from Doctor Weber's girlfriend. I've asked Frau Paack about food. Every day, if you want them to speak, that is, you put a few grains of 'talking seeds' under the little creatures' food. There's a whole lot to learn. I'm so pleased! If I get the yellow one I'm going to christen him Hänschen . . . I think it suits him . . . I must stop now! Will you write soon?

Masses of love and kisses from your Hänschen.

Hans or Hänschen was not only the budgerigar's name but Johanna's boyish nickname – so it really did 'suit'.

Ilse was more than usually worried about her mother at this time. Lilli was not equipped to withstand the cold that set in early during the autumn of 1943, and Ilse knew that she was only allowed to wear thin prison clothing: a shirt and trousers of greyish-brown sackcloth, although the temperatures were below freezing. On 7 October she wrote:

My dearest Mummy,

I wonder how you are! I hope so very much that you're all right. Just don't get cold. Put on all the warm under-clothes you have. Please do, so you don't become ill. And eat enough. Enjoy what we send you. I hope you'll eat enough. Don't be too terribly sad. Aunt Lore is looking after us again. She came back today . . . Daddy and Aunt Rita came over today, and Daddy took us four children to the Paulus. We each had two cakes and an ice cream. The ice cream and one of the cakes were very good, but the other tasted awful. It was very nice there otherwise. Marilis stayed behind with Aunt Lore and didn't come with us. Marilis will be sleeping at Immenhausen from tomorrow, because Aunt Lore is too scared. Then Aunt Rita will come here again every evening.

Gerhard has got leave on Saturday and Sunday . . .

Good night, sleep well, a big hug and lots of love from Ilse

Johanna, too, recounted their visit to the Café Paulus the same evening. She also made a jocular reference to the fact that some neighbours had asked 'if we didn't have any parents. Funny, isn't it?' The question was not so wide of the mark, either, because the four girls were often left by themselves, at least during the day, in spite of the worsening air raids.

Johanna's greatest preoccupation continued to be her budger-igar. On 10 October the bird caused a considerable flurry of excitement:

My very dearest Mummy,

It's Sunday evening, and I'm terribly tired, absolutely all in. Listen to this! Marilis and I went to see Gerhard this afternoon. When we got back, my Hänschen wasn't there. The cage was shut and the little bird gone. 'Marilis,' I yelled, 'here, quick.' When Marilis heard, she said: 'Quick, shut the door first.' Then we looked around the room. He was nowhere to be seen. Suddenly we spotted him perched on the curtain rod. 'Hänschen, you dear little fellow, please come down.' But no, Hänschen wasn't budging. Well, Marilis fetched a stepladder, and then it started. Marilis put a cap on for safety's sake, because you never know! When Marilis reached the top of the ladder and tried to grab him, whoosh, he flew off. Oh boy, Mummy, he kept whizzing over our heads really fast. There was quite a wind. He perched on the ledge above Ille's bed. 'All right, you naughty bird, please come down, please, please.' Not on your life, thought the little bird. Well, we threw a tablecloth over him, but – whoosh! – he soared off on to the blackout. We climbed the stepladder again and tried to grab him, but Hänschen hopped nearer and nearer the other end. 'Marilis,' I said, 'turn the light out.' But we couldn't shift the creature even in darkness. So we shooed him a bit lower down with the tablecloth. But, guess what, he flew back up on to the curtain rod. One grab and I had him, but 'Ouch, ouch,' I shrieked. He bit me, jabbed his little beak into my thumb really hard. I held him tight and quickly put him back in his cage. Heavens, was I exhausted! We had such a laugh. How did he get out, you'll ask. I'll tell you. On the sides are some little doors you can slide upwards. The naughty boy had kept on trying to push the door up with his head, and he succeeded, and got out in no time. But now the door is firmly tied shut, and the little rascal is happily pecking away at his seeds. But you've no idea the shock I got at first.

Gerhard was very tired today. They've had a lot of alerts. They'd just had one when we got there. His weekend leave is off. He'll now get his weekend leave on Wednesday, during the week. Gerhard told us there are mice in his locker. They've completely riddled his underpants with holes. During the night they shot down a plane and took two really young Canadians prisoner . . .

Now I shall close again, and think of you a lot, and wish you all the very best, so you come back home soon.

A million hugs and kisses, your loving Hannele

Gerhard's military achievements impressed his sisters. The same night, he himself proudly recounted the most recent success scored by his anti-aircraft battery at Obervellmar, near Kassel, in his regular Sunday letter to his mother:

Dear Mummy,

I send you my very best Sunday regards. How are you?

I'm fine. All is well at home, too. I hope you weren't too scared during the night of the 3rd/4th. I also survived the night unscathed. We even shot down a four-engined bomber. I'm sure you can guess how pleased we were.

Apart from that, nothing very special happened last week, except that we've had an awful lot of alerts. Two or three nights we managed to sleep right through, but then it started again, twice as badly.

That's why we aren't doing too much school work. In German we're now studying ballads. We're learning 'Die Kraniche des Ibykus' . . .

I should really be home today on weekend leave, but I had another stroke of bad luck: Twenty-three air-force auxiliaries were killed in the raid on Kassel. They all came from Eschwege and around there. The funeral was held at Eschwege yesterday. We had to send the twenty tallest members of our battery as a guard of honour, so I was there too . . .

It went like this. At 9.30 on Friday night we went to bed after the alert. At 12.30 we got up again – a second alert till 2.30. At 5 we were woken, moved off at 6, and got to Eschwege – eighty air-force auxiliaries and ten lieutenants in all – at 10 a.m. Overcoats off, steel helmets on, and away we went to the funeral . . . There was an alert when we got back, so I didn't get to bed until 10.30. There was another alert just as Hannele and Marilis turned up. Now I must finish this letter quickly.

All the very best and lots of love from

Your Gerhard

The girls were also harnessed to the war machine at this time. The authorities organized a large-scale campaign in aid of the victims of the 3 October air raid, and schoolgirls also had to take part. Ilse mentioned this in a letter dated 12 October:

We're on disaster relief duty tomorrow and the day after. We're glad to do it, because we're helping so many poor people who have very little left, some of whom have had relations killed. The poor things are so worn out by those terrorbombers, they're badly in need of help.

Like most Germans, Lilli's children failed to grasp the Allies' purpose in attacking civilian targets. At first, however, these air raids did little to demoralize the population. On the contrary, they tended to breed a sense of solidarity. Nor did Lilli's daughters ever suspect that the destruction of Kassel's munitions industry might benefit their mother by shortening the war. As for sixteen-year-old Gerhard, he had adopted the Wehrmacht's military logic. No one, not even his own father, pointed out to him that the British or Canadian bomber pilots whom he shot at so zealously were indirectly trying to halt the Nazis' genocidal activities.

On the other hand, even if Gerhard had fathomed their insane policy, he had no choice. Whether he wanted to or not, he had to serve as an air-force auxiliary.

On 14 October Ilse told Lilli about her 'disaster relief' duty:

Dear Mummy,

I've just had a nice day. I got to the swimming pool at

eight this morning, and we were bussed from there to Sandershausen. Only eight out of twenty girls had turned up. Rotten of them to shirk their duty like that, wasn't it? When we got to the village the woman in charge of operations wasn't there yet. We waited for a little while, but then we went off to our previous people. I went with Ellen to her woman because my own people hadn't put in another application. The house was all shut up when we arrived, but a man who was working there unlocked the door and told us to go into the kitchen. It was very cold in there, because it was two degrees below freezing this morning. We lit the stove and waited until the woman came. Her husband is the village schoolmaster, and she went to our school herself. She has a nice little house.

We'd only finished a few rooms when the woman in charge came and sent us off to some other people. Another nice girl from my form was already there when I got to the people – Friedgart, if you know her. I was made to have some noodle soup as soon as I arrived.

Then it started: washing dishes, scrubbing the bar parlour. The wooden floor of the bar parlour only gets scrubbed once a quarter. I had to do it all on my own, because Friedgart had to help in the house and fetch water. The water main is fractured, so it all has to be fetched from a stream, the Nieste. Every little bit of the floor had to be sluiced first, then scrubbed with soap powder, and then mopped dry. And so on, bit by bit. I slogged away at it for three or four hours, I should think.

When I'd finished there was bread, butter, cheese, and jam. After that the room next door had to be mopped again. Friedgart and I did that by ourselves. Friedgart played a waltz on the out-of-tune piano, and I danced with the broomstick. After that I had to oil the whole bar parlour. Some job!!! Then I mopped two kitchens and picked some carrots in the garden. Then it was five o'clock. We were given two sandwiches and a pear. Then we were driven home again.

I hope you're well. Sleep well and take a big, loving
hug from your Ilse Mouse

Ilse found such little adventures welcome because they helped to
take her mind off her troubles. No one else could compensate the
girls for the loss of their mother's love and the sense of security
she imparted, nor did anyone endeavour to do so. The most they
received was a little sympathy from Aunt Lotte in Leipzig, as Ilse
told her mother on 15 October:

I got an awfully nice letter from Aunt Lotte today. She
often writes, and her letters are always a comfort to me.
Because, oh, Mummy, it's *so* hard. But we'll bear our lot
together, however hard it gets. Are you really warm
enough? It's always so terribly cold in the mornings.

Ilse conveyed her fear and despair more and more clearly,
whereas Johanna masked those emotions by adopting a cheerful,
optimistic tone. Here is the letter she wrote the same night:

My dear darling Mummy,
    Oh, I've had another terrible time of it. Imagine, that
naughty Hänschen bit right through a wooden bar the
thickness of a spillikin, sneaked out of his cage, and
escaped on to the curtain rod. When I came home (the
others were at Aunt Maria's, it was around six
o'clock) the cage was empty once more. I fetched Julie
and the stepladder, and then we started all over again,
chasing and catching the poor little bird, who gets so
scared. He's back in his cage at last. Now there's a big
cushion lying on top of the cage. He'd have to push
the cushion off first. I don't think he'll manage it,
though.
    This morning was nice. The doll, Mummy, is a dear
little thing. She's wearing a pale blue floral silk dress and
a little bonnet. Long lashes and great big eyes that open
and shut. The head is made of china, the rest of cloth. But

really delightful. It'll make a lovely Christmas present for our little mouse.

I asked Aunt Maria if she had something for me to read, because Daddy still hasn't told me what I can read. So she gave me a book called 'Jungfrau Elise' by Ingeborg Maria Sick. I don't know if you know it. Then I asked whether she had some story books for girls, so she went to the bookcase in the living room beside the kitchen and looked. She came across an old book of Uncle Theo's, tales of the Great War, so I said: 'May I read that sometime?' All at once Aunt Maria said: 'I'll make you a present of it. You can take it with you as a memento of Uncle Theo.' What could I do? Then she said: 'Let's count how many mementoes of him there are.' But there were very few. There was a Bible I particularly liked. Almost brand new, completely un-used. I said: 'That's nice. If only I had one like that.' It wasn't supposed to be a hint, though, honestly and truly not. Then she said: 'Take it, and one moment, look here, take the hymnal as well. We don't need that.' It was a hymnal just like the one I had, you know, Mummy, with the cover coming to bits. But much nicer. Brand spanking new. I was speechless. I really couldn't, I said, I mustn't and I won't. So she went straight to the telephone and called Uncle Paul, and he told me over the phone to take it. But imagine, I was worn out. It's too much, don't you think? But I'm *so* pleased. Oh boy, Mummy, it'll soon be dangerous to go and see them. Tomorrow I'm going to Heidi's. At Hümme it takes longer for letters . . .

Johanna's letter has not survived in full and breaks off here. Her and Ilse's visits to their girlfriends were important to Lilli because they indicated, among other things, that her children were not being ostracized in spite of their Jewish mother – and Lilli had anticipated unpleasantnesses of that kind.

Throughout these months, Ilse acted as the channel for all information about the current state of affairs in Breitenau. She evaluated Lilli's letters and transmitted their contents to her father, Gerhard, Lore, Rita, and Aunt Lotte. Lotte also wrote a few times to her imprisoned friend, for instance on 17 October:

My dear Lilli,
I was delighted to hear today from Ilse that you had received my letter, and that it gave you pleasure. I'd write you one every day if I could.
If thoughts and good wishes could help someone else, even a little, then mine would be bound to do that for you. I think of you so often during the day, and often at night as well, and hope with all my heart that you come through this safely. I firmly believe you will. Keep calm and be patient. It seems that, after all your peaceful and harmonious years at Immenhausen, you were destined to be caught up in a whirlpool, and of this I'm quite certain: It will *not* drag you under!
I hear from Ilse now and then. She writes very sweetly, and she's so touchingly impulsive that I can always tell how she's feeling. Everything seems to be going well, so you won't worry too much on that score, will you? . . .
Goodbye for now, my dear, dear Lilli.
Chin up and be of good cheer!
Your Lotte

Lilli herself wrote a letter on the same day. The regulations in Breitenau did not entitle her to write another one at that time, so she once more contrived to get the closely written sheets of brown wrapping paper smuggled out of the camp and posted to Kassel illicitly:

My *dear, dear* children *all*, I'm going try my luck again and see if this letter reaches you. You know, of course, that you mustn't mention it.

The next few lines, written in pencil, are smudged and illegible. The letter goes on:

145

You really must believe me when I say I'm fine, and my gall bladder is behaving itself too, dear Marilis. The meagre fare and long hours of sleep are doing me good. We have to be in bed by half past eight and get up at half past five.

You dears, you've spoilt me so much this week, it really preys on my mind. I've certainly had plenty to eat every day, and today, Sunday, I've lacked for nothing thanks to your kindness, and many of my room-mates here have had some too. Thank you from the bottom of my heart for the parcel of tinned sardines, etc., and the sweets, which I'm sure you made yourselves. Also for the parcel of butter and so on – children, you really mustn't do it again, however kindly – very kindly – you mean it! I *forbid* you to send me any more butter. You mustn't stint yourselves of *anything*, and you must also keep your sweets for yourselves. I'm so very happy if you have everything, and *so* grateful to you for all the other things you send me. Your parcel with all those delicious things in it was almost like a Christmas parcel. A thousand thanks! The plum puree is really excellent! And many thanks to my Gerhard for his dear, sweet letter! And such delicious honey cakes! I was so *very* pleased with everything, but you really mustn't go on sending me so much of what you yourselves need so badly!

Please give Aunt Maria my fondest love. Her lovely fruit loaf was a great treat. It does one so much good to receive such tokens of true friendship. And your letters give me the greatest pleasure. I find it a real blessing that you let me share in all your doings, so I remain in touch with you. I'm only sorry I can't comment on every last detail.

Above all, my Ilse Mouse, don't worry about me so much. I'm being careful, and my one thought is to come back to you fit and well and, I hope, soon. Has my Dorle also caught a cold? Why does she need arch supports? Presumably she'll be getting some more little shoes? If

Dorle needs a dress, there's an old pale-blue knitwear dress among the winter things, a sleeveless one. You could sew on some cloth sleeves, then it would still serve. It's all right about the coats for Magda and Dorle. Do the leggings fit Dorle? I approve of all your other clothes arrangements too.

The good, big swansdown blanket is in the sideboard cupboard. Have the windows and blackout in the dining room been repaired, and are the apartments and furniture undamaged? Please let me know! Hasn't Armbrust delivered the bookshelf yet? Have you now got some shelves in the hall cupboard? If you need any more preserving jars, remember the jars in the cellar and the preserving jugs. I'm very glad you've now got the clothes washed and ironed and ready to be put away.

And you, my Ille, are working so hard to see that everything gets put back in the right place. How are your chilblains, my little Eva? Are you doing anything for them? I'm always especially delighted to get your letters, Hannele. I take an interest in *everything*, absolutely *everything*. And Gerhard's and Marilis's letters are always so sweet and nice. I hope you'll find some digs in Marburg. Has Aunt Paula written from Geneva? And Uncle Georg? Please send me a few photos of you all, if you haven't stuck them in yet. I don't suppose you've taken any new ones. Oh, but best of all I'd like to see you all again in the flesh.

I'm badly in need of hairpins too, if only two or three. Also, please send the other book by Pearl Buck when you can, and maybe you could get a set of spillikins? The girls get so bored on Sundays, but I don't. I read your letters and the newspapers and think my private thoughts, which wing their way *only* to you. Special regards to your Hänschen, Hannele. What grand books you're reading these days! And Gerhard, my *dear*, don't you ever get a chance to read? And what about you, Marilis? I don't expect Ille ever gets the time. Goodbye for today!

Thousands of affectionate, loving hugs and kisses, Gerhard, Ilse, Hannele, Eva, Dorle, and Marilis!

Your Mummy

The 'girls' Lilli mentions, most of whom were Russian and Polish labour conscripts, confided in her more and more. Lilli not only helped her fellow prisoners to pass the time. She also looked after the young women in a medical capacity and assisted at several births.

Lilli wrote another letter, probably the same night, to her sister-in-law Lore. She again used dark brown wrapping paper, a packet of which her daughters may have included in one of their parcels.

The date is missing, however. A subsequent letter to Ernst mentions that a longish letter to Lore had been 'posted' on 29 October, but the Lore letter itself mentions that she had been away 'seven weeks tomorrow'. This implies that it must have been written on 17 October but not sent off until twelve days later. Perhaps Lilli had failed until then to find anyone who could smuggle the letter out of camp.

My dear, devoted Lore,

I can never thank you enough for all you're doing for me and the children. My heartfelt love for you and Marilis is the only form of recompense I can offer. I owe it to you that I don't have to worry about the children's physical wellbeing, and how much easier in my mind that makes me.

You're going to so much trouble and effort over the preserving, and now over the children's winter wardrobe, and I know in advance that all is as it should be. I would naturally prefer it if you could look after the moth cupboard, just as you should keep a grip on everything else. Thank you also for your efforts as regards Eva's music and English lessons. When does she start them? I think you'll have to devote a little more care to Ilse than to the other children. My absence grieves her so much,

148

and many of her letters are heartbreaking. But *please* don't let her know I told you.

Many thanks for your sweet letter from Essen. I've been thinking of you a great deal, and can well imagine how worried you were. I felt just the same, and I thank God we were all spared on this occasion too.

It would have been Wilhelm's birthday this week! Oh, my dear, dear Lore, I'm with you in spirit and thinking of you with affection and sympathy. Please, at this time, take a little book from the bookshelf beside my sewing table called 'Der Traum des Gerontius'. Get Marilis to look it out for you and read it. I'm sure it'll do you good.

I wanted to ask you to ask the Labour Office again if they can't find a replacement for Julie. I put in an application in August, and it was endorsed by Frau Meyer of the Labour Front. Julie is entitled to some home leave in December, and I'm sure she won't come back, so it's better to be prepared.

I shall have been away seven weeks tomorrow. I often feel quite ill with homesickness. Couldn't you find out from the Gestapo how much longer I have to be away? Ernst could surely ask Herr Hoppach. If I'm to be allowed home soon, write that you 'hope to see me soon'; if not, say 'we must wait a bit longer' or, at worst, 'be patient for a long while yet'. This uncertainty and these tormenting thoughts are so gruelling. Things are naturally far worse than I say in my letters to the children. Less than adequate food, insufficient clothing. We aren't allowed to wear overcoats or jackets or gloves, and in the mornings we often have to stand waiting in the cold at the station for three-quarters of an hour or an hour because the trains are so late, and the same again in the evening. The building isn't heated yet, either. And being cooped up in general. You can't imagine what it's like.

Couldn't Ernst put in an application if I'm not released after two months (on 30 October)? Surely he could do something more for me? I feel so forlorn and rejected! I was arrested for contravening the police regulation of August 1938 (?), which carries a sentence of four weeks. That was up long ago.

He could also argue that Marilis has gone back to university and Rita can't always sleep in Kassel, so the children are all on their own at night. As for you, dear Lore, you're always having to go to Essen. Who's supposed to look after the children then? And isn't the work becoming too much for you, healthwise? Surely one could at least cite those reasons? Seeing that the boy is an air-force auxiliary and his father in the army, couldn't he request that his children get their mother back? Perhaps the request could be endorsed by the military authorities and made a matter of urgency?

Or could one try to achieve something through the youth welfare office? Oh, *please* help me to obtain my release. Work out what you can do, and have a word with Aunt Maria as well! I hope this letter reaches you both. Best regards to Ernst, and to you, my dear Lore, all my gratitude and love and good wishes, and an affectionate hug!

Your Lilli

Lilli, who was pinning all her hopes on Lore's assistance, believed that her sister-in-law would by now have taken over the children's care. In fact, Lore was still overwhelmed with despair at the loss of her husband and son in the air raid on Essen. Lacking the energy to shoulder the responsibility devolved on her by Lilli, she spent these weeks restlessly roaming the country in search of a new home. It did not dawn on Lilli until months later that Lore could be of little help to her and her children.

'Hänschen gets scared'
The war in the air draws nearer

The autumn of 1943 brought a renewed intensification of the air raids on Germany. Allied bomber squadrons carried out attacks on industrial centres throughout the Reich, and many aircraft traversed the air space over Kassel. Gerhard's anti-aircraft battery at Obervellmar was in action almost daily, and the sirens were forever wailing in Kassel itself.

Lilli had packed a few essentials in an 'air-raid suitcase', and there were many occasions when the children had to tote this down to the cellar several times a day, as Johanna recounts in a letter dated 18 October:

> My sweet little Mummy,
> It's half past nine. I meant to write earlier, actually, but circumstances have prevented me from doing so. At half past eight we had another alert. Another, because we'd already had one at four. But both times they were kind enough to fly past us. You know, Mummy, we've had so much practice when there's an air-raid warning. It all goes like clockwork, and we're nearly always the first to reach the cellar. Tonight I went back upstairs again to the Kunzes. It always takes the four of them a bit longer. I helped Pipa to put on her shoes and carried some bed-clothes down. You know what, Mummy? I've decided to take my violin downstairs with me and leave my dear little birdie Hänschen upstairs. I can only take one or the other because I have to carry an air-raid case as well.

I take my Hänschen down from the wall, then at least he's on the floor and shielded from the worst of the blast. If you write . . . please tell me what you think. I'm not quite sure, myself. The little creature is alive, after all. He senses things and gets scared. But the violin is a bit like that too, and I'm very fond of it. Oh well, I'll ask Daddy.

Tomorrow we've got a substitution, PE instead of music. That's fine with us. Aunt Lore is now finishing off my blue knitted sweater, I'm glad to say. We're unpicking the red sweater for Ille. I think it belonged to Aunt Hansel. I really enjoy doing that. I've got a fine old cold, so I've got a fine old thirst as well. It's awful, having to drink water all the time.

But there's something else that's much nicer. We haven't got [Frau] Jahns for geography and history any more, only for maths and biology. We all danced for joy in the playground. The little ones gawped at us like idiots. Well, it had to stop sometime, having that silly woman for four subjects. We got a new timetable on Saturday. Someone gave me some bacon. We'll send it off to you today. Please write and tell us if you receive it and if it's all right. Ille is just baking another cake, that's why she won't be writing a long letter tonight. Well, my best beloved Mummy, that's it!

A billion good wishes and kisses from your loving Hannele.

Ilse added the following postscript:

Dearest darling Mummy,

I've just finished my cake. Let's hope you like my baking too. There was another air-raid warning in the middle of it all. We're in practice now. We make it downstairs in two minutes if we're dressed, five minutes if we're asleep. Much love from your Ilse Mouse, who thinks of you constantly.

Ten-year-old Eva still hadn't settled down in Kassel two months after the move. She continued to go to Immenhausen every day, either before or after school. On 19 October she wrote her mother a lengthy account of her doings:

Dear, sweet Mummy,

How are you? Well, I hope. I've been going to Immenhausen the whole week. On Sunday Frau Rösch gave me some cakes to take back to Kassel. I helped at the Rösches one afternoon. I watered the cows, unloaded beet leaves, fed cows, rinsed the churns they sell the milk in and carried them outside and loaded them on to the milk cart.

Just imagine, Mummy, we now have afternoon school as well. This week is my first week of afternoon school.

Today I went to Immenhausen on the 9.17. First I went to Aunt Rita's and paid her a visit. Then I walked up Hohenkircherstrasse and collected Friedchen Rösch with the milk cart. We had to stop at Kersting because we had to unload some milk churns. When we got to the Rösches we carried in the churns for the milk. Then we fed the horses and the tiny little foal. The little foal can now walk properly again. Then we fetched some beets from the cellar, ground them up and carried them to the stable in a basket. We also fetched some wood. Hedwig and I fetched some potatoes from the cellar and peeled them for the pea soup.

Herr Rösch pumped some liquid manure into the manure cask, and Friedchen was in the stable rubbing down her beloved horses . . .

Then Frau Rösch called me and said I was to have lunch with them, so I did. After that I went to the Hirdes and said hello.

Many loving thousand millions of good wishes and kisses from Eva

Ilse and Dorle were also at Immenhausen that day. There were still some cupboards filled with children's clothes at their old house, and Ilse wanted to take some winter things back to Kassel. She wrote to Lilli the same night:

My dear, darling Mummy,
It's now been seven long, hard weeks for both of us. Oh, how I hope they'll let you see us again soon. The worry is often too much to bear. It lies on top of me like a dead weight, and I simply can't think of anything else. If only it would be over soon!!!
Yesterday morning Dorle and I went to Brandau's. The arch supports weren't ready to be tried on yet, needless to say. Then we collected Dorle's dress from the Dietrichs. It's red wool (Kübler) with white smocking on the front and blue embroidery. There's a little white bow on it too. Then I bought $16\frac{1}{2}$ pounds of flour on our ration cards, because there's a huge amount of white bread in the 55th distribution period, which we're in at present – 1400 grammes extra per person.
We all went back to Immenhausen today – all except Hannele but including Dorle. Dorle enjoyed the train journey immensely. Then we collected our winter coats from the mothball cupboard at Immenhausen, Marilis her fur coat, Aunt Lore's black overcoat, Hannele's muff, my fur bonnet, and the old red dress . . .
When we got home this lunchtime, loaded down with things, I put Dorle to bed, then quickly did my French homework and dashed off to school at the last minute . . . In biology yesterday we started on cytology. It's tremendously interesting. How lovely it would be if we could discuss it a bit together, and if you could tell me things. We've got a mass of things to do in German. (1) Read [Schiller's] 'Die Räuber', (2) Learn 'Morgengedicht', (3) Composition: 'German loyalty in Lessing's "Minna von Barnhelm"', and (4) 'The origins of the German word family'. A lot, isn't it?
Yesterday evening, when I was going off to my piano lesson, Dorle screamed like mad and clung to my dress,

begging me not to go. She's been clinging to me so much since you've been away. There's a hullabaloo every time I go out . . .

Herr Zschiegner wants me to give up taking lessons with him. That's because at seven in the evening it's so dark you can scarcely see your hand in front of your face. He thinks a 'little girl' like me might be accosted on the way home. It's really true, though. When I emerge from Herr Zschiegner's front door I can't see a thing. It's taken me a good five minutes to get from the front door to the garden gate. I've felt with my hands and feet for the two steps just before the garden gate, and groped my way along for twenty minutes before getting home. It's been suggested that I go to the same teacher Eva will be taking piano lessons from. I'm not altogether averse to the idea, because it isn't too pleasant, having to walk home in the dark every time. Please write and tell me what you think. I'll keep going to Herr Zschiegner till I get an answer.

Our living-room clock is hanging in the passage now, and it always sounds so homely when it strikes the hour. It keeps time very well. Well, my darling Mummy, are you overdoing it? Are you being careful? Are you sleeping? Are you receiving all our parcels? Hasn't any of them gone astray yet? All my love and kisses and hugs, your Ilse Mouse

All windows and sources of light had to be blacked out at night because of the incessant air raids. That was why Ilse could scarcely see a thing outside her piano teacher's front door, even early in the evening.

Now that the days were growing shorter, the girls became still more depressed. Johanna intimated this in a letter to Lilli dated 21 October:

How are you? I can't help thinking of you so much. Today, when the bell rang and I peered through the glass of the front door, I thought it was you, Mummy, standing outside. I've never had such a strange feeling. Oh, the disappointment when it wasn't you! It was Frau Kunze.

That same Thursday, 21 October 1943, Ilse too sat down at her desk and wrote to her mother. It was the last letter she would ever write in the Kassel apartment. There had been an endless succession of air-raid warnings in the preceding weeks. During one raid, probably on 3 October, the blast had smashed a small window. The sirens wailed several times more in the hours to come.

My dearest, loveliest Mummy,
I've been thinking of you even more than usual this week. I'm happy and sad at the same time. I felt so awfully depressed again this morning, as if something terribly heavy were trying to squeeze my heart. All the others are still asleep, but I can't sleep any longer. Julie has just got up and started to clean the rooms.
You may be worried about the dining-room furniture, but it's quite all right. The bomb blast broke the transom window, but that's all. No splinters. We'll get it repaired soon . . .
On Wednesday morning I took Dorle to Brandau's again to see about the arch supports for her flat feet. Dorle's plaits have grown, and she often asks: 'When is Mummy coming home?' Gerhard is coming this afternoon and staying till tomorrow morning.
Oh, if only you could be here. Mummy, console yourself like me. You're also probably sick with longing for us, and I'm quite sick with longing for you. So let's console ourselves with the thought that everything, absolutely everything, must come right again soon. Oh Mummy darling, I try to console the others in all kinds of ways, but I can't.
I'm going to Aunt Maria's later on. She's not working

because she's rather unwell. She takes good care of us all. After this I have to put the laundry away. Then there's Gerhard's bed to make up, and I still have some home-work to do. Masses of love and good wishes from your Ilse Mouse, who thinks of you constantly.

'Running for our lives'
The air raid on 22 October 1943

On the night of 22 October, a Friday, more than 500 British bombers headed for Kassel. Air Chief Marshal Sir Arthur Harris had decided that the city was to be destroyed once and for all.

The attacking aircraft had been located and the German anti-aircraft batteries were alerted in good time. A ghostly hush descended on the city once the sirens had died away.

All the occupants of 3 Motzstrasse had been down in the cellar since approximately 8.30 p.m. In addition to Ilse, Johanna, Eva, and Dorothea, they included Gerhard, who had been granted an extra day's leave, and Rita, who was due to spend the night with the children.

The British bombers appeared overhead. Neither night fighter interceptors nor anti-aircraft guns had managed to check the advance of this huge aerial armada. Between 8.55 and 9.11 p.m. Kassel was bombed by four waves of attackers. In all, more than 400,000 incendiary and high explosive bombs were dropped. The fire storm reached its peak in the city centre between 10 p.m. and midnight. Whole streets were transformed into a huge, blazing inferno. Some 10,000 people were burnt to death, asphyxiated, or crushed by falling masonry.

Incendiary bombs landed on the roof of 3 Motzstrasse. The occupants tried to fight the fire, but without success: the building was completely gutted, and the cellar had to be evacuated.

The glow in the sky above Kassel had been visible from Breitenau. It was days before Lilli knew whether her children had survived the raid. Ilse did not write again until 24 October, this time from Immenhausen:

My dearest, most darling Mummy,

I hope you also survived the raid unscathed! Unfortunately, our little home has been completely gutted by phosphorus bombs. Gerhard happened to be on leave, and he and some other people from the building tried to put the fire out, but it was impossible. Our cellar stood up all right, but we soon had to get out because the air was becoming too smoky. Our building was ablaze. The buildings to left and right of us had already collapsed. The ordinary, flimsily constructed houses opposite were on fire. The whole of Kronprinzenstrasse was in flames. A terrible shower of sparks came down all around us. Hannele and Eva carried the blankets and suitcases, Aunt Rita Dorle's pillow, and I our most precious belonging, our Dorle. That dash through the fire and heat was a dash through death for our lives.

Then we got to the museum air-raid shelter on the corner of Kronprinzenstrasse and Kölnische Strasse. We stayed there until eleven the next morning. Then the shelter had to be evacuated because the air had run out. Next we went to the town hall, where we were given thick slices of bread and butter. There were supposed to be some buses going to Immenhausen, but no, we had to trudge off to Wittich Barracks with all our things. There we were given some soup and got some sleep. No buses were running from there, so we went to Wilhelmshöher Station. There were apples there, and a car took us into Kassel. Then, with immense difficulty, we got hold of a another car and finally reached here after dark.

Dear Mummy, I know you can only write every four weeks, alas, but we really do enjoy getting your letters, even if it can't be more often. Well, tomorrow we'll go and fight for some requisition slips . . . Goodbye for now and lots of love. Daddy's fine. Sleep well, and a big kiss.

Don't be too sad about our things. Your Ilse Mouse, who never forgets you

Johanna also told her mother about the air raid in a letter dated 24 October:

My dear darling Mummy,

Now we're here at Immenhausen. Oh, Mummy, it's good it turned out this way. I can't believe that all our nice things are gone, but we must grin and bear it.

Aunt Lore and Marilis have already given me a nightie and a blouse that was too small for Marilis. I got a pale-blue pullover from Aunt Rita. I was wearing the skirt and the white blouse, you know, the dirndl skirt. Eva had her green check woollen dress on, and Ilse her blue knitted dress. Dorle was only wearing underclothes. She got a little dress from Aunt Rita right away, so she's also provided for. We all had our warm winter overcoats on.

Everything's fine here at Immenhausen. It's a bit of a squeeze, but all the nicer. Tomorrow, that's Monday, I shall go to Hümme because I'm getting so bored here. Our school has completely had it, both buildings. Eva's school too. The whole of the barracks in Westendstrasse is a heap of rubble. I hope I'll get a few old things of Heidi's at Hümme. Please don't be upset, Mummy. It happened, that's all, and it could be worse. Daddy's fine. Aunt Rita has gone to join him today. Herr Dr Schupmann's parents' house was also damaged. They managed to save their things . . .

It's an awful sight, but the organization was good. At the town hall we were given thick slices of bread and butter and milk and sweets. Gerhard worked *so* hard. He tried to save our apartment with Inge Gaugler from the first floor. Afterwards, when we left the cellar for the shelter because of the smoke and fumes, Gerhard came, and he was all back and grimy. He helped to put fires out everywhere. So don't worry, my dear little Mummy.

Lots of love and a thousand million kisses from your loving Hannele

Since Lilli's children had lost almost everything in the raid on Kassel, they had to obtain replacements. However, wartime shortages made it very difficult to procure clothing, furniture and food. Ration cards or requisition slips had to be produced for every item purchased, and these were the documents Ilse planned to obtain. She gave her mother an account of the days immediately following the air raid in a long letter written on 26 and 27 October:

My dearest darling Mummy,

I've a tremendous lot to tell you, but since that's impossible at present, I'm writing to you instead.

On Monday, yesterday, Marilis and I went to Kassel to get some requisition slips. The train only went as far as Obervellmar, so we went into Kassel via Obervellmar and Niedervellmar. I didn't see a single building from the beginning of Holländische Strasse up to Hindenburgplatz. This is the route we took: Holländische Strasse, Königstrasse, Hedwigstrasse, Mauerstrasse, the post office, and Königsplatz. From there we had to go back to Mauerstrasse at top speed because an unexploded bomb lying in the middle of Königsplatz could have gone up at any moment. Then we went home by way of Bahnhofstrasse, Kurfürstenstrasse, Ständeplatz, Hohenzollernstrasse, Kronprinzenstrasse, Motzstrasse, the barracks, Luisenstrasse, Hindenburgplatz, the town hall, and Harleshäuser station. Not a single shop has survived. Kassel no longer exists. Really, I'm not exaggerating. All the side streets running off all the streets I mentioned are also mounds of debris. You can see all the way from Königsplatz to Bettenhausen. The whole of the old quarter is gutted. Tens of thousands of people are missing, I'm afraid. Mummy, you often don't know where you are for ruins. On Gisela's house – it's also completely burnt out, of course – there's a notice saying that the Stephans are at Nienhagen. I haven't heard of any people we know being killed.

You can't buy anything in Kassel any more. The outskirts and suburbs are still standing, but the whole of the city centre and the old quarter are one big mass of rubble.

At our local branch headquarters, which have also been transferred to a shelter, I was given a certificate stating that we're 'totally' bombed out. From there we had to go to the Bürgerschule in Herkulesstrasse to get some requisition slips. There were several hundred people standing outside the entrance. We wormed our way forwards, and then, when our turn came after a very, very long time, it all began. First I was issued with a red 'bomb card'. That was in one room. In the next room we were given a certificate to the effect that we were moving out of Kassel. In the last room we got new milk ration cards, because the old ones had been burnt, travel vouchers for the cards where coupons had been cut off and, last but not least, a certificate stating that we'd signed off for foodstuffs. Requisition slips would be available at the place we were moving to.

After that we went to Aunt Maria's. Everything is still standing up there by the town hall, but Aunt Maria wasn't in. From there we went into the town hall to get something to eat. There was some good pea soup with a nice lot of meat in it. Then we walked to Harleshausen and caught the train to Obervellmar, where we went to see Gerhard and find out how his eyes were. He's fine again, and he can see properly too. The trains were so full when we got to the station, we couldn't get on, so we walked to Mönchehof. We couldn't walk any further, so we called Aunt Rita and she picked us up in the car. When I got to Immenhausen I simply fell into bed.

Next morning I got up at eight and put on my best clothes. Had some coffee, then went with all my children to see Armbrust and Daddy. We each got one pair of shoes there: Eva a pair of good black shoes with leather soles, Hannele a pair of brown lace-ups, really nicely patterned, and I myself a pair of very, very nice-looking brown lace-up boots, absolutely plain but nice-looking all the same.

From there we went to get hold of some requisition slips. At the town hall we were graciously informed that requisition slips had to be collected from the provisioning office in Hofgeismar . . . After coffee time, which is always very late, unfortunately, I . . . cut out a dress for Dorle with Dorle and Aunt Lore. The dress will have a coloured yoke, and the material itself is blue. After that I went back into the kitchen and helped again in there. For lunch we had noodle soup, potatoes, vegetables, and tinned liver sausage . . .

It's simply incredible, the mess the house is in – total chaos wherever you look. Magda cries and frets all day long. Rita has a really nice housemaid, Gerda, who's awfully sweet. The most important thing is, she's very, very neat. Aunt Rita doesn't take the slightest interest in her household, and she hasn't a clue about cooking. She expected us to make some tomato soup out of two tomatoes!!!

The rest of the letter has not survived.

Rita was not entirely responsible for the chaos Ilse complained of. There simply wasn't room enough at Immenhausen after the children had been evacuated from Kassel. The Gartenstrasse house, which wasn't large, now had to accommodate as many as twelve people: Ilse and her three sisters in two tiny attic rooms and a windowless cubby hole on the top floor; Dr Schupmann, Ernst's replacement, in Gerhard's room; Rita and Magda on the first floor; and Aunt Lore and Cousin Marilis on sofas in the living room and library on the ground floor. Gerda the housemaid must also have been housed somewhere, and it was a very tight squeeze when Ernst and Gerhard came home on leave.

There was no possibility of the children's returning to Kassel. Although the apartment house in Motzstrasse was still standing, being built of concrete, it had been completely gutted. Lilli's grand piano was just a mass of molten metal and charred wood.

Once the smoke in the city centre had dispersed, the survivors searched their ruined homes for remnants that might still be of use. Several little expeditions were launched from Immenhausen with the aim of salvaging any articles in Motzstrasse that had escaped the flames. On 27 October Johanna reported as follows:

> Aunt Rita went to our old apartment today. Gerhard, who had already been there, dug a few saucepans and a cup and a small dish out of the debris in the kitchen. Aunt Rita took that with her later on, also the bread-slicer, but that needs repairing. She also found a frying pan, and the little cut-out gnome above Dorle's cot was still there. Gerhard brought that back for her. The bedsteads in our room are still standing, but bare, of course, and all bent and twisted. Apart from that, nothing but mounds of debris. There isn't a sign of my dear Hänschen.

Two days later Johanna informed her mother of the results of another search: a large kettle and several saucepans had been unearthed 'with pick and shovel'. They had even discovered two pictures in Eva's bedroom, one of them a little head by Rubens.

Although the girls had already written several letters since the disastrous air raid, Lilli did not reply. They feared for their mother's safety once more. Had Breitenau also been bombed, or was it just that the postal service had been disrupted? Johanna doggedly continued to write, for instance on 4 November 1943:

> My most beloved Mummy,
>   How I long to see you. I wonder if you received our letters from after the air raid? Certainly not to begin with, so I'll tell you about it properly. I've now got the time and the peace and quiet, because Dorle and Magda are asleep.

I'm sure you'll have heard that the sirens went off at 8.20 p.m. The radio warning came ten minutes before that, so we had all our things ready. Marilis dashed off to the shelter and we all ran downstairs. I read, Ille and Dorle lay on the sofa, and Gerhard and Eva stood outside the front door, watching the searchlights! Five minutes after the sirens Aunt Rita came down to the cellar from the train. Five minutes after that the anti-aircraft guns opened up. Whoosh, you should have seen our two racing down the stairs like lightning. The cellar came to life when we heard the bombs go off. We moistened our mouth and nose masks, checked for cracks, and then silence returned inside, but outside an endless succession of loud, dull explosions. The blast made you feel quite suffocated every time. Suddenly things got serious. A terribly loud explosion. The door flew open, big clouds of dust rolled in, the light went out, and the pressure took our breath away for a few seconds. A moment's silence, then people called for someone to go and see if we were trapped. Gerhard and a girl of eighteen went upstairs but came down again at once because they couldn't breathe for smoke. They said we weren't trapped, but a bomb had landed on number 9. Fires were blazing outside, so everyone got ready to go up on to our roof. After a while Gerhard came and said: 'Quick, quick, we need some people, our roof is on fire.' That really scared us. The shooting stopped after a while. Thank God, everyone thought, but Gerhard came downstairs and said: 'We need people. Two on each floor, to make sure the sparks don't catch.'

The raid seemed to be over, but all we could see through the air holes was an even red glow. The smoke seeping through the cracks was unbearable, your eyes smarted terribly if you opened them. Dorle was very quiet and good. Then a man appeared and said: 'Come with me to the shelter in Kronprinzenstrasse, all of you.' 'Can we get through?' everyone asked. 'Yes, yes, it's all right.'

So we made our exit, Ille carrying Dorle, Eva and I the heavy air-raid suitcase, and Aunt Rita two bags. The smoke on the stairs was unbearable. Outside, swarms of sparks were whirling through the air. Flames were shooting out of the windows sky-high. It was very hot and as light as day, even though it was only 11 p.m. On we went. We all struggled along and reached the shelter utterly exhausted. Then we flopped down on a sofa, just like that. We slept now and then. Gerhard came in a few times and said: 'You could eat nice baked apples at our place.' So we knew it was on fire. At seven the next morning Aunt Rita went back to the cellar and fetched my violin, and the Kunzes collected a suitcase. After a great deal of trouble we got to Immenhausen at seven o'clock.

My poor little Hänschen must have burnt to death or died of the heat. The school is wrecked, Eva's and ours, Gerhard's, the department store, the town hall, the theatre, the Murhard Library, the Waizsches Haus on Opernplatz . . .

We've been put down for the school at Hofgeismar, so we'll have to wait and see. It's incredibly overcrowded already. Sixty children in one form, three forms in one year, we'll wait and see . . . I'll stop now. All the very best and many affectionate good wishes and kisses,

Your Hannele
Courage and hope!

At last, early in November, Lilli wrote the children another letter. She had not until then had a chance to smuggle another one out of the camp. After all that had happened in Kassel, she had no wish to remain at Breitenau a day longer: she simply had to get out of there and rejoin her children.

Her letter – it was probably mid-November before it reached Immenhausen – has not survived, except for the undated enclosure for Ernst it contained. As before, Lilli used brown wrapping paper. She wrote 'Vati' (Daddy) on the blank half of the sheet and sealed the letter with lengths of adhesive strip intended for use on boxes of Eu-med.

These strips prove where Lilli was made to work during her detention at Breitenau. Eumed, a headache remedy, was originally manufactured by Pflüger, a Berlin firm. When Pflüger's plant was destroyed by bombs, the production of Eu-med was taken over by the Spangenberg branch of Braun of Melsungen, a pharmaceutical company. It is possible that Sanatogen was also packed at Spangenberg with labels like the ones Lilli used for her letter of 3 October 1943, although no evidence that Braun manufactured Sanatogen can be found in the company's surviving records.

Braun employed female labour conscripts from Breitenau for years. Almost all the relevant documents were destroyed after the war, and no lists of names have survived. All that does exist is a memo from the office of the district administrator at Melsungen to the corrective labour camp at Breitenau requesting the allocation of 'approx. thirty workers' to the 'chem. factory D. Braun at Melsungen'.

The labour conscripts were taken there by train in the morning and brought back in the evening after twelve long hours of work. Lilli said little about the exact circumstances under which she carried out forced labour, and she never mentioned the name Braun. She did, however, make several references to the fact that she and her companions in misfortune got off the train at Malsfeld on their way to work. From there it was only a few kilometres by train or bus to the Braun subsidiary at Spangenberg.

'Your work is clean and not very hard, that's worth a lot,' her niece Marilis wrote in mid-October 1943. That much, at least, could be inferred from Lilli's allusions.

It is probable that some of her clandestine letters were posted with the help of Braun employees. Her appeal for Ernst's assistance may have been enclosed in one of these:

Dear Amadé,
    I want to ask you yet again to spare no effort to get me

released. A longish letter I wrote to Lore was posted on Friday night (29 Oct.). I hope you received it. In it I listed all the arguments you can adduce. If you're willing to put in an application, it should be addressed to the Gestapo at 9 Prinz Albrechtstrasse, Berlin SW. You will probably have to certify that the children and I have lost everything, and if the application could somehow be endorsed – perhaps by the military authorities – that would be better still. Do please help me once more!! You've no idea what I'm having to endure and undergo, mentally and in other ways, but that's nothing compared to my tormenting fear and concern as to whether I'll ever get out again.

Do also write and tell me sometime what's to become of the children temporarily. No one can hold it against you – the mail is only checked in the office here, not by the Gestapo. But please, never make any mention of my letters. I hope you're all right and feeling reasonably well. Remember me to Rita. I often think of you, Amadé.

Lilli

Much, much love to Lore and also to Marilis, who must surely have left by now.

'Oh, Mummy, often it's hard . . .'
The children establish a household of their own

At the beginning of November 1943, Rita took Ilse to Franken-stein, near Breslau, where her mother kept a shop that sold household goods. The purpose of their visit was to re-equip the children with essential articles of clothing. Ilse described the outcome of this trip on 7 November:

My best and dearest Mummy,
Today you're at last going to get a letter from your Ilse. You mustn't think I've forgotten you, but I couldn't write to you from Frankenstein. We had to unpack when I finally got back here at eight on Thursday night, and there was such a mass of work to do on Friday and Saturday, I could scarcely get through it – and still haven't.
Aunt Lore didn't get back from Essen until two o'clock on Friday afternoon. She went there on All Saints' Day to try to fix up an apartment for us. An apartment has fallen vacant in her own house, so she wants to use it as a bargaining counter. We're hoping we'll soon have an apartment to take us all, because there's no point in staying here with our beloved Aunt Rita, not in the long run.
She was very nice to me while we were in Frankenstein together, but here at Immenhausen her nasty character and attitude become noticeable again. We very often get into arguments, because I tell her whenever something

doesn't suit me. If I said everything I thought was unfair, I'd never stop grousing. I have to restrain myself all day long so as not to set off an explosion every five minutes. I could quote you a thousand things that set off explosions, but it's not worth the effort.

You've no need to worry about me on that score, Mummy, because it's now my duty to look after and protect the three younger ones. If they don't like something they come to me, and I tell Madame, and sometimes I get somewhere, but sometimes she gets her own pig-headed way. From that point of view I'm not as quiet as I used to be. Oh, when you're back with us you'll be amazed at how boldly I tell the silly goose to her face whenever I disapprove of her being so unfair. You've no idea the things she's had to hear me say, and I've always had the last word. My principle is: You must protect the younger ones the way Mummy did, and make sure they don't have any worries, mentally or physically, but shoulder them all yourself. And I think that all three are the way I want them. Oh, Mummy, often it's hard. You mustn't think I'm boasting, I'm simply telling you so you'll know that someone's taking good care of your three little ones. (I'm not impertinent, Aunt Lore has said that too.)

Often it's hard to console them when I'm feeling so sad myself. But if I summon up all my strength, it works because it's got to work, and it's nice when I see them romping around five minutes later and can tell that they're feeling comforted, and (I tell myself) it was a good thing you pulled yourself together, because now the two of them are feeling a bit happier. So we'll stick it out until they let you come back to us. You've honestly no need to worry about the little ones. I help them to the best of my strength and ability.

The clothes situation is very good. We brought back a lot of good stuff from Frankenstein and Breslau. It's very, very nice in Frankenstein. Aunt Rita's mother's shop is very big and nice. Her apartment is nicely furnished too. We got one vest and one pair of knickers for each of us four children. All warm, worsted things in white and pink. Very good quality. And an extra pair of knickers for Dorle and Eva and a white woollen vest for Hannele, all on coupons . . .

Ilse devoted the next two pages to a detailed description of all the other articles of clothing she had brought back from Franken- stein. She concluded:

I hope you'll be pleased too. (I am.) Letters are always opened at Immenhausen these days. Why, we don't know. (Everyone's letters to everyone.) A big, loving hug and a big kiss from your Ilse, the friend who never forgets you. Let's hope you can soon be back home with us!

Ilse's allusion to stricter postal censorship was intended as a warning. From now on, Lilli could not afford to assume that the letters she smuggled out of Breitenau would remain undetected. There was a risk that, sooner or later, one of them would find its way into the hands of the Gestapo.

Ilse's sisters were absolutely delighted with her consignment of clothes. Johanna wrote to Lilli the same day:

My dearest precious Mummy,
How are you? Oh, how I'd like to be with you right now. And you with us. It'll be Advent soon. Oh, how sad it'll be without you, dearest. But nothing lasts for ever . . . Let's hope you'll soon be able to come back to us.

It's Sunday afternoon, and I think everyone's thinking of you and writing to you. Gerhard is sitting writing at Daddy's desk, Ille is sitting writing with Dorle, and Hannele and Eva are sitting upstairs writing to you in what used to be the maid's room.

I've been brought some things from Silesia! Some

wonderful checked material, a sample of which I'll enclose. Definitely the kind of material that could hardly be bettered in peacetime, with angora wool in it, genuine woollen cloth. It's already with Frau Wittich, who's making me a dress out of it. The dress is going to be, you know, Mummy, Ille had a brown checked winter dress like that with a polo-neck, buttoned up behind, and a yoke with a frill below and a skirt cut on the cross. You liked it a lot. Well, that's how my dress is being made too. I wonder if you'll like it? . . . Oh, wait, I almost forgot the best thing of all: a pair of slippers, Mummy, better slippers than the ones I had before, really *soft* and *warm*, you know, checked ones. Oh, and something else: A lovely pale floral skirt, looking like this. Now I'll draw you a rough idea of it.

There follows a drawing.

Please, Mummy, you know I can't draw. You're allowed to laugh but you mustn't show it to anyone else. I'd be dreadfully ashamed if a stranger saw it. But it'll give you some idea . . .

Yesterday evening Ille and I baked a cake, a Rührkuchen. I had a letter from Daddy today, so I'm going to write back. Daddy's coming home on leave on Tuesday. Gerhard has weekend leave and is spending half of it here and half with Daddy.

Mummy, Professor Dr Hofmann, who came here once with his wife, was killed in the raid with his family. Terrible. Thirteen-year-old Ulrike was in my form, and Christiane two forms above Ille. Such nice, friendly girls. Old Herr Meuschel, who owned the Schwanen pharmacy, was also killed together with his daughters. It's terribly sad.

Well, Mummy, we're being brave and hoping.

Dearest love from your affectionate Hannele

Unlike his sisters, Gerhard often spent his hours off duty with Ernst at Lindenberg military hospital. At sixteen he already felt at home in military surroundings; more importantly, he was spared Rita's presence. Gerhard's dislike of his father's second wife was steadily intensifying. His letter to Lilli dated 7 November:

My dear Mummy,

Today I'm on leave again. That's because people who are bombed out go on getting their regular leave in addition to special leave. And today I've got my weekend leave . . .

Now I'll tell you everything I've been up to this past week. On Saturday night I got back to our battery position around 8 p.m. . . . We didn't have a single lesson all week, so we had the mornings off, of course, and I even got time to read. I've been reading Carossa's 'Eine Kindheit und Verwandlungen einer Jugend'. I enjoyed it very much indeed.

On Tuesday Wolf returned from leave bringing his squeezebox (accordion to you). That certainly livened the place up. Come the evening, though, the two of us slipped out. Wolf was well supplied with cigarettes. We went into the gun emplacement and sat on the parapet furthest away, smoking and chatting, and Wolf played some music . . .

On Thursday we pulled another fast one. We were absolutely sick of our barrack room, so we went up into the emplacement and talked. It was 12.15 when we came down again, but lunch is at 11.45. We sneaked into the canteen by the back way – we couldn't afford to let the sergeant see us – and got our food all the same. We were scared stiff when the CO, the lieutenants and the sergeant-major came in to have lunch, one after the other, but nobody said anything. We tried to get back to our barrack room just as surreptitiously, but the sergeant had ordered everyone to fall in because he had an announcement to make. He spotted our eating irons just as we were trying to sneak through the doorway. 'Carry on inside with the rest of them and listen to the performance,' was all he said, and he paid no more attention to us. We were very relieved when he finally dismissed us, because he once stopped someone's leave for the very same reason.

On Friday the general was due. No duties all day, and everyone went around festively attired in their number ones. That afternoon we really let our hair down in the barrack room. Wolf played, we sang. Anyone who could dance, danced. We were in such high spirits, not even the sergeant said anything. The sergeant-major joined us and celebrated too . . . This afternoon we'll be relieved of Aunt Rita's presence because she's going to the Lindenberg. That'll be really nice.

To end with, I wish you all the best and send you my very fondest love.

Your Gerhard

Lilli had noticed after a few weeks that her air-force auxiliary son was not doing much reading and neglecting his literary interests, so Gerhard did his best to dispel that impression. He always dutifully reported on his current reading matter and ended nearly all his letters to Breitenau with some poem he had read. The above letter concluded with one by Christian Hofmann von Hofmann Swaldau. Generally speaking, Gerhard tended to adopt the cocky, barrack-room tone typical of a youthful air-force auxiliary. He seldom revealed how much he genuinely missed his mother, seldom put himself in her place, and never asked when she was coming home.

Gerhard, then only sixteen, was clearly overtaxed by the new situation. He had always regarded his father, who was now repudiating his mother, as a shining example. He continued to seek Ernst's company far more than did Ilse and Johanna, often visiting him at the hospital and sometimes spending his weekend leaves there. Gerhard tended to identify with his father, whereas his sisters modelled themselves on their mother. Moreover, he was in a schizophrenic situation: on the one hand, being a 'half-Jew' subject to discrimination, he hoped that his service as an air-force auxiliary would gain him acceptance by military men loyal to the Nazi regime; on the other, that regime not only stigmatized and abhorred his own mother but – as anyone willing to recognize the truth could tell – was clearly intent on destroying her.

Gerhard had to allow for the probability that letters to his beloved mother would sometime be monitored by the Gestapo and forwarded to his superiors. Critical comments on her detention at Breitenau could have harmed him, and even overly outspoken expressions of sympathy for her might have been construed as evidence of political unreliability.

Gerhard knew that this could prove dangerous, especially to a so-called half-breed. Further sanctions against 'half-Jews' and 'quarter-Jews' were always being mooted during the war years. Even as things stood, they could no longer hope to pursue an academic profession.

But the girls, too, ran a risk. Although Ilse, Johanna and Eva never criticized the Nazi regime in their letters, they clearly found Lilli's detention incomprehensible.

Every contemporary letter-writer had to take refuge in diplomatically guarded language. This applied in special measure to Lilli's friend Lotte. Being a Jewess, she was protected solely by her marriage to Ernst August and her son Peter, so one injudicious remark could have cost her her life. On 8 November 1943 Lotte received Ilse's detailed account of the air raid on Kassel. She wrote to Lilli the same night:

My dear, dear Lilli,
    This morning I at last received a long-awaited letter from Ilse which conveyed all your messages to me. You can't imagine how delighted I was.
    Ilschen wrote me a card after the raid, and today I finally heard about it in greater detail. Above all, I now have your address, which I asked for, as I hear from Ilse

that you're being allowed more mail. I can also send you parcels, she writes. Forgive me if I don't send you one today, but I have to leave with Peter the day after tomorrow and still have so much to do. Peter is still running a temperature for no identifiable reason. Even his lung is quite all right. He's now to have a change of air and better food, if possible, because he's losing weight. So I'm taking him to Freiburg and from there to the Kinzig Valley, where our former maid Josephine is now living. I myself am better, and Ernst August is fine. So much, in brief, for us.

But you, my dear, have suffered another blow. You can't conceive how upset I was to hear that you've lost everything, and to imagine what it must mean to you. But you're glad in spite of everything, and entitled to be, that all the children are safe. At Immenhausen they're being as well cared for as humanly possible. I wrote to say they could come to us any time, but since Ille didn't comment on this, I assume it's neither necessary nor desirable. I must also admit that my offer wasn't entirely wholehearted because we're far from safe from the bombing here and recently underwent quite a heavy raid. But you can depend on our always being there for the children.

If only we could also do something for you, you poor dear! A few days ago I suddenly and quite by chance came across an empty box of Eu-med. Since then I've been carrying it around and hoping I could do something for you, but I know that's just a childish illusion! Still, it may please you a little to know that you're always in my thoughts. Don't let dark thoughts get the better of you – preserve your confidence. I believe it's justified. The sun will shine for you again, my dear, I'm quite sure. Keep your chin up and, above all, keep well.

There's so much I'd like to know about you and the whole situation. Ilse can't write and tell me what I need to know. She's still a child, after all, but I haven't heard from Rita or your sister-in-law, although I asked them to write. But they must have plenty of other matters to attend to. Please let me know if you need anything I can send you. You know I'd be happy to help you in some way. Are your bedclothes warm enough, and should I send you a warm blanket? Or anything else? Are you allowed to read and do you like to? Any requests in that line? When I come home, my first job will be to send you a parcel, even if I myself don't have much food to spare. You can tell that from the fact that I'm having to send Peter away because of malnutrition!

Things are particularly bad here too. I'll have to go to the Labour Office when I get home. A few days ago, after a very pleasant talk, they granted me deferment because of Peter. Well, if I have to work after that, I don't care. It doesn't really matter. I still have things to do – lots of them! – so I must stop now. Let me know if you receive this letter, and feel free to write and say if you need anything . . .

A big hug and kisses, my dear.

Your Lotte

Lotte's appeal to Lilli to 'feel free to write' shows how little she knew about the circumstances of her friend's detention in Breitenau and the conditions prevailing there. After all, Lilli could not even write to her children whenever she wanted.

Three weeks after the air raid on Kassel, the girls had to go back to school. Eva was simply sent to the elementary school at Immenhausen, although she should long since have been attending secondary school. After lengthy inquiries, Ilse was found a place at the secondary school in Hofgeismar, the nearby administrative centre. On 11 November she went there by train for the first time. Conditions at the school were chaotic, however. Years had been amalgamated because the older boys were liable for duty as air-force auxiliaries, and Ilse had a lot of catching up to do. The clergyman at Immenhausen tutored her in Latin. Johanna was initially supposed to be sent to a youth hostel in

Fulda, where many other girls from her bombed-out school in Kassel were being housed and taught, but it took another ten days to reach a final decision.

It was during this transitional and uncertain period that Lilli's long-awaited – and, sadly, no longer extant – letter arrived from Breitenau. Johanna's response to her mother's first sign of life since the air raid:

> Oh, what a joy it was when your letter came. Your letters are always a joy to us all. And they all get here. I don't understand why our letters don't reach you. We write every day. Letters leave here every day. They ought to arrive, they can't be lying around somewhere. We already wrote you two long letters about the air raid.

And so Johanna wrote her mother a third description of what had happened the night Kassel was devastated. Lilli later intimated that she construed these repeated accounts as her daughters' way of overcoming the trauma the raid had inflicted on them.

In the letter that has not survived, Lilli asked Ilse to go to Leipzig to see Lotte. She was to give her a detailed report on the situation at Immenhausen and Breitenau and enlist her help in replacing some of the household articles that had been destroyed by fire in Kassel. Ilse replied on 14 November:

> If you think it's right and would like that, of course I'll go to Leipzig. In that case I'll go during the Christmas holidays. I can't understand why you've received no mail from us. We've written so often.
>
> Everything's wonderful when Aunt Rita isn't at home, but it isn't nice when she's here. Oh, Mummy, if only I had you back again. There are so many times when I can't help feeling sad, and then it's like something squeezing my heart. But I have to keep going, mainly because of the younger ones. Otherwise they get sad too, and that they mustn't be – and they aren't, either.

'You must be very careful!'
Lilli tries to arrange a clandestine meeting

On 20 November 1943 a letter reached Immenhausen bearing the following sender's address: 'Gisela Stephan, Nienhagen, near Kassel.' The postmark indicates that it had been posted in Malsfeld, in other words, on the route Lilli and her fellow prisoners took to work.

Gisela was a schoolfriend of Ilse's, so it was she who opened the envelope. Inside it she found five small sheets of wrapping paper closely written in pencil on both sides. This illicit letter from Lilli was dated 14 November:

My dearest children,

To prevent the post office from noticing how often I write to you, I've got someone else to address this and named Gisela as the sender. I'll explain why. And before I forget, please ask Daddy if he can spare me a little money. If so, would he please send some to the institution for me. I need to get some shoes resoled, and if I were released sometime – who knows when!! – I wouldn't have any money for the fare. Many thanks in advance!

And now to you, my darlings. I think of you all the time, filled with love and longing, and believe me when I say that your love for me, our love for each other, is helping us to get through these difficult weeks and months. Alas, I haven't heard from you, my boy, for a very, very long time, and I've had no letter from my Ille, either, for two weeks, which I greatly miss, though it's bound to be because the postal services are still disrupted. I hope everything will get here by degrees, because I'm sure you also wrote from Frankenstein. I gathered that you weren't in Leipzig from a very sweet letter from Aunt Lotte, which I received the day before yesterday.

Yesterday, though, I did get the batch of newspapers you sent on 2 November, dear Hannele. Many thanks indeed, likewise for your letters of the 2nd and 9th, your two fine postcards, and also your letters of the 22nd and 24th October, and two sweet little notes from Eva. From before and just after the raid, in other words.

I still can't grasp what you must have been through, children, but I can sympathize with your gradual realization of what we have all lost. Don't be too sad, though; when we're all safely together again, you girls and Marilis, Aunt Lore and I, everything will be easier and all right again. I'm sure I'll soon hear how you got on at Frankenstein and what you managed to do there, won't I, dear Ilse? So did you get some requisition slips for tableware, etc.? Have you already bought some? So Eva's going to school in Immenhausen and Ille at Hofgeismar? How do you like it there, my big girl?

Hasn't my Hannele been found a place yet? I should be very relieved myself if you also found a place at Hofgeismar. Is Heidi staying at home for the moment? How sweet of her to bring some toys for Dorle. What's my little treasure up to? Was she pleased when Ille came back? Does she play nicely with little Magda? What is Aunt Lore doing, is she all right? Give her my fond love. Best regards also to Daddy and Aunt Rita. Are you letting your hair grow these days, Hannele?

Now listen, my dears, but don't breathe a word. We haven't had a railway carriage to ourselves since the raid, so we get into the same compartments as other people. If we were clever about it, we might be able to meet up. I was thinking of Ille and possibly Aunt Lore, or, if Daddy and Aunt Lore think it's all right, Ille and Hannele (then you could bring me a letter from Aunt Lore, if she had something to tell me that mustn't be censored!). But you would have to take great care that none of the wardresses noticed anything. You'll find I look very different in my institutional clothing, especially as I've lost a tooth that's always been loose. So don't be alarmed.

I wouldn't like us to meet on the evening train, not on *any* account. You might all too easily become involved in an alert or a raid, because the train doesn't get to Kassel until 8 p.m. There are two possibilities, and you can choose the one that fits in best with your connections. We leave here just after seven every morning, on the train coming from Kassel. You would have to be in the last carriage and look out of the window at Guxhagen. If I don't get in with you, change to my compartment at the next station. Then we'll go on to Malsfeld together. If it's not too difficult, it might be even better for you to come to Malsfeld on Saturday. We take the train back from there at about 2 p.m., then you could get in after me. It's only twenty minutes, but we could at least see each other!! Wouldn't that be wonderful??

But you must be very careful on the platform not to give us away. Then we can talk in the train. If it comes off, please bring me some notepaper, stamps, cigarettes, matches, some skin cream, and a razor blade – I don't suppose my little razor has survived. And perhaps Daddy or Dr Schupmann (please send him my best regards) could give me some tablets for the pains in my arms and hands, which are troubling me a lot again. The best plan would be to make a small parcel of everything and hand it to me in the big tunnel before Guxhagen. And if it's not asking too much, please bring me some white bread or a fruit loaf. That would give me a bit more to eat on Sunday. But only if you really can.

For days now, I've been picturing how happy I'll be during those few minutes. Don't drop any hints when you write. I shall keep my eyes open from now on. If it works, and if I have to be away for much longer, perhaps Marilis and Eva could come another time.

Goodbye for now, children all. When does my boy come home on leave again? Can't he sometime go to Marburg at the weekend to see Marilis? I clasp you tightly to my heart and give you a tender, loving kiss.

Your Mummy

This letter crossed with one that Ilse wrote to Breitenau on 15 November, in which she mentioned another meeting in Kassel with Lilli's friend Maria Lieberknecht:

I was at Aunt Lieberknecht's from this morning to this afternoon. We had a useful conversation . . . She was *so* nice to me again, and I'm sure you'll be back with us soon.

Lilli knew what this coded message signified because she herself had suggested taking advantage of Maria Lieberknecht's contacts with the Gestapo. It implied that 'Aunt Maria' had informed Ilse of how far she had got in her efforts to secure Lilli's release through her brother-in-law. If only to Ilse, she had conveyed that the chances were good.

Meanwhile, Johanna reported that her school problem was still unresolved. Four weeks after the raid on Kassel and the destruction of her school, she was still unsure of where she would now find a place: the youth hostel at Fulda or the secondary school at Hofgeismar. On 18 November she wrote:

Dear Mummy,

How are you? Today I went all over the place. At 9 a.m. Aunt Rita drove me to the school in Hofgeismar. It was very cold and the fog was dense, very bad driving conditions. At the school we asked whether they had a teacher for Form 3. The answer was no. Then we quickly drove home and on to Kassel at 10 a.m. for the school meeting, which was at 11. There we were told that anyone who wanted to, one of them being me, should report to their form teachers afterwards. There were a whole lot of grown-ups standing there with [Frau] Jahns, but they all asked: Why go to Fulda of all places, where all those factories and soldiers are? The Brits are bound to go there. No, we're definitely not sending our children there. They're all we have left.

Only four out of thirty-three children reported with me. Isn't that discouraging? Tomorrow Aunt Rita is going to withdraw my application. We'd sooner ask Superintendent Kölling if he can't send one or two more teachers to Hofgeismar. He wasn't there, but he will be tomorrow. Now we'll have to wait and see. We mustn't lose heart, dearest. Be brave and keep on hoping!

Fondest love and kisses, your Hannele

Two days later, Lilli's letter suggesting a rendezvous with the children arrived under the pseudonym 'Gisela Stephan'. On Sunday, 21 November, Ilse confirmed that it had been received and sent a coded reply, following her mother's example:

My dearest Mummy,

I couldn't write yesterday, I was so dreadfully tired. Please don't be hurt. I received a long letter from Gisela, which the postman gave me on his way from the station to the post office. She has asked me to visit her on Saturday, catching the train that leaves around 2 p.m. I'll be only too happy to. Let's hope it comes off.

On Saturday we had some maths homework. It was very difficult . . . Yesterday afternoon I baked a cheese-cake with short pastry. All my very own work. It tasted very good today. Today I took Dorle to see Gerhard. He was very pleased when I turned up with Dorle. We all had some cake and read letters . . .

Tomorrow I must go and have another talk with Aunt Maria. There's no school again tomorrow, which is always very nice. I may get my gold watch repaired at the watchmaker's in Hofgeismar. That would be very nice.

My dearest! How I long to see you. I'm sure you'll soon be back with us. Aunt Lore takes good care of us. She's very, very sweet. Are you getting enough to eat?? I do hope so!!! Our parcels aren't too plentiful any more, but are they still all right? We get a special allocation, being totally bombed out: up to now, some apples, 1 kg of onions, $\frac{1}{2}$ kg of poultry, $\frac{1}{2}$ kg of meat, 1 kg of bread, $\frac{1}{8}$ kg of sweets. Great, isn't it?

And now, darling, sleep well, don't worry, and a big hug from your Ilse Mouse

Lilli could therefore count on the fact that Ilse would be waiting for her at Malsfeld station on the following Saturday, 27 November. Ilse had sounded confident that her mother would soon be able to come home. The following letter, written after her meeting with Maria Lieberknecht the next day, was far less optimistic:

My dearest Mummy,

I went to see Aunt Maria this morning. She was feeling awful again. Today was the anniversary of her husband's death, and yesterday she took a look at the old quarter of the city. There were wreaths lying on a number of mounds of rubble because people were still underneath them. She was very sweet to me again, and gave me a lot of good advice . . .

Tomorrow I'll send you a parcel of all kinds of things, and the day after tomorrow, or possibly tomorrow, the bread that goes with them. This is just so you know, and don't think I'm not sending you any bread. Oh no, dear darling, I do as much and as well for you as I can, so you don't, I hope, have to go hungry. Because if I thought you were always hungry I'd be even more unhappy.

And Mummy, if we really have to spend Christmas alone and apart, us two friends, we *mustn't* give up hope.

I think of you and you alone with all my heart, and you of me. So we will, we *must* overcome it. We'll celebrate next Christmas all the better. I owe it to you to pull myself together, because of the little ones! As far as I can, I and Aunt Lore will see the children have as nice a Christmas as possible. You know, of course, that it can't be a 'proper' one, but you really mustn't worry about the little ones. You see, Mummy dear, that's how we've got to bear it now. I'm trying to do so with all my heart and soul. Oh, darling Mummy, if only I knew that you aren't utterly miserable – that you aren't being utterly crushed. All alone there! If only I knew of something that would comfort you, I'd gladly give it. I'm going to look out some poems for you, and you can read them at Christmas. I haven't got anyone anything for Christmas. Nothing for you either, Mummy.

You see? Now I'm trying to imagine I've been talking to you. I always find writing to you a pleasant activity.

Now I'll tell you what requisition slips we've got. Mummy, just imagine, there was another terrible racket just now. I grabbed Dorle and dashed into the library. We've had another awful forty-five minutes of it. Always this gnawing fear. I really can't take it any more, even when only the guns are firing (no bombs).

Sleep well now. A big hug and a thousand kisses from your Ilse Mouse, who thinks of you alone.

Ilse's thoughts constantly strayed to Lilli, even at school. Next morning she wrote again from Hofgeismar:

My dearest Mummy,

How are you, I wonder? I'm in the middle of a biology class. The teacher is a tiny little man. Dr Grupe, a professor. He's lecturing us on genetics. It's terribly boring. Now it's getting interesting!!! Now marks are being handed out. All the boys in Form 7 have to assemble. Everyone is wondering: This boy knows just as much as that boy, and what did that boy get? A 3. In that case, you'll also get a 3. What did those two get? And so on, till everyone's through. Now he's telling us about white beans.

I wonder what you're doing, and whether you're thinking of me too? I feel you are. Don't be too sad, my darling. I'm trying too! Goodbye till this evening.

Your Ilse Mouse

Ilse did in fact write Lilli another letter as soon as she got back to Immenhausen:

My dear, dear Mummy,

Good evening, darling! I hope you're resting after work now. I was terribly scared just now, because we had another alert. The sirens went at 7.15. I couldn't stop fidgeting. It's over now, thank God, and I can relax. No, not yet, there was another air-raid warning and I got twitchy all over again. I had to bring Dorle from the bedroom into the kitchen, where Aunt Lore was ironing a black suit jacket for me. When she was through I put Dorle in Daddy's (now Eva's) bed. I turned on a bedside light and draped something over it and sat down beside Dorle, and now I'm writing. Dorle has gone to sleep. I'm sitting at the table again and still writing. But it isn't over yet, unfortunately.

I had a quick bite when I got back by train at lunchtime today, then I baked you a honey cake. I hope you enjoy it. I also went to the basket down in the cellar and picked out one of the less nice tablecloths for Aunt Rita. She's always saying she's got so few, and asking if there isn't another downstairs she can use. But where's the key for the wicker suitcase? Tomorrow I'll take another look in the yellow wooden moneybox. I hope I find it.

After that I quickly made up a parcel for you with the following contents: one white loaf, one rye loaf, butter, cheese, jam, salt, a bottle of medicine for your rheumatism, which I'm sure you've got again, and some tablets for it, some soap, lots of apples, newspapers, the honey cake, and bon appétit! I hope you enjoy it all.

In the meantime, Helmut Rüdiger came here to copy my English. Finally, after masses of interruptions, I got the parcel to the post office. I spent the time before supper tidying my things. Then came this nerve-racking alert. Harmless so far.

Now to the requisition slips. For Gerhard: 1 suit, 1 shirt, 1 vest, 1 pair of socks, 1 nightshirt . . . For Ilse: 1 hat, 1 woollen dress, 1 vest, 1 pair of knickers, 1 pair of gloves, 1 nightgown . . . For Eva and Hannele, per head: 1 nightgown, 3 handkerchiefs, 1 raincoat, 1 pair of knickers, 1 vest . . . For Dorle: 1 pair of knickers, 3 handkerchiefs, 1 nightgown, 1 pair of gloves, 1 bonnet, 1 frock . . . Well, that's it. Are you pleased, darling?

Now I must do my German. Sleep well! Don't be too sad. Think of my letter yesterday, sweetheart. I think of you and you of me. A big hug and a big kiss from your Ilse Mouse, whose thoughts are all of you.

The wicker suitcase Ilse mentioned had been deposited at Immenhausen by Lilli's aunt, Tilly Schlüchterer. It contained large quantities of linen and clothing. Tilly had planned to emigrate, but the Nazis hauled her off to Theresienstadt. By this time, Lilli's daughters either guessed or already knew that Aunt Tilly would not be needing her suitcase any more.

Of the 800 girls who had attended the Jakob-Grimm-Schule with Ilse and Johanna before the destruction of Kassel, some 180 moved to the Fulda youth hostel that had been converted into a secondary school, among them Ilse's best friend Gisela Stephan. Johanna was eventually enrolled at Hofgeismar, as Lilli had hoped, but not at the same school as Ilse. A boys' secondary school had been evacuated from Bremen because of the bombing and transferred in its entirety to Hofgeismar, and this was where Johanna was now granted a place. Her letter dated 24 November:

My best beloved Mummy,

How are you, dearest? If only I could be there with you, or you here with us. How happy and thankful we would all be. And how much I shall miss you tomorrow, my darling, when I have to go to the boys' school for the first time.

In the end Aunt Rita managed to get Heidi and me enrolled there. School is from 2 to 6 p.m. I leave here at 1 p.m. and wait in Hofgeismar for Heidi, who gets there at 1.30 . . . I shall meet Ille in Hofgeismar, that's some consolation at least. Well, I'm happy to be able to go to school or be driven there, whichever. For a satchel, I'm taking a small suitcase I found in the surgery. It contained some old bottles (empty) and boxes (empty). I've got a better use for it. I can't wait to see how many boys there'll be in the form with us two girls. Got to stop now. My dear Mummy, we must pray to God, he'll help us.

A billion billion loving hugs and kisses, Hannele

Meanwhile, the planned rendezvous at Malsfeld station was drawing steadily nearer. On Thursday, two days before the appointed time, Ilse wrote:

My dearest Mummy,

What a nasty, windy day it was today. I hope you aren't cold!!! I really hope not!!! Today we wrote the long-awaited composition. The subject for the other girls, the ones who've always been in the form, was: 'The structure of a tragedy with reference to Goethe's "Egmont"'. And the new girls had to write on: 'What do good manners mean to you?' What a peculiar subject! I wrote four pages on customs like raising your hat, letting the lady walk on your right, being respectful to old people, and so on. I hope I'll get a reasonably good mark.

Alas, alas, it's impossible for us to visit Gisela. Today I got a postcard from Stephi, absolutely no news.

The last two sentences contained another coded message. By regretting that it was impossible for her 'to visit Gisela', Ilse was cancelling the rendezvous with her mother at short notice. And, to preclude any misunderstanding, she expressly referred to her friend Gisela Stephan by her nickname, 'Stephi'. Ilse did not explain why the rendezvous at Malsfeld could not come about, but Maria Lieberknecht had probably warned her against the imponderable risks of such a meeting. Her letter goes on:

> Today I've sent 20 Reichsmark by registered mail to the following address: 'District Labour Institution, Breitenau'. I hope that's all right with you. I shall try to see if I can get permission to visit you. I think I will. That would be lovely. I hope I'll get permission. Aunt Maria is very worried about everyone.
>
> On Monday I'm going to Frankenstein again. This afternoon I went down to the cellar and broke open the wicker suitcase – with difficulty. I took out a pair of white knickers. It's lucky we've got these things.
>
> Are you cold? That's my greatest worry. Oh, if only I knew. I hope you'll get our parcel soon. Parcels get terribly roughly handled on the trains these days. I see that again and again every lunchtime. Tonight you're getting another kiss from me. A goodnight kiss. Sleep well now. A big hug from your Ilse Mouse, who thinks of you constantly.
>
> Don't be too sad! Nothing lasts for ever!

Lilli, as her next letter indicated, did not receive Ilse's cancellation note soon enough and was very disappointed when nobody met her at Malsfeld. At the same time, however, a new possibility arose: with Maria Lieberknecht's help, Ilse managed to obtain a visitor's permit for Breitenau.

'A sack dress of coarse material and wooden clogs'
Ilse visits her mother in the corrective labour camp

All surviving victims of the air raid on Kassel had to submit precise inventories of destroyed and missing articles in order to obtain the corresponding requisition slips from the authorities. It was explained to the Gestapo that a complete list relating to the gutted apartment at 3 Motzstrasse could not be compiled without Lilli's help – hence the necessity for a visit to Breitenau. Further bureaucratic procedures had to be completed beforehand, however, because the camp made no provision for visits of this kind. Ilse deliberately refrained from mentioning the possibility of a meeting until she had actually obtained the requisite permit. Her next few letters were silent on the subject, for instance that of 26 November:

My dearest Mummy,
There was another long series of crashes and bangs just now. Oh, how scared I always get! It seems to be over now, but the all-clear hasn't sounded yet. I keep on listening for it. Dorle isn't asleep yet. She's lying rosy-cheeked beside my desk, playing with her little fingers, and she's bound to go to sleep in a minute. Whenever the guns start firing she says: 'But Ille, don't walk through the fire again.' So Dorle also noticed it. I'm sure you must have heard it too.
This afternoon I went to Resemarie's to ask for some textbooks, but she doesn't have any left, unfortunately. Then I went to the clergyman. I'm now learning the

future tense: laudabo, bis, bit, bimus, etc. I've got a lot to learn in Latin, but I'm so very short of time.

In school today we had two periods of art history. Dr Faust is a really fantastic person. He showed us 'Die Madonna im Rosenhag' by Stephan Lochner, and then 'Die Madonna mit der Wickenblüte', the Isenheim Altar, and commented on them in language which I, with my simple words, can't possibly reproduce. He's the greatest person I've ever met . . .

Oh Mummy, it's just too sad you probably won't be able to be back with the five of us for Christmas. We must put up with that too. We mustn't give up hope, however hard it will be for us two friends. But you can depend on me. I'll do my utmost to make it a 'relatively' happy time for the little ones. When things don't work out, I think so much of you . . . Goodbye for now, my dearest. Lots of love from your Ilse Mouse

Johanna wrote to her mother at the same time. She told her how she was getting on at the secondary school which had been evacuated to Hofgeismar, and it appears that her introduction into this boys' school, which she had been dreading, had gone well:

My very dearest Mummy,

There's a raid on, the guns are banging away like mad and it's bright as day. Up to now, Eva and I have been watching from the staircase window. Ille fears the worst, but I don't think it's meant for us.

It was really fantastic in school today. The boys are very nice. You just have to join in all their silly games. During break today they pinched Heidi's old, full composition book, so the two of us chased after them until we got it back, torn into a million pieces. Then they bombarded us with paper balls, but we threw them all back. That impresses them.

In history they had to write a composition about

Henry the Lion. Not being as far on as them, we had to read it up in the book. We told the boys in front of us everything we thought was important and significant, so that made us some friends right away. For maths and geography we have a very nice but strict young teacher named Fatthauer . . . For biology and religion we have one named Hengst [stallion], whom we just call 'Giddy-up'. Then there's our form teacher, Jachens, who's awful. He takes us for Latin, history, and English. Phew, Latin's quite something. I've got a lot of ground to make up.

Will they let you come home soon? I don't think we'll be together at Christmas. Oh, if only we knew. We must be brave and have faith. Lots of love and kisses from your Hannele

Meanwhile, Lilli's Freiburg friend Lotte Paepcke had returned to Leipzig. Her son Peter, whom she had left with her former maidservant Josephine, seemed to be in good hands. Although now obliged, like Lilli, to do forced labour, Lotte was allowed to go on living with her husband. She wrote to Breitenau on 26 November:

My dear Lilli,

I've just got back, and am quickly sending you a little something to eat. I meant to bake you something myself, but I don't have the time at present because I have to start work at a fur factory the day after tomorrow, and I've got such an awful lot left to do first. But you'll get something better as soon as possible, all right?

I found a sweet letter from Ilse waiting for me. I hope she'll come and stay with us. I have to work until either 2 or 4 p.m., but I'd have plenty of time for her after that.

It was really lovely in Freiburg! I recuperated and ate well. Twice I went for a walk in the mountains. I took you everywhere with me.

Peter is being well looked after and got some extra rations from the public health office because of his undernourishment. Now that I have to work, I'm doubly glad to know he's so well provided for.

In the next few days I'll send the children as many clothes, etc., as I can. I'd have liked to discuss it all with Ilse. I hope she comes soon. I imagine you received my query about a warm blanket? Write soon and tell me whether you need anything else.

Forgive this rushed letter, but I've so much left to do.

Ernst August sends his love, and a big hug and kiss from me,

Your Lotte

Lilli was positively inundated with letters during those weeks in the late autumn of 1943. Ilse and Johanna wrote every day. They assiduously sent off parcels, too, though not all of these reached their destination; some were probably confiscated by the camp authorities.

At the end of November 1943 Lilli managed to smuggle another letter out of the camp. Written on 28 November, this time in red ink on three sheets of brown wrapping paper, it patiently and exhaustively commented on all that her children and her niece Marilis, who was now a student at Marburg University, had told her in the preceding weeks.

My dearly beloved best of children,

Today is the first Sunday in Advent, and I very much hope that, in spite of all our troubles, you are feeling a touch of pre-Christmas excitement. I think of you so much the whole day long, with all my love and a great deal of longing. Ilse Mouse, my dear, you're being very brave and must continue to be so, and you needn't think I'm always just sad. I'm not that at all – in fact when I receive your dear, affectionate letters I'm really proud and happy and *so* grateful.

And I meet with a great deal of friendliness and affection and kindness, even here. Today someone actually gave me a little Advent wreath, and when we're all together again I'll tell you lots more about this place. If only it could be *soon*!

At Malsfeld yesterday I strained my eyes looking for you and was very disappointed you weren't there. I assume you hadn't got travel permits from the railway people, or was there some other reason? On the other hand, I received masses and masses of lovely mail – from you all, including two letters from Gerhard and a letter and a card from Marilis. I'm always *so* delighted to get it.

I've also received two parcels this week, one with sanitary towels, hairpins, etc., and Ille's really excellent biscuits, which were delicious. It contained everything you'd listed in your letter, and very special thanks to kind Gerda for the tasty things. It was really nice of her. And yesterday there came a big parcel from Aunt Lore containing two loaves, cheese, butter, jam, cakes, *lots* of apples and medicaments, and the set of spillikins. How can I thank you for all your kindness! But *please* don't send me any butter – please, please don't, because I can't eat it without feeling guilty. So, you dears, please accept my heartfelt thanks. Now I shall eat my fill, and I hope the tablets, etc., will help. I'm taking them like a good girl.

The previous week's parcel of bread never reached me, nor did any of the parcels mentioned by you and Marilis in recent weeks. But I expect things will improve, so let's not be sad about it, all right? Just remember how happy I am with everything I get from you. And special thanks, too, for the packet of newspapers and the two illustrated magazines.

Please send Marilis lots of love and special thanks for the *lovely* little book of poems by Mörike, which I'm much enjoying. And heartfelt thanks to you, my boy, for your Sunday bulletins and the beautiful poems! Hannele, how was it at Hümme? And how are your school arrangements progressing? I'm *so* glad you haven't gone to Fulda with the others. So Eva's doing well at arith-

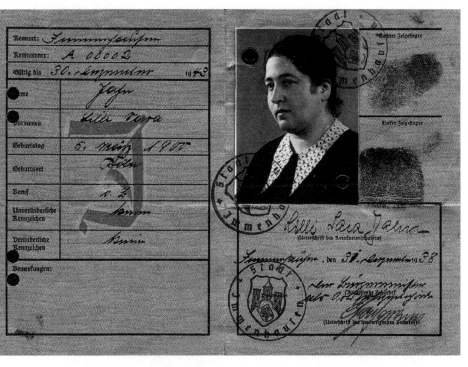

Identity card issued to Lilli 'Sara' Jahn, 31 December 1938.
(Note the large 'J' on the left.)

Lilli with Gerhard, Johanna, Ilse and Eva in the Black Forest, c. 1937.

Ilse, Lilli, Eva, Johanna, Ernst and Gerhard at Immenhausen, 1939.

Lilli in the Black Forest, summer 1939.

Ernst Jahn in his Opel at Immenhausen, c. 1939.

Johanna, 1942.

Ilse in 1942. The photograph was taken to mark her confirmation.

Guxhagen an der Fulda, Breitenau

View of the former monastery of Breitenau at Guxhagen. The Kassel Gestapo
used it as a corrective labour camp from 1940 to 1945.

Lilli's clandestine letter to her children from Breitenau, 3 October 1943.

Kassel, d. 19.10.43.

Mein Liebstes, Herz und Mütterlein!

Letter from Ilse to her mother Lilli, 19 October 1943.

Lilli's note to Ernst from Breitenau, late October 1943.

Gerhard Jahn as an air-force auxiliary. This photograph was enclosed
in his letter to Lilli dated 22 January 1944.

Johanna, Ilse, Eva and Dorothea, early summer 1944.

Auschwitz, den 5|VI·1944

Meine liebe Lore! Ich bin so sehr glücklich
Dir zu schreiben zu können. Es geht mir
gut, ich arbeite in meinem Beruf und
das ist sehr angenehm für mich. Nun er-
warte ich sehnsüchtlich Nachrichten
über Dich und Kinder. Was machen
sie alle? Ist Gerhard schon im Arbeitsdienst? Gehen Ilse und Hanele nach
Hofgeismar in die Schule? Was macht
meine kleine Eva? Und was macht
mein Allerkleinste? Und wie geht
es Dir selbst und Marielise. Ich er-
warte nun regelmäßig Nachrichten
von Euch. Ich danke Euch herzlich

Lilli's letter from Auschwitz to her sister-in-law Lore Sasse, 6 May 1944.

für die regelmäßige Geldsendungen.
Ich danke Euch für das letzte Packet
nach Breithenau. Die Kinder möchten
auch selbst schreiben. Meine Gedan-
ken sind ununterbrochen immer
bei Euch. Hoffentlich seid Ihr alle
gesund. Ich grüße und küße jeden
einzelnen tausend Mal. Ich bin in
großer Liebe als Mutter und Schwä-
gerin. Lilli u. Mutti

Lilli Jahn's death certificate, issued at Auschwitz on 28 September 1944.

metic? Keep it up, my dear. You didn't tell me anything about Dorle this week. What is my sweetheart up to? I'm very, very glad you all get on so well with Aunt Lore. Give her my fond love. I was tremendously pleased to get her message.

Ille my friend, I always treasure your long letters and find them reassuring, but it distresses me so much that *I* can't look after and take care of *you*. Do you really mean to go to Frankenstein again? I'd almost prefer it if Aunt Lore bought the beds and so on, because she runs the household more like me than Aunt Rita, and knows more about it. Couldn't you go shopping in Leipzig with Aunt Lore? I'm sure Aunt Lotte would be only too happy to put you up and help you. But if you think it's better the other way, don't be influenced by me. If you go and see Aunt Maria again, give her my fondest love. I'm so grateful for all her love and kindness to you children. How good of her to give you another dress, dear Ille, and such grand extras for me. Regards also to Aunt Rita, Dr Schupmann, and above all to Daddy. You were right, Ilse Mouse, to write to Münster for those books. You darlings, go on telling me about everything, about school and all you do. Are you having a cosy get-together today? Will you be going to Marburg sometime, Ille? Will I be with you at Christmas???? I send you all six thousand good wishes and hug and kiss you tenderly, gratefully, filled with love and longing for you!

Your Mummy

In the margin of the last page she added:

Gerhard's letters always give me a great deal of pleasure, even if lack of time prevents me from answering them separately. You understand, my boy?!

Lilli's children continued to write without flagging, even though the fundamental message embodied in every sentence, every incident described, was the same: Mummy, we miss you. When are you coming home?

Johanna was the only one who sometimes managed briefly to conceal this longing beneath her cheerfully recounted anecdotes. This letter was written, like Lilli's, on that first Sunday in Advent:

My dear, best, poor, sweet Mummy,

How are you? If the mail is back to normal again, you'll notice I'll have skipped a letter for once. That's because I've had a violent toothache these past few days, thanks to a thoroughly rotten but firmly embedded molar, top right. After I'd consumed an entire tube of Veramon, Aunt Rita dragged me off to see Dr Holland, the feeble old seventy-plus dentist. He promptly sat me down in his torturer's chair and injected my gum with anaesthetic. The pain was bearable, but after five minutes he took his forceps and started to prise the half-crumbled tooth out of the gum. Ouch, did that hurt. I thought I was being stuck with pins. Then he took another instrument and yanked and yanked, up and down, right and left, until I felt as though I had thirty-two teeth. I kept trying to jump up, and Aunt Rita had her work cut out to hold me down. Then, at long last, half the tooth came out, but what about the other half? Oh God, I thought, to the extent that I could still think. But then he summoned up all his strength, and heave ho, heave ho, out it came.

'That was quite an effort,' said the old thing. I didn't knew whether to laugh or cry or scream with pain. Ow, ow, was all I kept saying, and Aunt Rita said, there, there. But I was completely beside myself. He didn't get a goodbye from me, just a handshake and the sight of a rapidly receding figure. Then I was outside. But did I have toothache, oh Mummy . . . Then it was a cloth round my head and two tablets, one for the pain, one to make me sleep, and into bed. I cried awhile longer in bed.

Then *dear, kind* Uncle Dr Schupmann came in and comforted me and told me his own tooth story. You know, how he got his wisdom tooth at home with us. Then the toothache subsided and I fell asleep while he was still there. I love Dr Schupmann like a father. He comes immediately after you in my list of people I'm fond of.

Well, that was the tooth page.

Johanna took another sheet of paper and went on:

It's Advent today, but without you, darling. Oh yes – it was nice, but – far, far!!!!! less nice than with you. With you at least some Christmas spirit would have set in, but here, not a bit of it. Oh yes, she read out (or intoned) something from the Catholic missal which meant next to nothing to any of us.

And then there were some bits of paper on a little plate. Everyone had to draw one, and every bit had a name on it . . . If you drew 'Ille' you had to do something nice for Ille every day, like give her something or help her, clean her shoes, darn her stockings, make her bed, or something like that. A nice idea, but quite out of character with Aunt Rita. The other thing was, you weren't allowed to say whose name you'd drawn. When Aunt Rita went out of the room, we all showed ours. I'm sure you'll want to know whose names we drew. Aunt Rita drew me, naturally, and, because there was one too many, Eva as well. Aunt Lore drew Dorle, which is nice, Gerda drew Ille and Ille drew Gerda, a perfect match. Eva drew little Magda, fancy! Hannele drew Aunt Lore, which is fine, and Dorle – for heaven's sake! – drew Aunt Rita. And Magda drew Eva. The older ones have to help out with the younger ones, Ille with Dorle and Aunt Rita with Magda.

Today I did our room for Aunt Lore, made the beds, cleared the table, and swept the floor. Then we had an

Advent wreath as well. Ille is going to Frankenstein tomorrow.

That was the Advent page.

A thousand million billion hugs and kisses from your Hannele

A week later, on the next Sunday in Advent, Gerhard wrote to Breitenau:

My dear, dear Mummy,

I wish you all the very best on this second Sunday in Advent. How are you? Everything is fine here. I'm well. So are the children. They all come to see me in turn. Ilse was here on Sunday. She brought me a pair of gloves knitted for me by Marilis. I was particularly pleased to get them, because I didn't have any before, and that's not funny in this cold weather.

When Ilse had gone – it was already getting dark – I went up to a gun in the emplacement. Wolf, Ernst and Martin were already there, three Marburgers I get on with very well, Wolf especially. They're far nicer than the rest. I celebrated the first Sunday in Advent with them in the emplacement. At least we were undisturbed there by the others, who think it's merely ridiculous. We had an Advent wreath, a candle, a few biscuits, and a few cigarettes . . .

At lunchtime on Wednesday, 1 December 1943, the CO promoted us old air-force auxiliaries to air-force auxiliaries 1st class. After that he carried out a strict inspection which everyone naturally failed. Our insignia is an NCO's stripe running diagonally across the shoulder strap, like an NCO candidate . . .

We opened fire again on the night of Thursday/Friday. The Brits were coming back from Berlin, so we 'singed their fur with a couple of shots', as the CO likes to put it. A bit of gunnery once a week 'raises morale' and restores our good spirits. Even if there's quite a lot of work to do afterwards, the main thing is, we opened fire.

Yesterday I was duty NCO again till lunchtime, so I didn't get much peace. Yesterday evening I made my regulation report in my number ones adorned with my new badge of rank as an air-force auxiliary 1st class. He congratulated me and wished me all the best and lots of luck.

We were very busy again last night. An alert from 2 to 6.15 a.m. And the cold! I was well wrapped up except for my feet, and after four hours they were regular blocks of ice . . . Hannele was here briefly and brought my laundry. After four weeks I may get some leave tomorrow. My short leave has been cut to a day, but I may get my weekend leave next weekend. If would be very nice if I could get off tomorrow, especially as the lady of the house won't be there. I'm particularly looking forward to it after all this time! Much, much love and all the best
from your Gerhard

There followed a poem by Eichendorff.

Thirteen-year-old Johanna, who was impressed by her big brother's military prowess, wrote about it to her mother the next day:

Gerda quickly baked him a cake because he's now an air-force auxiliary 1st class. He now has a little silver stripe on his shoulder straps. I'm sure you'll be pleased. Not all of them were promoted, either.

In the meantime, Ilse had after all paid another visit to Frankenstein with Rita, primarily to obtain some clothes and towels for the household at Immenhausen. Her account of the trip is dated 7 December:

My dear Mummy,

It's been so long since I could talk to you in my letters, but now I'm home again. We had a really awful journey. The express left on time but got to Kassel almost eight hours late. The train was heated, so it was just bearable. We were at a standstill for a long time outside Halle because the Leipziger Bahnhof is completely devastated. That caused the first of our delays. Our longest delay occurred beyond Halle, where a goods train had been derailed.

So we didn't get to Kassel until 1 a.m., laden with two handbags, a school satchel, three heavy suitcases, and nine blankets. By degrees, we toted these into the slow train, which left at 4.25 a.m. We couldn't go into the waiting room because there isn't one any more. The slow train was cold as ice. I caught a lovely cold and got frozen feet after shivering for four hours.

They weren't expecting us when we got here in the morning, and the whole place was in chaos . . . Then we collected the bags from the station and unpacked them. All the new things were laid out all round the room on top of the mess that was lying around there already. After that we had a quick coffee. I got Dorle dressed between times. Everyone spent ages going through the stuff. Some things were borne off, others picked up and put down again.

Finally, when everyone had left, Aunt Rita came and asked for her things. So first of all I had to start looking underneath everything, including a packet of soap powder that had burst and deposited half its contents on the blankets. I ended up tidying continuously from 10 a.m. to 1 p.m., and still I hadn't finished.

Then I went to Kassel and only got through the barrier by the skin of my teeth. I went to the Gestapo and obtained permission to see you on Sunday morning to draw up the list of things we've lost in the bombing. I'm so looking forward to that. Then, at half past four, I went back to Immenhausen, where Aunt Lore had turned up with Eva. Aunt Rita had already shown Aunt Lore some of the things in the meantime, and started making a mess again.

Then Aunt Rita went off to see Daddy. We were alone, thank goodness. I showed Aunt Lore everything, and she was very pleased with it all, including the bedlinen and the hand towels for us and the kitchen. We'd also brought some things for Aunt Lore and Marilis on their requisition slips. After supper Dorle and I had a bath. Aunt Lore had helped me to put things away, so it didn't take us long.

When Dorle and Eva had gone to sleep – Eva is also sleeping in the children's bedroom at the moment – I filled a slipper for everyone. Aunt Rita hadn't remembered. I'd gone to see Gustchen that morning and asked her if she had anything for Santa Claus, so she gave me two bags of sweets. I'd also brought a few honey cakes from Kassel. So this morning Dorle and Eva were delighted to find that Santa Claus had been. I suddenly felt so terribly tired last night, I really couldn't write because I'd been up for nearly sixty-five hours . . .

I didn't go to Leipzig because Aunt Rita really wanted to go to Daddy's in Kassel on the return journey, and I would have had to travel on alone with the baggage. But it's a good thing I didn't go shopping in Leipzig, because I'd have been there during the air raid.

Oh Mummy, it's such a shame you can't be with us at Christmas. I can hardly imagine it. But I'll do my utmost to create a Christmassy atmosphere for the little ones all the same. It won't be my fault if there isn't one. I shall think hard of you, Mummy, and tell you all about it . . . Oh Mummy, I miss you so much. All my thoughts are of you, and then I always feel sad at heart. I can safely write and tell you all this because you know me too well to think I'm never sad. And writing to you is always a pleasure . . .

A big hug and a loving kiss from your Ilse Mouse

Ilse's letter also contained a long list of the articles of clothing acquired in Frankenstein. She had missed some more days of school because of the trip, but in her view there were more important considerations – for instance her forthcoming visit to Breitenau. On 9 December she wrote:

My dearest Mummy,
I went back to school today for the first time, and oh, there was lots of news. Holidays start on the 15th, next Wednesday. I'm very glad because I'll be able to devote more time to our little ones. As it is, my whole day is one long rush. The holidays last four weeks, until 18 January, and then it starts all over again. I'm afraid I only got a 4 for my composition on manners, but I hope I'll soon do better at school. I had another Latin lesson today. I'm making good progress. I'm now learning the perfect and pluperfect, laudavis and laudaveris, etc. He says I'm working well.
Several people were very nice again today, and gave Eva all kinds of things for you. They're all very sweet. This afternoon I sat with Aunt Lore for a short time and discussed all kinds of things with her. On Sunday!!!!, when you receive this letter, I'll have been there already. But then you'll have my visit to remember . . . Oh Mummy, how I miss you. No one could possibly gauge how much I miss you. I'm so glad Aunt Lore is here. With her at least I can have a proper conversation and tell her some of the things I'm unsure of. But only some of them. I can't do that sort of thing with Aunt Rita. It's better to keep my mouth shut.
So, my darling Mummy, sleep well! Don't be too sad and don't get cold!!! A big hug from your Ilse Mouse, whose thoughts are of you alone.
See you Sunday!!!

Ten-year-old Eva was rather proud of all the things the Immenhausen farmers' families had given her for Lilli. On 10 December, two days before Ilse's visit to Breitenau, she told her mother about them:

My most beloved and best Mummy,

This evening I'm writing you a quick letter. The first snow fell today, Friday. I did a lot of sledging this afternoon. I've got masses of nice things for you. Someone gave me a sausage and I'm having it smoked – for you, dear Mummy.

I hope you come home soon. How are you?

We're still fine.

Many millions of loving good wishes and kisses from your country girl, Eva

Ilse had already told her mother about the heavy air raid on Leipzig. On 10 December Lilli's friend Lotte Paepcke finally sent her a postcard:

Dear Lilli,

You've probably heard about the bombing raid on Leipzig. We're alive, and our house is still standing in spite of all the fires around it, but all our windows have gone. Still no gas or electricity. Ernst August's factory is still standing. It takes him four hours to get there and back every day. My own factory has been destroyed and the boss is dead. I don't know what's going to happen. I'll send you some sewing things as soon as one can send anything again. Did you receive a little parcel from me?

More soon, my dear.

Ernst August sends his best regards.

I send a kiss.

Your Lotte

On Saturday, 11 December, final preparations were made for Ilse's trip to Breitenau. The girls found some little presents for their mother, and each of the children wrote her a note, Gerhard included:

This will probably reach you in time for the third Sunday in Advent, because Ilse will be bringing you this letter. I hope and believe that this will be a very special day for you, but I'm so sorry I can't come too. If I'd known, I might have been able to get my leave pass made out for there. I hope you're as well as you possibly can be. I'm sure Ilse will give you all our news.

Sunday morning dawned. It was more than three months since Lilli had seen her children. Now, at long last, her eldest daughter was able to visit her. Today, almost sixty years later, Ilse preserves the following recollection of 12 December 1943:

> I dressed as smartly as I could. On a rainy morning I stood apprehensively outside the old, forbidding, ominous-looking walls of the prison. I waited for my Mummy in a small, dark room. She came in escorted by a wardress. How changed my well-groomed Mummy looked. She was wearing a sack dress of coarse material, wooden clogs without any stockings, and one of her incisors was missing. 'You've got ten minutes,' ordained the wardress, who remained in the room. I can't remember what we talked about. We held each other in a tight embrace. Frau Lieberknecht had impressed on me that I must whisper to Mummy not to write any more illicit letters. If that were discovered, it would be the end of her. I did as I'd been told. And suddenly I was once more standing outside the big gate.

In tears, Ilse took the train back to Immenhausen, where she told her brother and sisters what had happened. Gerhard and Johanna wrote their mother brief notes the same evening:

> My dearest Mummy,
> Ilschen has just got back, and I wanted to tell you quickly that I love you very, very much and think of you a great deal.
> Yours, Gerhard

My dear, sweet, dearest Mummy,

How glad and sad I am to know how you're getting on, and much more besides. Many heartfelt thanks for the little hankie bag, which is *so* sweet. You truly can't imagine how delighted I was. It's my *most favourite* Christmas present of all, believe me. It's really splendid! I'm so happy you're well. And perhaps you'll be able to come back to us soon.

Hannele

'Don't be too terribly sad'
The turn of the year, 1943/44

With the exception of a letter Lilli had written a week before the reunion at Breitenau, the children heard nothing more from their mother for over a month. Although Lilli had taken in Ilse's warning and wrote no more unauthorized letters for the time being, she naturally hoped that efforts to secure her release would continue. Ilse had, in fact, gone to see her father at the hospital near Kassel the day after the Breitenau meeting and begged him to make some move towards saving her mother. She could only hint at this in her letter of 13 December:

> My dearest Mummy,
> How happy I was to see you again. I hope you weren't too terribly sad for long when I had to leave. I got home safely.
> Today I went straight to see Daddy. An air-raid warning was in progress when I got to Kassel, so I had to go into the station shelter. The guns opened up in the distance, and I was awfully scared. When I was in the shelter it sounded as if bombs were landing right next door, but the fact was, it was only the shelter doors that kept banging, and no bombs landed nearby. You can't imagine how relieved I was when the all-clear sounded.
> When I got to Daddy after a rather tiresome journey, Aunt Rita was still there from Sunday night, so I couldn't put things the way I wanted to. All Daddy kept saying was: 'Everything remotely possible will be done.' I didn't

hear anything definite. If something doesn't happen soon, Aunt Lore and I will take things in hand within the next six days.

I've got hold of a small suitcase for Gerhard. He'll be delighted with it, I'm sure, because his briefcase got burnt too. I also paid a visit to the Bärenreiter publishing house today. You can still buy all kinds of things there, but only one copy. I bought a portfolio, 'Romanesque Buildings in France'. It's for you for Christmas from us all.

I ought to be slogging away at my Latin, actually, but I really can't. I'd sooner get up early tomorrow morning. Still no letter from you, and nothing at all from Aunt Lotte either . . . So, my dearest, sleep well and a loving hug from your Ilse Mouse

It was now the last week of school before Christmas. On Wednesday, 15 December, Johanna once more tried to cheer her mother up with an anecdote from the boys' school. The protagonist of the story was Johanna's friend Heidi:

My dear Mummy sweetheart,

How are you? We're fine. You've really no need to worry. It was great again in school today. It was Heidi's turn in maths, and she had to work out a sum on the blackboard for this really young maths teacher, thirty at most. While she was standing up at the front, nearly all the poppers on her skirt burst open and her slip peeped out. Fatthauer, that's his name, said: 'Heidi, your shirt's hanging out.' How the class roared. One boy, who's always trying to flirt, turned crimson and gave Heidi a look of commiseration. Then the stupid teacher said: 'Hassogen, stop making sheep's eyes.' The laughter started all over again. Then the teacher said: 'All right, put your maths things away, Heidi sit down, and we'll sing.' So we belted out one song after another . . . Some lesson, that was! But we join in everything, Mummy. It's really great.

With many loving good wishes and kisses, your Hannele

Meanwhile, Ilse went on trying to talk her father into launching a rescue operation on Lilli's behalf. He seemed reluctant to do so, as Ilse reported on 16 December:

No application has been lodged yet. But if nothing has happened by Monday morning, when Aunt Rita comes back from visiting Daddy, I, Aunt Lore and Marilis, who's coming today, will deal with the matter. On Sunday afternoon Marilis and I are going to see Aunt Maria, who I hope will be back from Bad Liebenstein.

Marilis, now a student at Marburg University, came to Immenhausen for Christmas. Lilli's children were looking forward to their cousin's visit. Marilis provided them with a certain amount of support in their altercations with Rita, which were always coming to a head. Gerhard was planning a return visit to Marburg. In January the sixteen-year-old 'air-force auxiliary 1st class' was due his first longish spell of leave.

To ensure that their Christmas greetings got to Breitenau in good time, the children posted their cards and letters on the fourth Sunday in Advent. On this occasion, Gerhard made some attempt to put himself in his mother's place. 'Please don't be too sad,' he told her on 18 December, 'but remember that it's much nicer for me, too, if I know you aren't crying too much.'

Ilse wrote her Christmas letter the next day:

My dear, sweet Mummy,
Today was Sunday. It's quite late already. Marilis is splashing around in the bathtub.
Saturday . . . was our last day of school. In the first period we had history. The second lesson was supposed to be maths, but the teacher didn't feel like teaching any more, so he made us sing carols. So we sang Christmas carols for the whole lesson. We spent the next period

with our form teacher. It was his birthday on Friday. Two of the girls had baked him a cake, and we'd got a cyclamen for him. We'd put it on his desk together with a poem, decorated with candles and sprigs of fir. When he came in, some girls played the flute and we sang him a birthday canon . . . He was really touched and said he didn't know how to repay us. He couldn't do so with good marks – that would be bribery, he said – but he wanted to thank us for our affection by reciting a poem he'd 'perpetrated' himself. The poem was about a picture of an old woman with her hands over her eyes. He said it would give us a deep insight into himself. The poem was indescribably beautiful, just as the teacher himself is a fine and exceptional person. After that we got our reports, and that was it.

When the bell went we filed out and dashed off to the station to catch the train. Marilis got in at Immenhausen, and we went on together to Aunt Maria's. She'd got back from her trip long ago. First we had sandwiches, then fruitcake and ersatz coffee [made of barley and rye], and then Madeira cake and biscuits and real coffee!

Aunt Maria's advice was thoroughly sound, as usual. She gave me fresh hope. Then she gave us everyone's Christmas presents: Dorle's doll and a little parcel for everyone except Magda and Aunt Rita. She gave them to me to take home, although we'd really meant to go there with Dorle over the holiday. I'm far too nervous, though, and I couldn't answer to you if there was an air raid. The younger ones are very annoyed with me, but I can't help it. I'm sure you understand.

Aunt Maria intends to write Daddy a proper letter. She isn't *entirely* satisfied either! . . . This evening I had a fine old row with Aunt Rita over the butter, and from tomorrow we'll each have our own butter on a separate plate. Then each of us will get our fair share, at least . . . Gerda's husband came after supper, and we had a nice time. Meantime, the heating had gone off. Aunt Lore,

Marilis and I got it going again. By the way, I've a confession to make: I smoked my first cigarette today. Are you cross?!?!

Your letter dated the second Sunday in Advent came on Saturday. Could we send you a pair of gloves and a scarf? Please write and say. We've already got something.

Dorle is being very good. She has written a list of requests for the Christ Child: A little sister for Gretel (Gretel is the curly-headed doll you gave her), a pussy cat, a music (mouth organ), and lots of biscuits. Eva is blissfully happy that the holidays are here. Hannele is making things for Christmas. But I'm very worried that you're cold. I hope it doesn't get too cold. Now you must sleep too. Don't be too terribly sad. I'll try not to be either. A thousand good wishes and kisses from your Ilse Mouse

Johanna also wrote the same night, using another Madonna postcard appropriate to the occasion:

Dear Mummy, sweetheart,

I'm sending you a little Christmas greeting in the shape of this card.

Perhaps it will reach you by Christmas, and tell you that we're all being brave and not crying, but hoping and trusting to God that we won't be too sad and will be really brave. It's easier for Dorle and Eva, but Ille and I . . . I can honestly tell you that we think of you every hour, in fact almost every minute. But Mummy, we're being brave, so please don't brood too much yourself. Oh Mummy, it's very, very hard for us all. Fondest good wishes and kisses, your Hannele

Gerhard had not been granted leave on Christmas Eve 1943, so he had to spend a rather boring night with his battery at Obervellmar. 'In desperation, we played hit tunes for hours, Wolf on the squeezebox, me on drums,' he wrote to his mother on Christmas Day. His sisters spent Christmas at Immenhausen with their father, Rita, and Magda. Ilse's letter dated 25 December:

My dearest Mummy,

My goodness! It's been quite bearable. I'll tell you about it all in chronological order. Present-giving was at 7.45 on Christmas Eve, and beforehand it was all such a rush. For supper we had potato salad and a sausage Eva had brought. Daddy was awfully irritable, and my dear little Dorle had tummy-ache and wasn't at all well. She didn't eat anything, just wanted to sleep, and I was very worried about her.

When the Christ Child rang downstairs, we all went down. I was feeling thoroughly unfestive. It was only when Daddy read the Christmas story that I felt Christmassy too. Then we were supposed to sing a Christmas carol. Eva was told to fetch Aunt Rita's mouth organ, but she couldn't find it upstairs. (Daddy was becoming more and more irritable.) So Aunt Rita went upstairs with Magda. While Aunt Rita was upstairs with Magda, Magda did it in her pants. (Daddy became even more irritable.) We all stood waiting on the spot for at least five minutes. It was awful. Then, when ten minutes had gone by, Daddy said we should look at our things. So by tonight we still hadn't sung a carol. The children weren't too sad. Eva cried a bit, but I soon managed to cheer her up.

I hope you weren't too sad. Did you get something to eat? Did you light the candles on your little Christmas tree?

First I devoted myself to little Dorle. She got a home-made yellow teddy bear from Lene Hirdes, the doll from Aunt Maria, from you – so I told her – an oilcloth ball and a squirrel, from Daddy a big picture book, from Marilis a black pussy cat she'd made herself, and from Aunt Lore a little white pinafore . . . She's delighted with them all.

From Daddy I got a Weigele art history book; from Aunt Lore a book of engravings and a handkerchief plus hankie bag; from Lene Hirdes some biscuits and a handkerchief; and from Aunt Rita a Hammer book on Caspar David Friedrich, a girls' book, a scarf, and the boots. So now you know everything.

This afternoon we went to see Gerhard. He was very pleased with my suitcase, and they'd had two enjoyable days. Well, sweetheart, goodbye till tomorrow evening. A big, loving hug and a big kiss from your Ilse Mouse

Johanna also wrote on Christmas Day and told her mother about her presents. They included a 'negro baby' doll, a sewing box, a nightgown, several adventure books, and, from her father, a book of drawings by Moritz von Schwind.

The Christmas-present table was sumptuous but sad. But Mummy, you'll get a lovely Christmas-present table when you're allowed to come home. I've nearly finished all your presents.

The children viewed the coming year with apprehension. On 28 December Johanna sent her New Year's greetings to Breitenau:

Dear Mummy sweetheart,

Warmest good wishes for the New Year from me. Let's hope the New Year will be better than 1943, which has brought us – and mainly you – a great deal of worry, fear and sadness. Let's hope and pray that we'll all be able to be together again in the New Year, perhaps even in a new home. I have here a nice card that's meant to bring you, too, a little pleasure. I wish I could send and write you far nicer things.

I'll stop now. A million million loving good wishes for 1944.

Your Hannele

Ilse also wrote her mother a brief letter on 31 December.

Dear, sweet Mummy,
Today is New Year's Eve. The first one without you.
Aunt Rita has invited us all downstairs with Dr Schupmann. Dorle is still up too. We'll see how it goes. I slept
late this morning, then did my usual chores . . . If only
you could be with us soon. I'm missing you again so
much today. All the best, sweetheart. Will you be allowed to write again soon? I shall look forward to your
letter so much. Let's hope that next year brings us
something good. A loving hug from your Ilse Mouse

Finally, on 3 January, a New Year's card from Leipzig reached
Breitenau. Lotte had posted it at the end of December:

Many loving good wishes and kisses!
Did you receive the sewing things and sweets, plus a
card and a letter? . . . Ilse wrote and told me that she'd
visited you. Was that lovely, but was it awful afterwards?
I shall think of you when the New Year begins – it's got
to be a better one for you.
Goodbye, my dear. Your Lotte.
Everything's still very difficult here.

'If you were back with us'
The children wait for news of Lilli

On the night of 1 January 1944 Ilse wrote her mother an account of New Year's Eve:

Dearest Mummy,
I'm sure you slept the New Year in. I finished all my sewing but didn't do any more knitting. Gertrud played ludo with Eva. When I'd done my sewing I played rummy with Aunt Rita. We had red wine, apples and biscuits. It was a miserable New Year's Eve. At midnight we clinked glasses, but that was all. Hannele and I had a bath afterwards. Dr Schupmann kept us amused upstairs.

We slept late in the morning . . . After breakfast Aunt Rita went to the station with the intention of visiting Daddy, but her watch was slow. The train had gone, so she didn't leave until 4.30 and said she'd be back at 8.30. It's 9.30, and she still isn't here, so she definitely won't come back till tomorrow morning. Hurrah! . . .

Dr Schupmann had been given a whole mountain of cakes to go with his coffee, and he shared them with us. We got three sausages from the Münchs. We fried two of them this evening and secretly made some potato salad to go with them. We invited Dr Schupmann to supper . . .

After supper Hannele helped Dr Schupmann to put the card index in order. I darned some stockings. Gerhard had a hole big enough for me to put my hand through. I gave Dorle a bath and washed Eva's hair. Now I'm off to bed too. Well, goodbye till tomorrow night. A thousand good wishes and kisses from your Ilse Mouse, who thinks of you constantly

The children were now left more and more to their own devices. Ernst seldom got leave from the hospital, Lore's house-hunting trips took her away for weeks at a time, and Marilis was at Marburg University.

Only two adults lived permanently in the house on Gartenstrasse: Rita, who sporadically looked after the children and was anyway disliked by them, and Dr Schupmann. The girls had taken their father's locum to their hearts. He was a cheerful character who felt sorry for the family of 'orphans', and became a major source of support to them.

The four girls increasingly detached themselves from Rita's household and led a life of their own on the top floor. A small stove was installed there, and Ernst provided Ilse with the requisite housekeeping money. The children kept their contact with the lower floors to an absolute minimum. They still had lunch with Rita, but that was all. Gerhard seldom came to Immenhausen for reasons which he explained to Lilli on 2 January 1944:

My dear Mummy,
    You're now getting my first letter of the New Year. Let's hope there'll only be a very few to follow. How are you?
    I hope to start my second spell of home leave on Tuesday. I shall spend most of the time in Marburg with Marilis. At Immenhausen there'd only be a row sooner or later. I know she says I'm the most sensible one, and that she's awfully fond of me and plans to make my leave as nice as humanly possible. (Even though I got ten cigarettes pinched from one of my Christmas parcels.) I'll spend a few days there for form's sake, of course . . .
    I was duty NCO again on Monday, so I had plenty to do. We've taken to playing chess again lately. We really

enjoy it. Apart from reading and writing, all we do is play chess.

On Tuesday and Wednesday the CO got his own back on us for making fun of him at Christmas by holding two really awful drill parades. We christened the drill parades 'reprisals'. On New Year's Eve we rubbed his nose in it again . . . I had to play the drums in our band on New Year's Eve, as a stand-in, so I had put in a lot of practice. I took some lessons in the afternoon . . . Come the evening, away we went. We musicians only wore trousers, air-force shirts, and ties. They'd made up our faces, too, with moustaches and all the trimmings.

We had to eat first, of course. Potato salad and meatballs – terrific! At eight the battery turned up. We struck up and never stopped from then on. In between we were given real coffee and fizzy drinks . . . Air-force auxiliaries were forbidden to smoke and drink, of course, but the soldiers happily plied us with punch on the sergeant's orders. The only proviso: We mustn't let the CO catch us. At midnight the CO delivered a speech. Twelve drumbeats, then everyone shook hands, CO and air-force auxiliaries included. The CO was so plastered, I actually wished him Happy New Year with a cigarette in my hand. At 1.30 the air-force auxiliaries had to go to bed. Only the band stayed behind. Then there was white wine, of which I managed to get my share. When some schnapps appeared, various sergeants and other NCOs gave us far too much to drink while we were playing . . .

Evchen has just paid me a brief visit, and now I'm sitting in the canteen, listening to some decent music at last, Mozart and Handel sonatas for violin and piano.

Fond love and all the best,

Your Gerhard

While Gerhard largely kept out of family affairs, Ilse had entirely accepted her role as a surrogate mother. Although Ernst made several attempts to integrate three-year-old Dorothea into his new family, he was there too seldom to succeed in doing so. Ilse's letter dated 3 January reveals the extent to which Dorle had by now become her 'daughter':

My dear Mummy sweetheart,

I've plenty to tell you today, my darling. A great deal has happened again. At 4.30 this morning there was a wild burst of anti-aircraft fire. Eva started crying, and Dorle called 'Ille, Ille'. So I raised the blackout curtain and saw the anti-aircraft guns blazing away over Kassel. I thought I'd die. We all jumped up. When it was over we went back to bed.

I got up early. Brushed our Sunday things and put them away, had some coffee, but first got Dorle dressed. After coffee I got Dorle into her tracksuit and wanted to take her with me to . . . Armbrusts to get some butter, but the shop was stuffed with people, bombed-out refugees. They had some china. I went home, fetched a laundry basket, and queued up. Gustchen and Herr Armbrust were very nice. I got twelve mugs, nine white and three coloured. A set of six deep plates, one soup tureen, one gravy boat, one small fish platter, two bowls . . . One coffee service: one coffee pot, one milk jug, one sugar bowl, six plates, six cups and saucers – cream-coloured and sprinkled with little red flowers, really pretty. Last of all, a solid white stoneware pot. I'm sure you'll like the china too.

Eva and I unpacked the stuff when I got it home. Then I had to strip our beds and put clean sheets on. For lunch we had fried potatoes and red cabbage. After lunch I put Dorle to bed and went to Toni's to get a perm. Guess what sort of hairstyle I've got??? A roll. But it suits me. I hope you'll like it too . . .

Before supper I called Hildchen Rüdiger and spoke to Herr Rüdiger. I only wanted to tell Hildchen she didn't have to go to school until the 5th. Then Herr Rüdiger said I should give Hildchen some tuition in English. I'm really proud of that. I ought to be able to manage what Hildchen is learning in Form 2, I'm sure you agree??

I re-read your last letter earlier on. It's always such a pleasure. Now, my sweetheart, sleep well and don't be too sad. Let's hope we're all together soon. A thousand good wishes and lots of love from your Ilse Mouse, whose thoughts are of you alone.

When the Christmas holidays ended on 5 January, the two older girls had to resume their daily journeys to school in Hofgeismar. Their standard of work had clearly deteriorated over the past months, because the prevailing situation made it hard for them to concentrate. Johanna found the pressure particularly hard:

School started again today. Oh Mummy, I'm so scared of not keeping up. As you know, they expect much more of you in the boys' school than in our old dump. You know how bad I am at maths, and it's very hard to grasp in one lesson what used to take five. My Latin could be worse.

Ernst took little interest in his daughters' educational concerns. His conscience pricked him for having divorced Lilli, especially as his marriage to Rita was going far from smoothly, so he solicited his eldest daughter's understanding of his conduct in writing. Ilse informed her mother of this on 7 January:

Daddy has written me an awfully long letter. If I told him what I thought, I'd be bound to hurt him, and I've no wish to do that. I won't send him a letter at all.

But Ernst did not give up. Two days later Ilse wrote:

Yesterday I received another eight-page letter from Daddy. Horrible. Oh darling, if only you were back with me. I can never, never be truly happy.

The children found the tension in the house hard to cope with. 'If only you were back with the five of us,' Eva wrote plaintively on 11 January. 'It's really awful when you're not here with us.'

The next day Ilse wrote again:

My dearest Mummy,

It was quite a rush this morning. I got up at six again, translated some English and copied out vocabularies. It was ten past seven before I knew it. I still hadn't done my hair or cleaned my shoes or made my sandwiches. I didn't get to the station until three minutes after half past and only caught the train by the skin of my teeth.

But I still hadn't learnt any history. We had the whole of the Thirty Years' War to do, and I only knew the battles and wars up to 1635, the end of the Swedish War. The rest I learnt at school. In the first period I had our beloved and respected Dr Müller again for German. In the second period we had 'Keller' for maths. An awful man. He's got flabby cheeks, an almost bald head, a thick lower lip, and a beard. Miracles still happen: I understood the maths. In the third period we and another form had physics again with 'Cellarium'. That was very boring. In the fourth and last period we had history with 'Mohammed'. I wasn't asked any questions, thank goodness.

After school a girl from Form B at Fulda came and told the six of us from Kassel what conditions in the camp were like. It's possible to pay the girls a visit, so I'll go and visit Gisela on Saturday/Sunday.

Yesterday afternoon I gave my first lesson. I think Hildchen learnt something. On Friday I'm supposed to be going to Aunt Maria's to pick up my birthday cake. That'll be nice.

I hope you received the picture and parcels. The letter you wrote on the 3rd, according to my calculations, hasn't arrived yet. Aren't you hungry? Are you cold still? Oh, if only I knew. My thoughts are with you day and night. We've now been apart for 18½ weeks. Let's hope the bulk of the time is behind us. One lonely day follows another . . . without you! Oh Mummy, if only they would release you soon!!

Aunt Lore has gone off to Tübingen and the Black Forest, so we're all on our own. But we'll stick it out to the end. 'What do our dismal cares avail, and what our melancholy cries . . .'

A loving hug and a thousand good wishes from your Ilse Mouse

The children were once again becoming very worried. They had not received a sign of life from their mother for exactly one month, or since Ilse's visit to Breitenau, yet she should have been entitled to send another letter on 1 January at the latest. 'What's happened to your mail? You should have written again long ago,' Johanna wrote on 12 January. 'I'm uneasy that you haven't written for so long,' Ilse complained the following day.

Ilse eventually did what Lilli had suggested back in November: one morning, she caught the same train as the labour conscripts from Breitenau. She actually spotted her mother in the distance but refrained from making herself known for fear of putting her in danger.

Gerhard, who knew nothing of these latest worries, was spending his leave at Marburg with his cousin Marilis. On 16 January he wrote Lilli a detailed account of his visit:

My dear, good Mummy,

This time I'm sending my Sunday letter from Marburg. I've already been here a whole week, and I've had a wonderful time. Marilis has gone to church with her friend Ilse, so now I can really write to you in peace. How are you? I'm thinking of you so much, especially now I'm on leave.

Last Sunday Marilis and I left Immenhausen at 7 a.m. We were in Marburg by 11.30, and the first thing we did was have lunch at a very nice restaurant, 'Der Ritter'. I've eaten there all week, whereas Marilis has been eating in the students' dining hall.

Then we went to Marilis's digs. The people there were very nice and fixed me up with a couch to sleep on. Then Marilis showed me round Marburg. We went to a café a couple of times in between, had supper, and then went to the cinema: 'Gekrönte Liebe', a terrific Italian film, though not particularly significant. That evening we sat in Marilis's digs and talked and read.

On Monday morning we went to my first lecture: Professor Mommsen, a grandson of the great Mommsen, on the period 1890–1914. It was really impressive and terribly interesting. I had civvies on, so I didn't stand out. Then came a lecture on German fairy tales, which was awfully boring. We spent the afternoon in the university library, very interesting . . .

On Tuesday morning we attended a soporifically boring lecture on medieval history. Marilis and Ilse don't normally go to it. Then we listened to a legal lecture with the economists. Dull as ditchwater. Virtually all they do is learn the civil code by heart. Then Mommsen again on 'The post-Bismarck period', excellent. After that, Professor Kommerell on nineteenth-century novelists. Very interesting and really great, but I've noticed I'm quite incapable of concentrating properly. I feel terribly tired all of a sudden, even in the most interesting lecture, and I stop listening. And afterwards I always have a stupid headache. You get very out of practice in the armed forces.

But now, these last few days, things have improved. In the afternoon we went to the university library and then to Marilis's. In the evening the two girls had to do sport and I read: at Daddy's suggestion, Fontane's 'Der Stechlin', which I liked a lot. On Wednesday I got some passport photos done. Then I went to look at the Elisabethkirche. It's very beautiful, but all the important things have been either bricked up or removed . . .

On Friday I went to Mommsen and Kommerell again. In the afternoon we visited the castle and went inside. But there too, nearly everything has been safely stowed away. In the evening we went to the cinema: 'Meine Freundin Josephine'. Very moving! There was an air-raid warning and a raid in the middle, so I didn't see the film right through. We had a long natter at Marilis's after that.

On Saturday morning the three of us went on a lengthy window-shopping tour of Marburg. In the afternoon I saw the end of the film and then accompanied the two ladies to the cinema again: 'Reisebekanntschaft' – nothing special, but we had a good laugh at one point.

After that we had some splendid blancmange at Marilis's and nattered again for ages. It's really great here, and I'm glad I came. It was worth coming. I get some company in this place, which is mostly what I miss at Immenhausen.

All the best and a loving kiss from your

Gerhard

Lilli's eagerly awaited (but not extant) letter arrived at last. Ilse, who had turned fifteen the day before, confirmed this on 16 January:

My dearest, best Mummy,

Yesterday was my birthday. It wasn't at all nice. In the morning, before I left for the station, Aunt Rita came and wished me many happy returns. She showed me my presents. From Uncle Josef, Ricarda Huch's 'Vom grossen Krieg in Deutschland', two Hammer booklets ('St Stephen's Cathedral in Vienna', 'Three Imperial Cathedrals'), a little coloured glass bowl, an album I can stick pictures in or write in . . . a bag of almond biscuits, which I'm giving to you, two cheesecakes and a chocolate gâteau. Nobody wrote to me, but your letter came this morning . . .

In the evening we sat downstairs for a short while. Daddy had also turned up in the afternoon. Then

Hannele, Eva and I had a bath. We went up to Dr Schupmann's room and demolished the chocolate gâteau. It was fantastically good. Dr Schupmann had also brought a whole mountain of apple and sponge cakes. We could only eat two slices of gâteau apiece, it was so filling. We'd hardly been up there half an hour when Daddy came storming upstairs. He said it was late and we had to be in bed in three minutes flat. It was only twenty past ten, but what choice did we have? We quickly hid the rest of the gâteau and went to bed. Hannele and I finished off the gâteau this morning . . .

Daddy has put in a request. He intends to lodge the applications for bomb-damage compensation. You've no need to worry about that or me either . . . Your letter was written on the 1st but only franked on the 13th. I found it a long wait. Well, my dear, I'm very glad you also had a nice time at Christmas. A big hug and masses of good wishes and kisses from your Ilse Mouse

This letter contained two items of news that must have been of particular interest to Lilli. For one thing, Ilse's reference to the book she'd received on her birthday implied that Uncle Josef's Halle estate was now being distributed among the children bit by bit. More important, however, was her brief but unmistakable allusion to Ernst's having lodged a 'request' with the Gestapo that Lilli be released. So Ernst had actually roused himself sufficiently to launch a rescue operation. Lilli's hopes must surely have revived a little.

Meanwhile, the inhabitants of Immenhausen passed the time by devoting themselves to such minor attractions as the war still had to offer. One was a celebration at the local inn, where German PoWs repatriated in exchange for Allied prisoners recounted their experiences in North Africa. Johanna's letter dated 18 January reveals that she was highly impressed by this:

Dr Schupmann, Gerda, Ille and I were there. We enjoyed it a lot. They performed some African negro belly-dances and sang and played some very nice music for piano, violin and cello. The music was by Beethoven and Mozart. Afterwards the soldiers were regaled with coffee and cakes. But there was so much left over that Dr Schupmann brought back a big plate of sponge cakes and gooseberry cakes. We polished them off in secret on Ille's birthday. He's a nice man – joins in everything.

Although Johanna relished these brief moments of happiness, she too was finding the situation at Immenhausen almost unbearable, as she confided in a letter to her mother four days later:

Aunt Lore has written to say there's no chance of an apartment in Tübingen, but prospects in the Black Forest are better. I hope something turns up there, because staying here much longer *without you*, Mummy, would be awful. But please don't worry, everything will work out. I'm being brave.

Meanwhile, Gerhard had returned from leave to his anti-aircraft battery at Obervellmar. Also writing on 22 January, he reported that military routine had reclaimed him the very first day:

A five-hour alert from 8 p.m. till 1 a.m. We fired a few rounds too – may even have shot one down – so that's a good start.

Gerhard ended his letter with a long quotation from Rilke and enclosed a photograph, probably one of the passport photos taken in Marburg. One week later he and the other air-force auxiliaries born in 1927 received their call-up papers. He proudly informed his mother of this development:

Naturally, I'm classified as employable for war service, Class I Reserve, mobile troops. Fit for employment in the Arbeitsdienst [labour corps] too, of course.

Ilse was also able to leave Immenhausen for a few days. As previously planned, she went to see her schoolfriend Gisela Stephan, who had been evacuated to Fulda. On 24 January she wrote Lilli an account of this brief visit:

My dearest darling Mummy,

Now I'm back home again. It was very enjoyable. I had a very long walk ahead of me when I got to Fulda on Saturday morning, because the youth hostel is up the hill a long way out of town. When I . . . got there I asked for Gisela's room. I hadn't even made it to the room when I spotted Gisela in the washroom. We were tickled pink to see each other again. Then came a lively reunion with the whole form. The girls were all very nice. Gisela shares a bedroom with three others.

In the afternoon I went down into the town again and got something to eat. Thank goodness the old principal wasn't there. (1) I wouldn't have been able to sleep at the youth hostel. (2) Gisela would never have got time off . . . After supper Gisela and I got into Gisela's bed and talked for hours. The next morning Gisela and some of the other girls in her form had a fencing lesson. I went along too and watched. After lunch Gisela and I went into town. First I bought myself a railway ticket. Then we went to the National Socialist Public Welfare Office (NSV) and asked if I could spend the night there. They were very kind and said I could sleep there.

Gisela had to be back by half past five. I went with her part of the way but soon turned back and had some supper. At the NSV, I and two women and a man from Düsseldorf had to share a room where the window had been open all day. I was chilled to the bone.

An air-raid warning was in progress when I got to Kassel this morning. I was scared stiff, but nothing happened, thank God. It's not so easy for me to go to Kassel in the morning these days, only in the afternoon. After lunch I went for a rest with Dorle. Then I tidied away my travelling things and did some sewing and homework.

I've just been listening to 'Eine Kleine Nachtmusik' on the radio. I thought of you so much. If only you could be back with us again!!! Nobody here cares when you go away, and there's no one to listen to your stories when you come back. How much longer will this last? Things *must* change sometime. Well, darling, a big hug and thousands of good wishes and kisses from your Ilse Mouse, who thinks of you alone.

Ilse child

Johanna had looked after little Dorothea while Ilse was in Fulda. She accepted this as a matter of course. 'When Ille is away, I have to take her place,' she had written in October 1943, when Ilse went to Frankenstein for the first time.

As soon as her big sister returned, however, Johanna renounced her maternal duties and concentrated on school again. On 27 January she wrote:

My dear, good Mummy,
The sirens have just sounded – the lights went out, and we all sat there in the dark. There's a little light now, though. The weather here is frightful, stormy and rainy. It was no fun, stumbling around outside.

School was interesting today. The kids from Hofgeismar and Bremen fight like cats and dogs. When school finishes at 6, five or six kids are waiting on every street corner, and there's a fierce scrap when the Bremen kids come along. Direk got to hear of this, so he worked out a plan of action. School now finishes at five to 6 instead of 6. A few boys from Form 5 are sent on ahead, as scouts. Then come half of Form 4 and Form 3 (minus girls), and so on, always in small groups, three deep, with some big boys bringing up the rear . . . But just imagine, someone gave a whistle and the Hofgeismar kids suddenly charged from all directions. Then the fun started: satchels, jackets, caps, sticks, shoulder straps – a seething mass of all that stuff. We still don't know who won.

At school we're now practising constructing compositions. We're learning a tremendous lot at school. We never stop swotting, it's simply awful. And it's no fun when you don't understand everything properly. Never mind, though, I'll manage.

Now I must darn some stockings, so good night, Mummy. God is bound to help us, I'm sure.

A big hug from your Hannele

The division of the household into two separate communities was also evident in matters of detail. The four girls on the top floor were no longer woken in the mornings. Ilse, being responsible for getting them up, borrowed an old alarm clock of Lilli's. She did so with a bad conscience, because this act of usurpation somehow acquired symbolic significance: Did it mean that she was ever so slightly abandoning hope of her mother's return? The following extract from a letter dated 29 January 1944 betrays her misgivings:

I completely forgot to tell you yesterday that I've taken your red alarm clock. I'm sure you won't be cross, will you? Or will you? I really had no choice, Mummy. We never knew what time it was in the mornings. It rang so nicely this morning, and I got up.

The next day, a Sunday, the fifteen-year-old surrogate mother continued her report:

Dearest darling Mummy,

I had a lie-in this morning – slept till half past eight. Then my little alarm clock went off. I got up, got Dorle dressed and then myself. Went to church with Hannele immediately after coffee. When we came home, Dorle and I did some house-cleaning, or rather, room-cleaning. We got all the bits and pieces out from under the beds and chest of drawers, then swept and dusted and tidied up, so everything's looking perfect. Now I feel really at home in my tiny kingdom. It's very small, but nice for all that. In the evenings I always sit on the edge of my bed, doing my homework and writing. Like tonight. There's a child's desk and chair in here, but I find them too uncomfortable.

When I sit on my bed like this, I often, so very often, think of our dear apartment in Kassel, and of our nice things, and of this little house where we used to live together. And of how things are now. And of who it now belongs to. How different everything is!!!! And most of all I think of you. But when I'm still up, at 10, 11 or 12, you're bound to be in bed already.

I've arranged my little room really nicely. My bed is where Hannele's used to be. Dorle's bed and a toy cupboard, now a clothes cupboard, are where my bed was. The chest of drawers is back where it used to be a very long time ago. Between my bed and the radiator stands Eva's bed. Beside Eva's bed is Dorle's doll's bed with your old doll in it, now Dorle's Gretel. On the chest of drawers are my jewel box, a little wooden bowl, and a lace mat of Daddy's. Then there's a small chest of drawers belonging to Aunt Rita. On the right of this is a doll's bed with a little man doll and a little woman doll in it. The bed has 'Serene Happiness' written on it . . .

The preliminary all-clear has just sounded, even though the searchlight beams are still in the sky and there's quite a lot of gunfire in the distance. Those sinister bombers are over Germany night after night, day after day . . .

After lunch I went to fetch Gerhard. I'd only just got to Obervellmar when I saw Gerhard standing there, waving and calling. Up the steps to Obervellmar on one side, down them on the other and into the train for Immenhausen – it all went perfectly. The first thing I did back in Immenhausen was give Gerhard something to eat. Gertrud, Gerhard and I smoked and talked in Gertrud's room . . .

With coffee we had a cake like the one I sent you. It was very dry, but not bad apart from that. Better than nothing. How I'll manage a parcel for you next week is a mystery to me!!

I still have to write to Aunt Lore and sew an armband on Gerhard's greatcoat. I'm very tired today, I don't know why. Another Latin lesson tomorrow morning. I've taken a pair of green pyjamas and a pair of blue leather gloves out of the suitcase.

The sound of the guns is coming steadily closer.

Well, darling, will we be able to see each other soon?

Masses of love and kisses and a hug from your Ilse Mouse

Although Lilli had now been imprisoned for five months, word of her fate had not reached all who knew her. Among these was 'Fräulein Frieda', Grandmother Paula's former housemaid in Cologne, who was very fond of the Jahn family. On 31 January Ilse informed her mother that Frieda had got in touch after a long interval:

Fräulein Frieda recently sent you a registered letter which Gerhard and I opened. Frieda is very worried because she has heard nothing from us. I wrote and told her that we were on our own, and that you were prevented from writing. Now I must write to her in more detail – and without delay. First I shall have to think carefully what to say.

Ilse could not tell her the truth. A letter like that would never have got past the censor and might have put the children in a difficult position.

Lilli's daughters felt more and more at a loss as the first few weeks of 1944 went by. They sensed that all hopes of their mother's release were being repeatedly dashed. What should they do? What *could* they do?

They continued to write almost daily, to be with her in spirit at least, but their letters were becoming briefer and more routine. The contact they needed so desperately was turning into a ritual. Besides, the monotony of life in wartime did not produce much news. On 1 February 1944 Ilse wrote:

> My dearest Mummy,
>
> This morning was another mad rush. I still had to buy myself a rail ticket, but I made it. School was very enjoyable again. From our German lesson: 'Tragedy exists to move the soul.' Or: 'It holds sway over our emotions.' Dr Müller said the first thing, and Lessing wrote the second in his 'Hamburgische Dramaturgie'. I think our 'Müller' put it very nicely. Your Ilse is a completely different person these days. Her head is awhirl with masses of different things. I enjoy debating such questions while I'm darning. But if only you could tell me things again. This afternoon I did my homework and went for a Latin lesson. I made a terrible fool of myself, but I'll make up for it.
>
> Good night now! Daddy's here. A big hug and a thousand kisses from your Ilse Mouse

The girls' situation was made somewhat more tolerable by their father's presence, mainly because they could lodge an occasional complaint about Rita's behaviour. Ernst avoided rows as a rule, but this time, as Johanna reported the next day, he intervened:

> Daddy was here last night. He gave his old lady a bit of a talking-to. I wonder if it'll do any good?

The children's relations with Rita were as strained as ever. Only during her early days at Immenhausen had she ever shown Lilli's daughters anything akin to affection. It is impossible at this stage to reconstruct what ultimately led to the breach between them – her peculiarly harsh and intolerant attitude, or the children's dislike of a woman they came to see as their mother's rival – but they could hardly expect her to treat them with compassion, far less love.

Lilli's usual monthly letter, which has also disappeared, reached Immenhausen on 4 February. Ilse replied that same night:

Oh my dear, sweet darling, how glad I am that you're not too disheartened, that you're still getting enough to eat, and that you enjoy our letters. For me too, the best part of the whole day is talking to you (in spirit).

'Help to get me released soon!'
Did Ernst make an application to the Gestapo?

Only a few days later the children received another letter from their mother dated 6 February 1944. Lilli had got hold of a sheet of paper from somewhere – probably from an address book, because it bore the letters 'PQ' – and had written on it in pencil. The envelope was postmarked Malsfeld, and the sender, for safety's sake, purported to be 'Eva Beisse' of '19 Grosse Kirchstrasse, Gera'. Neither the name nor the address meant anything to the family.

Lilli had complied with Ilse's warning and refrained from sending any clandestine letters for two whole months, but her homesickness now outweighed any fears of further official harassment.

My dearly beloved children,

I wrote to you via the institution only last Sunday, but who knows when you'll get the letter. And my longing for you today is again *so* great, and it depresses me so much to think I've been away from you for *six* months. I simply have to unburden my heart a little by writing to you. But don't go imagining that your Mummy is always merely sad. All the work at the factory leaves me no time for that, and besides, there's always something or other that cheers me up.

Most of all it's your sweet, loving letters that always give me such immense pleasure, and I thank you for them from the bottom of my heart. I was especially pleased this week by your photo, my dear boy. I was so delighted to see your face again, and heartfelt thanks for your dear long letter with the *beautiful* Rilke quotation at the end!

The lovely cards from Hannele, Ille and Marilis also gave me a great deal of pleasure. It does me so much good to be reminded of what is fine, good, and important. Has Marilis completely recovered by now, and what is my dear, dear little Dorle up to?

Oh, children, when will they let us be together again? I can hardly bear to wait any longer, and I'm becoming more impatient every day. Daddy must go to the Gestapo and *insist* on my being released at last. And he must go *soon*! Please, please, please! It so often breaks my heart to think how little care is being taken of you, and how very much you're left to yourselves. We shall never have as lovely a life as we used to, but *how* happy we'll be together, even in the simplest surroundings, won't we?? I wonder if I'll be with you on my birthday? How long will Aunt Lore be away, and where is she?

I received *all* your parcels, your kind, sumptuous, lovingly wrapped parcels, and you wouldn't believe how much good they've done me. I've never gone to bed hungry, and my forewoman at the factory, with whom I'm on very good terms, and who has been in Berlin for the past four weeks, was delighted to see how much better I'm looking. I owe that to you!

Evchen, please convey my warmest congratulations to the Rösches on their little girl. How is Wilhelm Hirdes? How is Hannele's bad finger, and what's happened to the drawing of dear Dr Schupmann? Ille, my friend, your accounts of school always give me special pleasure, but please don't always go to bed so late. You need your sleep *so* badly. Of course you must use the alarm clock, I'm glad to hear you do. Hannele, how did the 'Battle of Immenhausen' turn out? Dear, dear, sweet children, goodbye for now and help to get me out of here soon.

I miss you so much, and I kiss you a thousand times in spirit and hug you very tight.

Your Mummy, who loves you immensely!!

Ilse had written to tell her mother that Ernst had already lodged a request – so far without success, as Lilli must have realized. Hence her renewed appeal: 'Daddy must go to the Gestapo.'

According to the Gestapo's murderous logic, however, there was absolutely no point in releasing Lilli. If they did, where would she go? She had already been expelled from Immenhausen and rehoused in Kassel, but Kassel was in ruins, and she would never have been permitted to move back into her ex-husband's home.

To that extent, Lore's months-long search for a new abode for herself and Marilis, Lilli and the children, was thoroughly sensible – indeed, essential. For whatever reason, however, Lilli's sister-in-law had no success.

Ilse had spent the weekend with Lore's daughter Marilis, so Johanna had once more assumed responsibility for looking after Eva and Dorothea. She mentioned this in a letter to her mother dated 7 February:

My dear, sweet Mummy,

How are you? Are you keeping well? We're all fine apart from a cold that's going around. The lights went out just now. Ille, Eva and I ate some cake by candlelight (left-overs from the Christmas tree) . . .

Ille had a very good time with Marilis. Now I've been stripped of my post as Vice-Mama. I grow fonder of children every day, Mummy, no matter whether they're clean or dirty. If I ever take up a profession, it must definitely be to do with children. I'd like to have a big house where I can take in sick, poor, or even orphaned children. But for that you first need money, so I want to – I must – practise a profession. I think there's still time for all that. Do you approve of my plan? I'd like to discuss it with you. Let's hope the time will soon come.

For today, loving good wishes and kisses from your
Hannele

The following night Ilse herself wrote an account of her time in
Marburg:

Dearest and best Mummy,
   Now, at last, you're getting another line from me.
   It's late again, but now there's no excuse. Some biscuits for you are in the oven. First I must take a look at
them. – Well, the first tray is done and the second tray
has gone in. They taste really good.
   I had a very nice time in Marburg. Marburg is a pretty
little town. The first night we went to the cinema: 'Ein
weisser Traum'. A really terrific film. We slept late the
next morning. On Saturday we went to the theatre in
Giessen to see Lehar's 'Graf von Luxemburg'. It was very
nice. We couldn't get in anywhere in Giessen beforehand
– all the cafés had shut because they were full. We had
half a mind to take the next train back, but in the very
end, when we were blue with cold, we got into a small
café. We sat there for a long time till the show started.
Giessen is a deadly boring town.
   Oh, how annoying! I just went to look at the biscuits,
and the second batch are slightly burnt. Still, I'm sure
you'll enjoy them all the same . . .
   I've bought a whole heap of things. Butter, cheese, jam,
and so on. Tomorrow you'll be getting another parcel.
There wasn't any bread left today. I hope you still have
enough to eat . . . I've just written to Gerhard – he also
gets two letters a week. I don't want him missing out
either. Dorle is well and merry as a cricket. She talks so
often of our apartment in Kassel. How lovely it was. Eva
and Hannele are also blooming.
   Loving good wishes and a thousand kisses from your
Ilse Mouse, who thinks of you very often

Ilse, who knew how much Lilli was pinning her hopes on Lore, always kept her informed about the house-hunting situation. But the news was bad again: 'Aunt Lore gets back from Waldkirch on the 20th. She hasn't managed to find anywhere to live yet,' Ilse wrote on 9 February. 'We'll simply have to wait,' Johanna commented the following day:

My dearest, most darling Mummy,
It's winter now. Is there as much snow where you are? It's slippery, too – pretty unpleasant.
Do you know where the most beautiful women on earth live? I didn't know either. On the island of Java, apparently. Only Fatthauer could ask such stupid questions. He was trying to catch us out, us girls.
Today a woman at Hofgeismar dropped a bag of clothes-pegs and braces and cooking spoons under the train. Heidi and I scrabbled around under the train and picked up all the clothes-pegs except four. Then the train pulled out. Quite something, that was. This morning I'm going to Hümme and I've got Latin, which I'm looking forward to.
Aunt Lore has written from Waldkirch. We don't have any great hopes yet, we'll simply have to wait and put our faith in God. For today, loving good wishes and kisses from your Hannele

Ilse wrote again the same evening:

Dearest, best Mummy,
It's so cold again, and when I walk to the station in the morning I can't help thinking you must be cold. How much longer!?? I've just re-read your last letter. Only then does everything really become clear to me. I get a good mental picture of everything.
When I came home in the old days I couldn't wait to talk about all the things that were going round in my head. Now there's nobody here I can talk to. But I'm

willing to bear everything and take it upon myself as long as it helps you. I've written to Daddy. But Daddy!!!! Poor Mummy!!! God's ways are wonderful, and that's the only thing that always helps me . . .

A thousand good wishes and kisses and loving hugs from your Ilse Mouse

Ilse went on trying to persuade her father to make another application to the Gestapo, but she was beginning to doubt whether he had made one in the first place. She had told Lilli so in a letter dated 16 January, but she was no longer certain. Although a request of this kind would probably have been fruitless in any case, Ernst's daughters resented his prevarication. During the day Ilse was largely distracted by her duties as a surrogate mother, but at night she was more and more often haunted by fears for her mother's future – as, for instance, on 12 February:

Peace at last. The other three are asleep. I'm also off to bed in a minute, but first I'll go to the window and look out towards you in Breitenau. When will the day come? I wonder how you are? A hundred such questions and thoughts go round in my head. At night, when I can't sleep, I think of you. We five, little Dorle included, never forget you . . . Goodbye till tomorrow night

And the following night:

Hannele and I went to church. I'm trying now more and more to derive a sense of security from it. Perhaps I'll succeed soon. I shall do some more Bible-reading tonight.

This letter also contained a brief mention of Julie. The Belgian housemaid had vanished without trace during the air raid on the night of 22 October 1943. Now she suddenly reappeared in Immenhausen.

When we got to the station, there was our Julie!!! She looked hungry and dirty!!! Dorle was beside herself with delight.

Julie either couldn't or wouldn't tell the children what she was doing at present. She may simply have been trying to avoid further employment as a labour conscript. After nearly four years, the Nazi war economy was starting to show signs of disintegration. Some days later Ilse reported that a sizeable number of Russian labour conscripts had escaped. The children were forbidden to leave Immenhausen on security grounds. As for Julie, they never saw her again.

Despite such problems, members of the general population were still considerably better off than the millions-strong army of labour conscripts and prisoners. 'We're fine. I don't have any more asthma attacks, and I'm swelling like a lump of yeast,' Johanna wrote jocularly on 15 February.

Lilli's friend Lotte was still having to do forced labour, even though she was utterly exhausted and forever falling ill. On 17 February she wrote from Leipzig:

My dear Lilli,

I was so very pleased to get your messages, I had to drop you a quick line right away. My letter to the children will go off today too, of course.

I'm so sad that I can't write to you more often and, above all, that I can't do more for you. But for some time now I've had to work again, shovelling debris in the factory, which is completely gutted, without doors, windows, or walls. Just big, open factory bays full of rubble, ash, filth, and water or snow depending on the weather. It's terribly cold, as you can imagine. We always make ourselves a little fire out of burnable odds and ends, but we're cold just the same. I'm working with another two women.

Then, when I've raced through the housework in the afternoons – still without gas – I'm so utterly exhausted after shopping, ironing, darning, and so on, that I simply can't write any more. I know you'll understand, but it hurts me that I can't do as I'd like.

Don't you have any requests at all? You never send me any. Let me know what you need via the children. I'm afraid I can't send you any food, though. I simply can't spare any, and I'm always hungry myself!

But I mustn't complain, not to you! I keep imagining what you're going through! This eternal waiting to be released and these constant disappointments.

Ernst wrote and told us that an application on your behalf was under consideration. Ilse wrote saying that she doubted it, but I'm quite sure it's true. Whether more could be done, I naturally can't judge from here. Ernst said that everything possible would be done. I'm convinced that something can be achieved in your case provided the right steps are taken. It must happen in the end. Oh, my dear, if only my innumerable thoughts and wishes were of some use!

I'm glad you're being treated decently. That must make the whole business much easier, and I'm sure you'll stick it out to the end. Don't allow yourself to be eaten up with impatience – that sort of thing can undermine and debilitate one more than having to endure the hard times themselves. And preserve your marvellous courage. You've stood up to this so wonderfully well, you'll see it through to the end.

Peter is fine, but how I miss him! Ernst August has largely recovered from a bad bout of flu and pleurisy, but he shows it too.

I know he sends his warm regards – he isn't home yet, and I'm going to post this right away.

Hugs and kisses!

Your Lotte

When Ernst wrote to Lotte that 'everything possible' would be done, it might have meant everything or nothing. Ilse received another 'very odd letter' from her father at this time. 'I'm getting sick of it,' she told Lilli on 18 January. 'I never reply to those letters.' Ernst besought the children to see his point of view, but they simply couldn't.

Ilse's letter dated 20 February, a Sunday, is the last extant letter from one of Lilli's children to their mother:

Dearest and best Mummy,

Now another two days have gone by. I miss you more and more every day. Sometimes I think I really can't stand it any more, but I always find new strength.

Gerhard is home on leave. That's always very nice. It was also very nice at school yesterday. In German one of the boys came out with such a funny answer, we spent nearly all the lesson laughing.

Our train was an hour late at lunchtime. I'm sure your trains are late every day too. You must be frozen stiff every morning, dear Mummy! You poor, dear sweetheart! How much longer will you have to endure it? Let's hope you're released soon!

We went to church again this morning. I'm not happy with our clergyman. I'd like a decent sermon for once.

This afternoon I baked us some oatmeal biscuits. Hannele, Eva and Gertrud visited Gerda in the hospital, so Gerhard, Dorle, Magda and I were on our own. We had coffee with Herr and Frau Dr Schupmann. After coffee I did some sewing and darned Gerhard's blue sweater again. We listened to Beethoven's 5th, but I only half enjoyed it because the little ones were there.

I had a lot of mail yesterday and today: Gisela, Aunt Lotte, Aunt Lore, and Daddy. Aunt Lore is staying in the Black Forest for the time being. Aunt Lotte is having to work half-days again, shovelling debris.

There was another air raid on Leipzig tonight. They shot down eighty-three.

Good night now, and a thousand good wishes and kisses from your Ilse Mouse

Lilli was particularly alarmed by news of the raid on Leipzig, as her last letter from Breitenau indicates. Written on notepaper sent her by Lotte and dated Sunday, 27 February, it bears the handwritten censor's note '29/2.44 St' in the top right corner but was not postmarked until 2 March 1944.

My dearly beloved children, all six of you,

Another Sunday here in Breitenau, but at least it's a Sunday on which I'm allowed to write, and although you know that all my caring and loving thoughts are with you every day, it's a joy to have a little chat with you none-theless. As ever, thank you from the bottom of my heart for all your sweet letters, though my last news of you is a week old already; I presume that all these air raids are disrupting the mail again.

And a thousand thanks for the wonderful parcels: the oatmeal biscuits were absolutely delicious, and you sent me *so* much butter that I can only eat it with a bad conscience. Last week's cake was quite scrumptious. My Ilse Mouse is an efficient little housewife already. The liver sausage was excellent too. Children, children, how do you manage to spare me so much! The soap was also very welcome, and I was particularly pleased with the toothbrush case.

And now I've got some more requests. Can you send me these things if possible? Toothpaste, skin cream, and black shoe-polish.

But your letters have always been, and still are, my greatest pleasure of all. I haven't heard from you, dear Marilis, for quite some time, but I'm sure you've a lot of work to do, preparing for your examinations. It was awfully sweet of you to give Ilse such a nice weekend. I very much hope that no harm came to you during the air raid last week, and I'm waiting a trifle anxiously for news of you. Will you be staying at Marburg for the summer semester as well? Do you have good news of your mummy?

You, my dear boy, have been very much in my thoughts. You poor fellows never get any rest with all these alerts. It's been an awful week, and I'm sure you're dog-tired. It's no wonder your school work is suffering. Binding's books are very, very fine, aren't they, and I've always read them with pleasure. And how nice that you went to 'Fidelio'! I'm so happy and thankful you all have such a love of music and art and literature! Believe me, the mental possession and knowledge of those things has often helped me to surmount all the unpleasant and depressing aspects of these difficult months.

We've now been apart for half a year, and I'm growing impatient. I'd hoped so *very* much that it wouldn't last any longer. I shall still be here on my birthday in a week's time – please don't be sad about it, children, I won't be, and we'll make up for everything later on. But I'd so *very, very* much have liked to be there for your Confirmation, my Hannele. *Please ask Daddy to go to the Gestapo again.* There's absolutely no one to take care of the barest essentials, especially with Aunt Lore still away. If I'm not mistaken, there's a plain but sporty black dress of two different materials hanging in the wardrobe with the dark clothes. Get Frau Wittich to make you a dress out of it, my dear.

How wonderful that you don't get asthma any more!

Your purchases, my dear Ilse, are just what I myself would have bought. You've already got together such a lot of things for our new home, and you look after everything else with such loving care!! Go to church as often as you can. I look forward *so* much to being able to talk about all your concerns. May it be soon!

How are my little Eva and Dorle faring?

And now, take a *big* weight off my mind and write *at once* to Aunt Lotte and then let me know whether she and Uncle Ernst August are safe. It's preying on my mind *so* much. And give her my most heartfelt thanks for her sweet, comforting letter of 18 February, which gave me great pleasure. Today I've been able to write to you using the notepaper she enclosed. Please send her my fond love and good wishes. And to all of you, many thousands of good wishes, hugs and loving kisses from your Mummy

In the margin of the first page Lilli had added:

Affectionate regards to Daddy, Aunt Lore, Aunt Maria.

At some point during March 1944, Ilse took an early morning train to Malsfeld to ascertain whether her mother was still at Breitenau corrective labour camp. She actually caught a last glimpse of Lilli in the company of her fellow labour conscripts. But, as before, she made sure that Lilli did not catch sight of her.

Death in Auschwitz

'I shall go on being brave'
Deportation to the East

If the Nazis had been consistent in implementing their brutal penal policy, Lilli would have been released four weeks after her arrest. Contravention of the police edict dated 17 August 1938 would hardly have warranted a longer term of imprisonment. As the war went on, however, the system of intimidation lost its veneer of legality. Only one major aim could be clearly discerned: the annihilation of the Jews. Without any official explanation, Lilli eventually spent nearly seven months in detention at Breitenau.

In the spring of 1944 this state of affairs was brought to an end. The Gestapo decided to send Lilli to Auschwitz, an extermination camp, and not – like many other Breitenau detainees – to a concentration camp such as Ravensbrück, Sachsenhausen, or Buchenwald. The usual preliminaries for deportation were put in hand. A doctor had to certify Lilli fit to travel and the Central State Security Bureau in Berlin, which was responsible for deportations, had to be informed, as did the district administrator at Melsungen. Finally, she was issued with her civilian clothing and personal belongings.

Before leaving Breitenau, Lilli secretly entrusted most of the letters she had received to either a fellow prisoner or a wardress, who sent them on to the children at Immenhausen. None of the letters they wrote to her during her last four weeks in Breitenau has survived. She must have taken them with her as keepsakes on her journey to Auschwitz.

The Breitenau authorities forwarded only a few of Lilli's

effects to the house in Gartenstrasse. These included one or two books, for instance Adalbert Stifter's novel *Der Nachsommer*. Lilli had inscribed the latter with a dedication to her eldest daughter: 'To my dear Ilse Mouse, who is so touchingly concerned about me, in love and gratitude from her Mummy. Breitenau, March 1944.' Johanna, Eva, Dorothea, and Gerhard also received books containing dedications. Gerhard's, a collection of essays by the theatre critic Rudolph K. Goldschmit-Jentner entitled *Die Begegnung mit dem Genius*, was inscribed: 'To my boy, for his pleasure and mental stimulation, in heartfelt remembrance from his Mummy, March 1944.'

The time came on 17 March 1944. The Kassel Gestapo, who had transferred their headquarters to Breitenau after the large-scale raid on Kassel, transported Lilli to the station and assigned her to a group of prisoners bound for Auschwitz. How long the journey took is uncertain. From Dresden, an intermediate stop, she sent a postcard to Immenhausen which has not survived. On 21 March 1944, when the deportees were still in Dresden, waiting to be moved on, Lilli sent her family another brief bulletin, this time in the form of a letter:

My dearly beloved children all,

This is a long and tedious journey. On Day 1 we travelled via Halle to Leipzig!! How much I would have liked to see Aunt Lotte once more! Ille, Leipzig looks quite, quite awful – Augustus-Platz and the whole of the city centre *nothing but* mounds of rubble. On Day 2 we got to Dresden. We've been here for three days, and I wrote you a card which I hope you'll soon receive. I hope you get this letter too. I'd be so pleased.

We've now been stuck here on Dresden station for three hours, and have just heard that the train won't be leaving until ten o'clock tonight. So tomorrow night we'll be in Auschwitz. Reports of what the place is like are very contradictory. It's possible that I won't be allowed to write for four or even eight weeks, so *please* don't worry if you don't hear anything for quite some time. However long it is, do try to write to me first – perhaps I'll get it. We'll now have to wait and see how everything turns out. I shall go on being brave and gritting my teeth and thinking of you all and holding out, no matter how hard it gets.

If you're allowed to send me parcels, please always remember toothpaste, hairpins and talcum powder. And please don't be too sad, my children. I find it so reassuring to know that you have your routine and are looked after and have your Daddy, who cares for you and loves you very much. Never forget that, even if you can't understand his behaviour at the moment. Daddy will always show you the way to all that is fine and good and noble – for man does not live by bread alone.

I greatly regret the fact that Aunt Lore isn't looking after you as I'd hoped and expected. Also, Aunt Rita complained to me that you were giving her a hard time. For Daddy's sake be good and obedient, then everything will be easier.

In the past few days I've envied the families who were all taken away together. On second thoughts, though, it's easier for me, in spite of my profound longing for you and the pain of separation, to know that you lead settled lives and are spared the sight of all that's objectionable and unpleasant. My one burning desire is to see you *all* again in good health. Give him [Ernst] my love and tell him this: *He himself*, and he alone, must again spare no effort, even if he has to go to the very top in Berlin.

In the train I met a former district attorney and lawyer from Freiburg who knew Uncle Max well, also Uncle Ernst August and Aunt Lotte. His is a mixed marriage too, and his son is a prisoner of war in England. This gentleman told me that all *single* Jewish persons from mixed marriages get deported, in other words when the other party is dead or divorced, but *only* if their children are over eighteen. He was very surprised when I told him about you, and simply can't understand it. It's unprecedented, he says, and shouldn't really happen. Daddy must double-check the accuracy of this information and then make it the basis of his application. He must *demand* my release, especially as he's also a member of the armed forces.

I do so hope you receive this letter! Did you get the parcel containing the letters, the spoon for my Dorle, and the other little things? And the parcel of books? If not, ask Breitenau for it (for the books! I sent the letters off secretly!).

And now goodbye again, all of you – Gerhard, Ilse Mouse, Hannele Child, little Eva, and my precious Dorle! May God protect you! The bonds between us are indissoluble. Heartfelt good wishes and kisses from your devoted

Mummy

In the margin Lilli added:

Fond regards again to Aunt Lotte and Uncle Ernst August, also from Herr Homburger.

Lilli's reference to the lawyer's comments merely accorded with the information Ernst had received before divorcing Lilli. In 1942 the Jewish mothers of 'half-Jewish' children were still protected; now, in the closing stages of the war, there could be no further question of this. Even if Ernst had approached the Central State Security Bureau in Berlin in March 1944, his appeal would probably have fallen on deaf ears.

Lilli guessed what awaited her at Auschwitz. Her remark, 'How much I would have liked to see Aunt Lotte once more!' betrayed more than she meant to burden the children with. In stating that reports of living conditions in Auschwitz were 'very contradictory', too, she was using a form of words that made light of the rumours and conjectures that were already circulating among the deportees. She must have taken it for granted that her children knew there was a camp at Auschwitz, because her letter gave no explanation of that place name. But what really went on there she was either unable or unwilling to commit to paper.

'My thoughts are with you'
Lilli's final months at Auschwitz

On 22 March 1944 another trainload of prisoners pulled into Auschwitz. As usual, those who were sick, frail, and unable to work were 'selected' for extermination in the gas chambers. The rest were assigned a number and a place in a hut.

Although we cannot say for certain that Lilli was a member of this particular batch, everything suggests so: Lilli was given the number 76043; a female prisoner had been registered as No. 76037 on 21 March, the previous day; and there is documentary evidence that the numbers 76076–76131 were allocated on 25 March.

The trains bound for Auschwitz during this period brought smallish groups of prisoners from the Reich and the occupied territories of Western Europe, notably Dutch Jews. The extermination of Polish and Russian Jews was largely complete, and most of the death factories were already at a standstill, but at Auschwitz the industrialized killing continued. One last major operation, the liquidation of the Hungarian Jews, began that spring.

Lilli's children received no more news of her for weeks. Not knowing what address to write to, they stopped writing and waited with mounting anxiety for a sign of life. In June 1944 a letter actually reached Immenhausen from Auschwitz-Birkenau, the central extermination camp which the Nazis had built next door to Auschwitz itself. The letter was addressed to Lore, Lilli's sister-in-law, and the sender's name and address were given as 'Jahn Lili Sara', Prisoner No. 76043, of 'Block 24, Women's Camp, Auschwitz, Post Office No. 2'.

In addition to the address, the letter form bears the instructions to be observed 'for correspondence with preventive detainees'. Point 1 states that 'All detainees may receive from their relatives, and send to the same, two letters or two postcards a month.' Point 5: 'Applications to the camp authorities for release from preventive detention are pointless.' Point 6: 'Speaking with or visiting prisoners in the camp is strictly prohibited. The Camp Commandant.' The front and back of the letter are stamped 'Mail Censorship Office KL Auschwitz'.

The letter itself, dated 5 June 1944, was written in pencil and probably dictated. Only the somewhat shaky signature 'Lilli o. Mutti' (Lilli or Mummy) seems to be in Lilli's handwriting. The text, on the other hand, was probably written by some fellow prisoner with an imperfect command of German, because the original contains a number of spelling mistakes. Lilli was evidently too debilitated to write herself. The choice of words sounds curiously stilted, though all such letters had to confine themselves as far as possible to non-committal stock phrases. Thus the writer of the letter may simply have tried to convey the sense of what Lilli had told her beforehand.

My dear Lore,

I'm so very happy to be able to write to you. I'm well, I'm working at my profession, and that's very pleasant for me. Now I'm eagerly awaiting news of you and the children. What are they all doing? Has Gerhard already joined the Labour Service? Are Ilse and Hannele going to school in Hofgeismar? What is my little Eva up to? And what is my littlest one doing? And how are you yourself and Marilis? I now await news of you at regular intervals. Cordial thanks for the regular remittances. Thank you all for your last parcel to Breitenau. The children may also write themselves. My thoughts are with you constantly. I hope you're all well. I greet and kiss each one of you a thousand times. With much love as mother and sister-in-law.

Lilli or Mummy

Lilli's daughters have no recollection of the 'remittances' she mentioned. On the other hand, it is not beyond the bounds of possibility that she worked as a doctor in Auschwitz, at least to begin with. Suitably qualified prisoners were, in fact, assigned to the camp hospital at this period.

It is probable, however, that Lilli herself was ill by the time this last letter was written. Living conditions in Auschwitz, where the sanitary facilities were in a catastrophic state, bred diseases and epidemics. The prisoners lived in grossly overcrowded huts, each containing hundreds of inmates, and slept without blankets or pillows on palliasses and plank beds several tiers high. Originally shared by five persons, each of these bunks later held as many as fifteen. Those prisoners who became ill and unfit for work under such conditions ran the risk of being 'selected' by the camp doctors and sent to the gas chambers.

Some 67,000 people were detained at Auschwitz at the beginning of April 1944, shortly after Lilli's arrival. Guarded by only 3000 SS troopers and policemen, they were compelled to work in the most appalling conditions, either in the camp itself or in the surrounding factories.

Lilli had already known and endured hunger in Breitenau, where parcels from Kassel and Immenhausen were all that kept her adequately, though temporarily, supplied with food. Worse was in store at Auschwitz. Jewish prisoners were generally fed during the day on watery turnip soup, and at night on a meagre portion of sawdust bread with a scraping of margarine and jam or a slice of – often rancid – sausage.

The whole system was geared to the extermination of the camp inmates, most of whom were Jewish. Anyone not killed in the gas chambers died of malnutrition, disease, or sheer exhaustion, and quite a few fell victim to sadistic treatment by the guards. More than a million people were murdered in Auschwitz alone.

A few days after Lilli's letter from Birkenau reached Immenhausen, the Gestapo telephoned Ernst Jahn's house. Rita, who took the call, was informed that Lilli had died. The cause of death was not specified. Today, Lilli's daughters recall that their stepmother conveyed the news without emotion. Only Dr Schupmann tried to comfort them. That they were informed at all was unusual, but they refused to accept the truth. They had little idea of what concentration camps were like and absolutely no knowledge of the barbarism practised at Auschwitz. Ilse wrote several letters to the camp authorities requesting precise details of her mother's fate, but it was months before she received a reply.

Instead, the children themselves were subjected to further discrimination. Ilse and Johanna had to leave their Hofgeismar school in June 1944 because Jewish 'half-breeds' were now debarred from a secondary education. Gerhard was discharged from the air-force auxiliaries on 11 September and conscripted into the Labour Service a week later. Ernst Jahn had to relinquish his post at the military hospital near Kassel and was sent to the Baltic front as an army medical officer.

Meanwhile, the war drew closer still. On 2 October some 140 high explosive and several thousand incendiary bombs carpeted the outskirts of Immenhausen, their intended target being the Henschel munitions factory in Kassel. Like the other inhabitants of the small town, Lilli's daughters escaped with a bad fright.

At about this time they finally received official confirmation of their mother's death in the mail. A death certificate in engraver's script, numbered LXXXX26/44 and issued on 28 September 1944 by Registry Office II, Auschwitz, it read as follows:

The physician Lilli Sara Jahn, née Schlüchterer – no religion – resident at 3 Motzstrasse, Kassel, died at Kasernenstrasse, Auschwitz, at 11.25 a.m. on 19 June 1944. The deceased was born on 5 March 1900 in Cologne (Registry Office . . . No. . . .). Father: Josef Schlüchterer, Mother: Paula Sara Schlüchterer, née Schloss, resident in Birmingham. The deceased was divorced.

The municipality of Immenhausen was also notified by the concentration camp. On 16 October 1944, quoting Reference

No. IVa 3/66d (14 KL7) F/10.44-76043, the 'Administration of KL Auschwitz' returned Lilli's ID – and, to ensure that this final bureaucratic formality was carried out to the letter, sent it by registered post:

To:
The Mayor – as District Police Authority –
Immenhausen
The enclosed Identity Card No. A 00002 belonging to Jahn, Lilli Sara, born 5.3.00 and died here 17.6.44, is forwarded for your disposal.
1 encl.
Head of Administration, Auschwitz Concentration Camp.

p.p. . . .
SS-Obersturmführer

This bureaucratic punctilio was obviously just a façade. The date of death given in the above communication did not even match the one on the death certificate – did Lilli die on 17 or 19 June 1944? – and there was still no information about the cause of death.

To this day, Lilli's daughters have no idea how their mother died. Of debility and disease, or in the gas chamber?

Epilogue

Lilli's children were also threatened with imminent deportation towards the end of the war. They were not allowed to leave Immenhausen, and Gerhard was discharged from the Labour Service on 13 November 1944. The Nazis had declared him 'unworthy to bear arms', so he was not drafted into the armed forces. He later wrote that the Gestapo had planned to arrest him, and that all that prevented them from doing so were the incessant air raids and the chaos prevailing in the closing stages of the war.

Lilli's friend Lotte was also in grave danger. No longer able to do forced labour because of illness, she feared the worst. With the help of a non-Jewish woman doctor, she took refuge with some friends in Freiburg. Admitted to a hospital but bombed out there, she survived the final days of the Nazi reign of terror in the protection of a convent near Freiburg.

The first American troops marched into Immenhausen at 3 p.m. on 5 April 1945. Lilli's persecutor, Mayor Gross, was removed from his post and arrested the same day.

The Nazis had previously buried some of the documents that incriminated them. Gerhard, who took charge of the mayor's official records on 1 June 1945, soon managed to lay hands on the letters Gross had written with a view to driving Lilli out of Immenhausen. He even proposed to bring Rita to trial for complicity in his mother's death, but Ilse, who did not want to exacerbate the situation, begged him to abandon this plan.

So Lilli's children continued to live with Rita under their

father's roof. It was not until the summer of 1946 that Gerhard went to stay with the Lieberknecht family in Kassel. There, after taking a preparatory nine-month course, he passed his school-leaver's examination, and in 1947 he became a law student at Marburg University.

Ilse and Johanna were able to return to school in Hofgeismar. Eva, after initially attending a Waldorf school in Kassel, switched to Hofgeismar as well.

Although Ernst was released from a Russian PoW camp in the summer of 1946, this did little to allay the tension between Rita and Lilli's children. At the request of Grandmother Paula and Aunt Elsa, the girls eventually joined them in Birmingham. Johanna and Eva emigrated to England in February 1948, followed a few months later, after Ilse had passed her school-leaver's examination, by Ilse and Dorothea. Before long, however, Ernst insisted that eight-year-old Dorothea should return to Immenhausen. He sought his children's love and understanding to the last, rejoicing in every visit and every token of affection, especially as he and Rita had been shunned by most of their friends, notably the Barths of Mannheim and the Paepckes, who had moved to Karlsruhe. He died of a stroke in 1960.

In England Ilse and Johanna trained as nurses and Eva as a physiotherapist. Lilli's daughters were already considering a further emigration to Israel, but early in the 1950s Ilse and Johanna met and married some German students. They returned to Germany in 1953 and 1954 respectively. Eventually, a few months after her father's death, Dorothea also left Immenhausen and moved in with her brother at Marburg. She later founded a family of her own.

Eva, who remained in England with her grandmother, ran a school for physiotherapists in Birmingham until she retired. Paula died in exile in 1972, at the age of 97, never having set foot in Germany again.

Gerhard made a career in the SPD as a young lawyer. He was elected to the Bundestag in 1957, later becoming a parliamentary undersecretary and a minister. He was appointed a freeman of the city of Marburg in 1977, and died of cancer in 1998.

On 25 September 1962, Dorothea's twenty-second birthday, Gerhard planted two trees in memory of his mother in the Martyrs' Grove at the Yad Vashem memorial in Jerusalem. Thirty years later, in 1992, a display cabinet containing Lilli's photographs and letters was installed in the former corrective labour camp at Breitenau. Lilli Jahn was also ultimately commemorated by the citizens of Immenhausen: in 1995 a street in a newly developed area of the small town was named after her, and in 1999 the local primary school was named the 'Lilli-Jahn-Schule'.

Since the summer of 1998 Lilli's name has also appeared on the tombstone of her father, Josef Schlüchterer, in the Jewish cemetery in the Bocklemünd district of Cologne. Her children had an inscription with her dates engraved on it so as to create a definite place of remembrance.

Lilli's friend Lotte stated at the end of her memoirs, *Unter einem fremden Stern*, that her own relations with non-Jewish Germans had never returned to normal, even after the collapse of National Socialism. 'They never recovered,' she wrote in 1952, and she adhered to this bitter conclusion until her death in August 2000.

'Normality' is feasible only for subsequent generations. Today, thirteen grandchildren and twenty-three great-grandchildren of Lilli's are living in Germany, England, and Israel. Ilse's daughter Beate, who emigrated to Israel in 1978 and has since converted to Judaism, named her second daughter Sarah Lilly. All of Lilli's great-grandchildren are still minors. Some were baptized Lutheran Protestants, others are Roman Catholics, and others Jews, but one thing unites them all: the memory of Lilli's 'wounded heart'.

Appendix

Lilli Jahn's Chronology

5 March 1900	Lilli, the daughter of businessman Josef Schlüchterer and his wife Paula, née Schloss, is born in Cologne
2 June 1901	Birth of her sister Elsa
1906–1913	Attends Fräulein Merlo's private school for young ladies in Cologne; goes on to the Kaiserin-Augusta secondary school; takes her school-leaver's examination at Easter 1919
Autumn 1919	Begins to study medicine: two semesters at Würzburg, three semesters at Halle, intermediate examination at Halle in November 1921, one semester at Freiburg, four semesters at Cologne
1924	Public examination and doctorate, Cologne
1924–1926	Employed as a physician by various practices and at the Jewish Hostel for the Sick and Infirm, Cologne-Ehrenfeld
12 August 1926	Marries Ernst Jahn in Cologne
August 1926	Moves into an apartment at Immenhausen, near Kassel, and builds up a joint practice with her husband
10 September 1927	Their son Gerhard is born
Winter 1928–9	The Jahns move into their own house at Immenhausen
15 January 1929	Their daughter Ilse is born
26 July 1930	Their daughter Johanna is born
12 January 1932	Lilli's father, Josef Schlüchterer, dies
1933	She ceases to practise medicine
10 April 1933	Her daughter Eva is born
1933	Her sister Elsa emigrates to England
May 1939	Her mother Paula joins Elsa in Birmingham

25 September 1940	Her daughter Dorothea is born
8 October 1942	Her marriage to Ernst Jahn is dissolved
February 1943	Her son Gerhard becomes an air-force auxiliary at Obervellmar
Summer 1943	Ernst Jahn is conscripted into the armed forces as a medical officer
21 July 1943	Lilli and her children move to an apartment in Kassel
c. 30 August 1943	The Gestapo arrest Lilli and detain her at Kassel police station for having contravened a police edict dated 17 August 1938
3 September 1943	She is interned in Breitenau corrective labour camp
22 October 1943	The Kassel apartment house is destroyed during an air raid. Lilli's children move back to Immenhausen
17 March 1944	Lilli is deported from Breitenau to Auschwitz
17 or 19 June 1944	She dies in Auschwitz-Birkenau concentration camp

Lilli's family, friends and contemporaries

Änne, friend of Lilli in Cologne
Änne, hairdresser in Immenhausen
Anna, Jahn family's nanny during the 1930s, later owned a grocery in Holzhausen
Annekathrin, girlfriend of Ernst during the 1920s
Gustchen Armbrust, daughter of a shopkeeper in Immenhausen
Dr Benjamin Auerbach, Privy Councillor for Health, and director of the Jewish Hostel for the Sick and Infirm, Cologne
Dr Liesel Auerbach, doctor, daughter of the Privy Councillor and friend of Lilli
Hanne (or Johanna) Barth, wife of Leo Barth, Cologne, later Mannheim
Leo Barth, nicknamed Posa, journalist, student friend of Ernst
Johannes, Michael, Ursel and Veronikia Barth, children of Leo and Hanne
Frau Becker, seamstress in Immenhausen
Dr Bonsmann, director of the tuberculosis sanatorium in Immenhausen
Brandau, shop in Kassel
Franz Bremer, patisserie and coffee shop in Cologne
Dr Fritz Cahen, medical councillor, consultant surgeon at the Jewish Hostel in Cologne
Evelyn Crosskey, friend of Lilli's sister, Elsa, in Birmingham
Dr John Henry Crosskey, doctor, husband of Evelyn
Lise Diekamp, wife of Leo Diekamp, Bochum
Dr Leo Diekamp, student friend of Ernst, lawyer in Bochum
Dietrichs, children's clothing shop in Kassel
Ellen, schoolfriend of Ilse in Kassel
Fatthauer, Johanna's teacher in Hofgeismar
Dr Faust, Ilse's teacher in Hofgeismar
Fiebig, owner of a small shop in Kassel
Johanna Forell, née Henning, known as Tante Hansel, schoolfriend of Lilli
Dr Martha Franken, doctor in Cologne
Fräulein Frieda, housemaid of Lilli's mother Paula in Cologne
Berhard Friedemann, grocer in Immenhausen
Johanna Friedemann, wife of Bernhard
Friedgart, schoolfriend of Ilse in Kassel
Inge Gaugler, neighbour of Jahn family at 3 Motzstrasse, Kassel

Gerda, housemaid of Rita Schmidt and Ernst Jahn in Immenhausen
Max Goldin, chemist in Immenhausen
Karl Gross, deputy district director of the NSDAP in Immenhausen, held office of Mayor from 1940
Hans, boyfriend of Lilli's sister Elsa during the 1920s
Hengst, Johanna's teacher in Hofgeismar
Lene Hirdes, daughter of publican Wilhelm Hirdes in Immenhausen
August Hoppach, director of the 'Jewish department' of the Kassel Gestapo
Ilse, schoolfriend of Marilis in Marburg
Jäger, garage in Immenhausen
Maria Jahn, née Breuer, Ernst's mother (1864–1913)
Oskar Jahn, Ernst's father, director of Kaiserlicher Telegraphen (1854–1905)
Greta Jahn de Rodriguez, Ernst's half-sister
Jahns, Johanna's teacher in Kassel
Dr Janik, Ernst's locum in Immenhausen
Dr Julie Janssen, gynaecologist and paediatrician in Cologne
Josephine, housemaid of Lotte Paepcke in Freiburg
Jachens, Johanna's form teacher in Hofgeismar
Jung, patisserie at Friedrichsplatz in Kassel
Ilse Kasten, schoolfriend of Ilse in Hofgeismar
Keil, medical councillor and doctor in Immenhausen, Ernst's predecessor
Kersting, farmer's family in Immenhausen
Prof. Bruno Kisch, cardiologist at Cologne University
Marie Klein, née Schloss, Lilli's aunt (born 1877, transported to Theresienstadt)
Resemarie Kressman, schoolfriend of Ilse in Immenhausen
Heinz Kroh, artist in Cologne and Lilli's friend in the 1920s
Prof. Dr F. Külbs, Director of first clinic of medicine at Cologne University, and head of the Augusta Hospital
Kunze family, neighbours of the Jahn family at 3 Motzstrasse, Kassel
Maria Lieberknecht, acquaintance of Lilli in Kassel
Paul Lieberknecht, clergyman in Kassel, husband of Maria
Dr Anna-Therese Lobbenberg, doctor at the Jewish Hostel in Cologne
Dr Eugen Löwenstein, medical councillor and ENT specialist in Cologne
Magda (a pseudonym), daughter of Rita and Ernst Jahn
Julia Maguestiaux, known as Julie, Belgian housemaid of the Jahn family, foreign worker
Max Mayer, husband of Lilli's cousin Olga, leather trader in Freiburg (1873–1962)
Neuman, farmer's family in Immenhausen
Helene Nördlinger, née Schlüchterer, Lilli's aunt (born 1862, transported to Theresienstadt)
Frau Paack, neighbour in Motzstrasse, Kassel
Dr Ernst August Paepcke, husband of Lotte, literary historian (1898–1963)
Lotte Paepcke, née Mayer, daughter of Lilli's cousin Olga, writer (1910–2000)
Dr Peter Paepcke, son of Lotte Paepcke (1935–1995)
Pankow, doctor in Düsseldorf
Tanta Paula, friend (or relative?) of the Jahn family in Geneva
Paulus, a café in Kassel

Pfleging, a publican in Immenhausen
Alfonso de Rodriguez Mateo, husband of Grete, Ernst's half-sister, journalist and government official in Madrid
Friedchen, Hedwig and Hilde Rösch, farmer's children in Immenhausen
Dr Lilly Rothschild, doctor, a friend of Lilli
Helmut and Hildchen Rüdiger, children of a landowner in Immenhausen
Lutz Salomon, acquaintance of Lilli in Cologne
Lore (or Leonore) Sasse, née Jahn, Ernst's sister (1896–1963)
Marilis Sasse, Lore's daughter and Lilli's niece (born 1924)
Dr Wilhelm Sasse, known as Willy, Ernst's brother-in-law, a doctor in Essen (1879–1943)
Wilhelm Sasse, Lore and Wilhelm's son, Lilli's nephew (1925–1943)
Schäfer, fellow student of Lilli in Cologne
Ellen Elise Schloss, née Wormser, Lilli's grandmother (1841–1927)
Eva Schloss, wife of Lilli's uncle Simon (transported to Theresienstadt)
Georg Schloss, Lilli's cousin and son of Julius Schloss, businessman in Cologne (1912–1990)
Dr Josef Schloss, Lilli's uncle and Ilse's godfather, medical councillor and paediatrician in Halle an der Saale (1867–1940)
Julius Schloss, Lilli's uncle, landowner (1879–1918)
Margarete Schloss, née Wiesengrund, wife of Lilli's uncle Wilhelm (transported to Theresienstadt)
Moritz Schloss, Lilli's grandfather, cattle dealer in Halle an der Saale (1839–1907)
Anselm Schlüchterer, Lilli's grandfather, gentlemen's tailor in Zeitlofs (1832–1896)
Dr Elsa Schlüchterer, Lilli's sister, chemist (1901–1949)
Josef Schlüchterer, Lilli's father, manufacturer in Cologne (1863–1932)
Ottilie Schlüchterer, née Marx, known as Tilly, Lilli's aunt (transported to Theresienstadt)
Paula Schlüchterer, née Schloss, Lilli's mother (1875–1972)
Siegfried Schlüchterer, Lilli's uncle, emigrated to the USA
Theodor Schlüchterer, Lilli's uncle, emigrated to the USA
Rita Schmidt (a pseudonym), Ernst Jahn's second wife
Professor Dr Kurt Schneider, Professor of Psychiatry at Cologne University and consultant at the Neurological Clinic at Lindenberg
Dr Karl-Werner Schupmann, doctor and locum at Ernst Jahn's practice in Immenhausen
Professor Dr Ferdinand Siegert, medical councillor, Professor of Medicine at Cologne University
Professor Dr Erwin Thomas, Professor of Medicine at Cologne University
Toni, hairdresser in Immenhausen
Ulla Ullman, schoolfriend of Ilse, daughter of a doctor in Kassel
Frau Wittich, seamstress in Immenhausen
Wolf, air-force auxiliary and friend of Gerhard
Professor Dr Ferdinand Zinsser, Director of the University Clinic for Skin Diseases, Cologne
Fritz Zschiegner, Ilse and Gerhard's piano teacher in Kassel

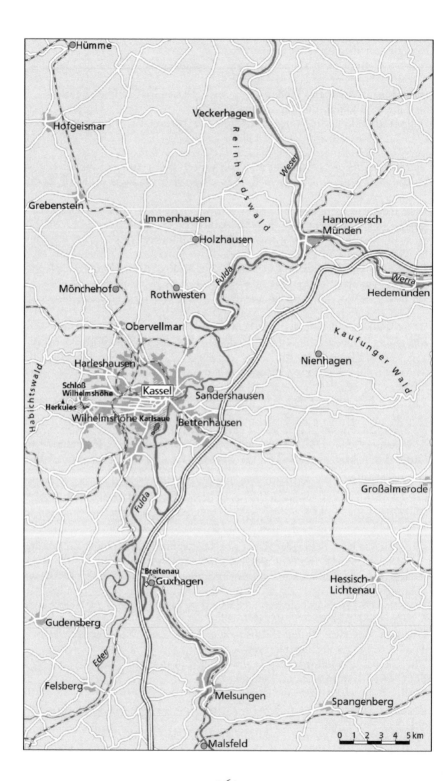

Acknowledgements

Lilli's daughters bore a heavy burden, but my mother Ilse, the eldest, bore the heaviest burden of all. She followed the genesis of this book for three long years, assisting me by offering suggestions, asking questions, contributing the first-hand knowledge of a contemporary observer and one who was closely affected, and, above all, by exercising patience. It often distressed her to come to terms with her own past. Although she wanted this book to be published, there were times when she found it almost unendurable to rake over her mother's story again and again.

Lilli's daughters Ilse, Johanna and Eva made available to me the letters they wrote their mother during her detention in Breitenau corrective labour camp. Together with Dorothea, their youngest sister, they strove to assemble as complete a collection as possible of all the other documents and photographs pertaining to their parents. In addition, they described their childhood in National Socialist Germany in autobiographical notes and numerous conversations.

But this book also owes its existence to suggestions and research contributed by colleagues and friends. Dietfrid Krause-Vilmar of Kassel University has since the 1980s published several books and essays on the history of Breitenau camp. Gunnar Richter of the Breitenau Memorial and the manufacturer Ludwig G. Braun of Melsungen were a great help to me in reconstructing Lilli's months of imprisonment. Information about her early years in Cologne was supplied by Barbara Becker-Jákli of the NS-Dokumentationszentrum, Cologne. Thorsten Wiederhold of Kassel evaluated the Immenhausen files in the 'Judaica' regional museum at Hofgeismar and the Immenhausen inventory in the Hessisches Staatsarchiv at Marburg. Further material was made available by the municipal records offices of Kassel and Marburg.

Other tips and bibliographical pointers were supplied by Volker Hage of Hamburg, Ursula Jahn of Marburg, Helga Paepcke of Karlsruhe, Resemarie Petersen of Immenhausen, Heinz Recken of Cologne, Monika Rudolph of Immenhausen, and Sybille Steinbacher of Bochum.

My friends Erwin Brunner, Thomas Kühne and Cornelia Rauh-Kühne, and the DVA editors Julia Hoffmann and Michael Neher read the manuscript and suggested numerous improvements. I was further assisted and advised while revising the text by my father Jürgen Doerry, my wife Inge, and my daughter Katja.

My sincere thanks to one and all.

Editorial Note

This biography is based on more than 570 letters and numerous official and private documents spanning the period 1882–1962.

Lilli's son Gerhard kept the letters he and his sisters had written their mother during her detention at Breitenau in 1943 and 1944. In addition to this batch, which numbered approximately 250, there were 45 letters written to Lilli in Breitenau by her sister-in-law Lore, her niece Marilis, and her friend Lotte Paepcke.

After Gerhard Jahn's death in October 1998, the children's letters were returned to his sisters Ilse, Johanna, and Eva. In the course of 2000, in response to a request from the author, Lilli's daughters transcribed nearly all of them into typescript. The author then selected from these transcripts those that lent themselves to publication. Finally, the sisters re-read their letters and checked them for transcription errors. Gerhard's letters were transcribed and selected by the author himself.

Also found among Gerhard's papers were Lilli's last letter sent from Auschwitz in June 1944, certified copies of the two letters concerning Lilli written by Mayor Gross of Immenhausen in 1942, and some family documents dating from 1939–62.

Of the letters Lilli herself wrote from Breitenau and Dresden (while en route for Auschwitz) in 1943 and 1944, there still exist ten handwritten originals, three of which were in the 'air-raid suitcase' salvaged from the burning building in Kassel's Motzstrasse on 22 October 1943. Some five more dating from the winter of 1943–4 have probably been lost.

Lilli's letters are now in the possession of her eldest

daughter Ilse. They were transcribed in 1988 by Dietfrid Krause-Vilmar and placed at the disposal of the family and various research institutes in the Kassel district. The above biography is, however, based on the originals. There are instances where the new transcripts diverge from the versions already published, for example where dates and the spelling of names is concerned.

Some 200 of the letters written by Lilli in 1923–6 and 1930 to Ernst, her friend and future husband, were preserved by him and did not pass to Ilse from his estate until the 1990s. She also possesses three letters written to his future son-in-law by Lilli's father, Josef Schlüchterer, in 1926.

Another 60 letters written by Lilli and Ernst to their Mannheim friends Hanne and Leo Barth between 1929 and 1943 are in the possession of Lilli's daughter Dorothea. Of these, 48 were entrusted to her by the Barths and 12 were found among their effects in the autumn of 2002.

A typewritten version of the letter written in 1935 by Lilli's sister Elsa to Ernst's half-sister, Grete Jahn de Rodriguez Mateo, is now with Lilli's daughter Johanna, who also possesses a photocopy of Lilli's 1942 letter to the 'Aunt Paula' resident in Geneva. Several copies of Max Mayer's letter to his grandson Peter are owned by members of the family circle. The original is in the possession of Peter's widow, Helga Paepcke, and was recently published for the first time in the appendix to Lotte Paepcke's book *Ein kleiner Händler, der mein Vater war* (Herder-Verlag 2002).

Those documents and private photographs reproduced in this biography which cover the years 1882–1930 come from the estate of Lilli's mother Paula. Most of them are owned by Johanna, who also preserves the Jahn family's photo album, which Lilli probably started in 1941.

With the exception of the children's letters, all the correspondence and family papers reproduced here have been transcribed by the author himself. It seemed advisable to abridge many of the letters, include brief excerpts or quotations from others, and dispense with some altogether. In two cases, pseudonyms have been used out of consideration for persons still living.

Finally, the explanatory and transitional passages are based on other archive material, on the results of historical research and, above all, on the recollections of Lilli's daughters.

A NOTE ON THE AUTHOR

Martin Doerry, one of Lilli Jahn's grandchildren,
was born in 1955. He studied German Literature
and History in Tübingen and Zürich, and
completed his Ph.D. in Modern History. He has
worked at *Der Spiegel* since 1987 and was
appointed Deputy Editor in Chief in 1998.

A NOTE ON THE TRANSLATOR

John Brownjohn is one of Britain's leading
translators from the German and has won critical
acclaim on both sides of the Atlantic. Among
his most recent awards are the Schlegel-Tieck
Prize for Thomas Brussig's *Heroes Like Us* and
the Helen and Kurt Wolff Prize for Marcel Beyer's
The Karnau Tapes. He is also a screenwriter
whose credits include *Tess, Bitter Moon* and
The Ninth Gate.

A NOTE ON THE TYPE

The text of this book is set in Linotype Sabon,
named after the type founder, Jacques Sabon. It was
designed by Jan Tschichold and jointly developed by
Linotype, Monotype and Stempel, in response to a
need for a typeface to be available in identical form
for mechanical hot metal composition and hand
composition using foundry type.

Tschichold based his design for Sabon roman on a
fount engraved by Garamond, and Sabon italic on a
fount by Granjon. It was first used in 1966 and has
proved an enduring modern classic.